LEGISLATION IN CONTEXT: ESSAYS IN LEGISPRUDENCE

Series Editor's Preface

The objective of the Applied Legal Philosophy series is to publish work which adopts a theoretical approach to the study of particular areas or aspects of law or deals with general theories of law in a way which focused on issues of practical moral and political concern in specific legal contexts.

In recent years there has been an encouraging tendency for legal philosophers to utilize detailed knowledge of the substance and practicalities of law and a noteworthy development in the theoretical sophistication of much legal research. The series seeks to encourage these trends and to make available studies in law which are both genuinely philosophical in approach and at the same time based on appropriate legal knowledge and directed towards issues in the criticism and reform of actual laws and legal systems.

The series will include studies of all the main areas of law, presented in a manner which relates to the concerns of specialist legal academics and practitioners. Each book makes an original contribution to an area of legal study while being comprehensible to those engaged in a wide variety of disciplines. Their legal content is principally Anglo-American, but a wide-ranging comparative approach is encouraged and authors are drawn from a variety of jurisdictions.

Tom D. Campbell
Series Editor
Centre for Applied Philosophy and Public Ethics,
Charles Sturt University, Canberra, Australia

Legislation in Context: Essays in Legisprudence

Edited by

LUC J. WINTGENS
*Centre for Legislation, Regulation and Legisprudence,
Katholieke Universiteit Brussels, Belgium*

Assistant Editor

PHILIPPE THION
*Centre for Legislation, Regulation and Jurisprudence,
Katholieke Uniiversitiet Brussels, Belgium*

ASHGATE

Published by
Ashgate Publishing Limited
Gower House
Croft Road
Aldershot
Hampshire GU11 3HR
England

Ashgate Publishing Company
Suite 420
101 Cherry Street
Burlington, VT 05401-4405
USA

Ashgate website: http://www.ashgate.com

British Library Cataloguing in Publication Data
Legislation in context : essays in legisprudence. -
   (Applied legal philosophy)
   1. Legislation 2. Jurisprudence
   I. Wintgens, Luc
   340.1

Library of Congress Cataloging-in-Publication Data
Legislation in context : essays in legisprudence / edited by Luc J. Wintgens.
       p. cm. -- (Applied legal philosophy)
     ISBN: 978-0-7546-2667-1
   1. Legislation. 2. Law--Philosophy. 3. Jurisprudence. I. Wintgens, Luc.

   K284.L42 2007
   340'.1--dc22

                                                                    2007009689

ISBN: 978-0-7546-2667-1

Printed and bound in Great Britain by MPG Books Ltd, Bodmin, Cornwall.

Contents

List of Contributors

Bruce Anderson, *Saint Mary's University Mount, Halifax, N.S., Canada*
Wojciech Cyrul, *University of Krakow, Poland*
Linda Gröning, *University of Lund, Sweden*
Tatsuo Inoue, *Graduate Schools for Law and Politics, University of Tokyo, Japan*
Philip McShane, *Mount St Vincent University, Halifax, N.S., Canada*
Marie-Francine Moens, *Catholic University Leuven, Belgium*
Philippe Thion, *University of Brussels, Belgium*
Hanneke van Schooten, *Tilburg University, The Netherlands*
Peter Wahlgren, *University of Stockholm, Sweden*
Pauline Westerman, *University of Groningen, The Netherlands*
Luc J. Wintgens, *University of Brussels, Belgium*

Introduction

Luc J. Wintgens and Philippe Thion

Current legal theory is increasingly concerned with the study of legislation. In today's major debate about the future of the social welfare state, with its emphasis on the quality and quantity of regulation, the growing instrumentalization of law and the juridification of social relationships, legal theorists have an important role to play. A milestone in this evolution, no doubt, was the publication in 1973 of Peter Noll's *Gesetzgebungslehre*.[1] The monopoly of the judge as key figure of theoretical reflections on law has been slowly but surely brought to an end since, so as to include the legislator and the creation of law. This book seeks alliance with this new field of study. It is the result of a long-run research project, uniting a considerable number of scholars who explore legislation by using the theoretical insights and tools characteristic of legal theory.[2]

Legislation does not pop out of itself but is, from an epistemological point of view, always already constrained by the framework of an analytical theory. This framework not only devises legislation as a *legal* phenomenon, but also provides the potential of model solutions for problems the same framework allows to conceive as *legislative* problems. The very recognition that legislation, as part of the legal system, is necessarily preceded by a constraining context in which it 'makes sense', is what clears the way for the theoretical study of legislation or *legisprudence*. This also involves that legisprudence avails itself essentially of an interdisciplinary method.

This volume contains three parts and ten chapters. The first part analyzes some fundamental questions concerning the various crossroads between legislation and legal theory. Luc Wintgens' paper on 'Legitimacy and Legitimation' examines whether, instead of the irreversible character of democratic legitimation, other patterns of legitimation can be thought of, in which the subject qua subject gets more weight, while avoiding, at the same time, the trappings of a de(con)struction of legalism. Wintgens argues that although democracy substitutes substantive legitimacy for active legitimation, the very first step of legitimation, that is, the identification of a specific content, is still pushed out of sight. The dynamics of the legitimation chain, as a result, has a unilateral character, so that earlier stages of the chain can no longer be questioned later on. Wintgens then substantiates these

---

[1]   P. Noll, *Gesetzgebungslehre* (Rowohlt, Reinbek, 1973).

[2]   See also L.J. Wintgens (ed.), *The Theory and Practice of Legislation: Essays in Legisprudence* (Aldershot, Ashgate, 2005); L.J. Wintgens (ed.), *Legisprudence: A New Theoretical Approach to Legislation* (Oxford, Hart, 2002).

assertions by focusing on Hobbes' and Rousseau's respective theories on the organization of political space. Both theories involve a proxy version of democracy in which the legal system contains *ab initio* its own principle of legitimation. Wintgens concludes his article with a brief analysis of four reversals that can be identified even in the proxy model of legitimation and which may give some idea of how the subject can actively enter into the process of legitimation, as legisprudence advocates.

Wojciech Cyrul's contribution deals with the complex problems connected with transforming legal discourse into legal text. His basic claim is that instrumental and technical understanding of legal text is too narrow and should also take into consideration inherent, structural and ontological determinants of textuality. Cyrul distinguishes 'discourse' from 'text' by arguing that the notion of discourse stems from the phenomenon of live dialogue, which inherently is a process, covering contextual elements that do not belong to textual categories. A text, on the contrary, is a finished product, recorded on a carrier, with an autonomy of its own and showing a monological disposition. This makes that 'discourse' is opposed to 'text' in the same way as 'utterance' is opposed to 'sentence'. The difference between both is not simply a matter of the signs' complexity, but regards their very ontology and social status. This distinction allows the author to explain in the last section of this chapter why the major requirements lawmaking currently imposes on legal text are in many respects unrealizable.

The primary claim put forward in Tatsuo Inoue's exposé is that in a pluralistic society a strong structural conception of the rule of law can offer an adequate basis for the legitimacy of legislation. According to Inoue, adequate legitimacy requires independent normative constraints on democratic process such that all losers in democratic politics can respect its outcome as worthy of their deference. It also requires that the normative constraints are independent of and binding on specific conceptions of substantive rights that compete for victory in constitutional politics. In order to meet both conditions, Inoue develops a concept of law as 'a project for justice'. Law, in this view, is understood, first, as an enterprise of subjecting human conduct to the governance of *just* rules, second, as a commitment to subject itself to constant critical review of its congruity with justice by all the people it governs, and, third, as a guarantee that judgments about justice are justified by *public* reasons that can also be accepted by those who are disadvantaged by them. In the final section, Inoue explains how this concept of law informs a strong structural conception of the rule of law and what specific conditions this conception involves. These conditions are extensionally identified as those structural principles put forward by Hart and Fuller, but Inoue intentionally reinterprets them as protecting justice-review of law.

The second part of the book deals with the particular shape legislation takes in contemporary societies. Peter Wahlgren's contribution discusses legislative techniques that can be developed to remedy the many shortcomings of traditional, black-letter lawmaking, especially in the light of the challenges brought about by information technology. Wahlgren identifies the following possible (speculative) approaches: the quantitative *ad hoc* procedure, the hands-off strategy, a potential reorganization of the legislative preparatory process, undertakings to develop the legal language, the employment of 'knowledge representation languages' in analytical phases, utilization of sociological methods to learn more about legislative impact, the elaboration of means to implement laws in physical mechanisms, the introduction of pattern recognition, the development of proactive risk analysis tools and, finally, the suggestion that biotechnology may function as a social instrument. These approaches, Wahlgren emphasizes, should be looked upon as complementary strategies, requiring further investigations as to the development of a functional typology for problem areas and related legislative solutions.

Philippe Thion's contribution aims to map out the principal conditions of possibility for the emergence and current predominance of alternatives to legal regulation. Law, therefore, is linked up with the legal mentality in which it appears and through which it is reflected upon. Characteristic of the current legal mentality, for Thion, is that it questions law and legislation primarily through society itself, that is, society as depicted by the social sciences in terms of what is believed to be normal and abnormal. As law is increasingly deployed as a strategic means in the hands of governments to normalize the inclinations of citizens and to manage the statistical features of the population, legislation, correspondingly, takes more and more the shape of alternatives. The legal mentality, what is more, is part of a wider network of power relations, which presents itself in a certain code of power. Alternatives, in this code, are said to foster individual freedom because they reduce the repressive character of state action. Thion criticizes the one-sidedness of this negative power model, since there actually has been, not at least through the very endorsement of alternatives, an intensification and extension of productive power relations through which the state precisely constitutes and disciplines its citizens. In the final section, Thion puts into perspective the recently growing demand formulated both by civil society and state authorities to enhance citizen participation in the regulatory process.

Pauline Westerman discusses the major effects aspirational norms and result-prescribing norms have on legal decision-making and our individual lives. To clarify her position, Westerman examines in detail the nature of both types of norms by comparing them to the paradigmatic mandatory rule. She argues that these new types of norms belong together, in that both are outcome-oriented and can be seen as the legal form of output management (the legislator is not interested in the actions of the norm-addressee as long as the desired effects are brought about). By elucidating, subsequently, the relation between rules and aims, Westerman shows that once people start thinking of aims as end-states or 'things' to be concretized into more concrete 'things', a dramatic change takes place that is mainly beneficial for the legislator and detrimental for the citizen. This change involves three problems, namely overregulation, inconsistency and the stifling of political debate. However, because these new norms minimize, at the same time, the risk of unintended side-effects, they are highly appropriate to regulate groups that are traditionally hard to control. Her position is close to Thion's in showing how these new types of norms severely limit freedom in that there is no space or time left for citizens to be free.

Hanneke van Schooten puts into perspective the constitutional protection known as the 'primacy of the legislature' by analyzing the new war terminology and the new war categories. Although most constitutions suggest a solid guarantee for citizens' rights against the arbitrary wills of rulers, van Schooten shows that seemingly unimportant shifts in political terminology may provoke the very undermining of the protective function of the constitution. The claim is elaborated within the theoretical framework of institutional legal theory. Van Schooten develops, mainly drawing on the work of Ruiter, a tripartite conceptual framework that extends MacCormick and Weinberger's dichotomy between socially existent norms and observable features of social life with another concept, namely the observable patterns of social conduct as an expression of indiscernible common belief. This sophisticated model of legal communication is applied to the Dutch case of Eric O. It shows that, contrary to the classical 'top-down' view in which the legal rule is seen as the legitimate basis both for its official application and rule-conform social behaviour, the acts of officials and the facts of social practice influence the meaning of the rule. That is, the facts of reality determine the fiction of the law, to such an extent even that the rule's projected meaning is turned into its opposite.

Central in the third part of the book is the relationship between legislation and the disciplines. Bruce Anderson and Philip McShane question in their article on 'Groundig Behaviour in Law and Economics' the particular view of economics adopted by most scholars interested in law and economics. They argue that laws regarding dysfunctional economic behaviour are not based on some grasp of sane economic behaviour. To explicate the 'natural rhythms' of economic behaviour, Anderson and McShane draw an extended analogy, as suggested by the Canadian economist Lonergan, between operating a car and operating an economy. After having enumerated the significant parts of an economy, Anderson and McShane examine how these parts fit together, what the norms are of a properly functioning economy, and what the role of law is in running economies. From this analysis, the neo-classical view on 'law and economics' as emblematically elaborated by Posner is criticized, as Posner's view, expressed in terms of driving a car, saying that the real function of cars is teenaged racing. According to Anderson and McShane, neo-classical economics mistakenly emphasizes that exchanges should be potential Pareto superior, because no clear view has been developed on the normative demands of the economic process. Any legislation, they maintain, that fails to take into account how the economy works will merely remain manoeuvrings in the economic dark.

Marie-Francine Moens' articulates the relationship between information technology and the format, function, and application of legislation. It focuses, more precisely, on the management, advantages and side effects of 'digital legislation' and how the science of informatics can help to solve legislative problems. Moens starts her analysis with explaining the advantages of using legal drafting systems and mark-up languages that allow enforced verification and translation of the document contents into formats readable by machines. Then attention is paid to the technologies currently used in legislative databases, search engines and so-called 'ontology research'. In the future, Moens explains, information technologies will much more incorporate information synthesis and reasoning so that information systems will evolve from a simple search engine to a proper problem-solving machine. Moens then shows on the basis of concrete examples that legal theory, and especially the theory of legal reasoning, has a crucial role to play in the development of intelligent information systems able to translate natural legal language into a language understandable by the machine.

In the final chapter of the book, Linda Gröning investigates the democratic legitimacy of European penal law. In Western political systems, the legitimacy of penal law traditionally is intimately connected to parliamentary majority decisions. Due to a growing regulation of penal law at the European Union level, however, the traditional claim of a parliamentary anchorage of penal legislation has become highly problematic. Gröning's basic claim is that the ideal of democratic control of penal legislation can be reconciled with the development of an autonomous penal decision-maker at the EU level, given that democratic legitimacy is separated from a state-based model of democracy and not *per se* identified with a claim that penal legislation must be enacted through parliamentary majority decisions. The meaning of democratic legitimacy, for Gröning, must be analyzed in the light of the purpose and underlying values of democracy. In the penal-law context, where the fear of abuse of state power is most articulated, the theory of constitutionalism, with its emphasis on the safeguarding of the autonomy of the individual, should prevail over the theory of popular sovereignty when defining the hard core of democratic legitimacy. This makes it possible, according to Gröning, to seek the roots of democracy both beyond the state and beyond parliamentary majority decisions, provided that legislative penal power remains controllable and that human rights are genuinely protected by superior constitutional norms and judicial control.

Part I

THEORY OF LEGISLATION

Chapter 1

Legitimacy and Legitimation from the Legisprudential Perspective

Luc J. Wintgens
University of Brussels, Belgium

Introduction

In earlier work[1] I have proposed a distinction between strong legalism and weak legalism as a starting point for the elaboration of a theory of rational legislation. After the diagnosis of the absence of a theory of legislation, resulting from strong legalism, some alternative, weaker version of legalism was proposed. This weaker version primarily aims at taking the subject qua subject seriously, in that the subject's freedom proposed as the principium of law.

In addition to that I have proposed an interpretation of freedom that better fits with its reflexive characteristics. Freedom that is, requires freedom to be realised. Freedom, that is, cannot, and even less than any other thing, be fully represented without destroying itself. Insofar as freedom is represented, it exists as the realisation on conceptions about freedom. In proportion to this representation, freedom in the moral sense is reduced in favour of freedom in the political sense.

I have further argued that the substitution of acting on conceptions about freedom for acting on conceptions of freedom seems unproblematic in the Modern philosophical project. The main argument that justifies it is of an epistemological character. In doing so, freedom in the moral sense is reduced in favour of freedom in the political sense. Consequential on this reduction, moral freedom can be outweighed without further justification.

In this chapter, I will focus on the problems of legitimacy on the one hand and legitimation on the other that come with this conclusion.

Strong legalism, in relying on representationalism, excels in its impossibility to provide a theory of freedom. A theory of freedom is crucial for freedom to make any moral sense at all. Instead of a theory of freedom, in which the subject qua subject occupies the places he deserves, the Modern philosophical project has supplied variants of a theory about freedom. Within a theory about freedom the subject shows up as a legal subject, that is, a subject defined through the rules that

---

[1]   *See* L.J. Wintgens, 'Legisprudence as a New Theory of Legislation', in L.J. Wintgens (ed.), *The Theory and Practice of Legislation. Essays in Legisprudence* (Aldershot, 2005), pp. 3-25, esp. 6-11.

he is supposed to edict himself.

Self-legislation as the political celebration of the autonomous subject, it must be conceded, is held one of the major products of this project. Self-legislation has all there needs to be in order to get a full theory of freedom. At least, that is what it seems to be.

That is what this chapter is about. Self-legislation as the core of most Western institutional designs is not well served, as I will argue, if it is taken from the mere perspective of an institutionalisation of truth as strong legalism does. Representationalism entails the institutionalisation of truth. In doing so, the institutional design we call 'democracy', leads its life as a representation of reality, although democracy is not a natural fact. Democracy is a matter of public justification resulting in valid norms; it is not a matter of truth.

From the very 'moment' the social contract enters into force, so to speak, the subject qua subject fades into the background. The suggestion could be made that, as a matter of course, he is still a subject qua subject at the moment of elections, moment supreme of democracy. But even there, he can only act on political rights, defined in and by the political space he is called to sustain, in some variants even under the threat of punishment.

The main claims I will argue for in this chapter include the irreversible character of democratic legitimation in the rationalistic version. As a consequence, so I will further argue, the question can be raised as to whether other patterns of legitimation can be thought of, in which the subject qua subject gets more weight, while avoiding the trappings of a de(con)struction of legalism altogether.

It is not however because strong legalism turns out to be defective that any form of legalism is to be criticized. The claims argued for in the pages to come are projected on the framework provided by weak legalism. This will assist us in the construction of a rational theory of legislation or legisprudence.

From the very beginning, a distinction must be made between deliberation on the one hand and justification on the other. Deliberation as a process of legitimation is considered to be political in nature. Justification for its part consists of a process of argumentative support for decisions, judicial or otherwise. The distinction does not claim to be a grand dividing line of opposition. As a matter of course, deliberation has justifying effects, while justification in turn may refer to deliberation in support of a decision. Both are processes contributing to some similar effects when it comes to decision-making.

Without denying the merits of deliberation in decision-making, I will mainly focus on justification as a distinct process. Deliberation, roughly speaking, has to do with the making of decisions, i.e. legal rules. Justification, in my view, comes after that. In the process of justification, the rules that come out of a deliberative process are to be connected to the social environment in which they will operate. This is what justification in my view comes to.

I will begin with a clarification of another distinction, that is, between legitimation and legitimacy. A familiar starting point is the distinction between positivism and jusnaturalism that for reasons of clarity I label 'non-jusnaturalistic' and 'jusnaturalistic' respectively.

Jusnaturalistic and Non-jusnaturalistic Models of Legitimation

In this chapter I will focus on the differentiation of the organisation of the social bond from its jusnaturalistic and theological roots, thus giving rise to a political space that has grown to be independent of these sources. The proper aspect of independence suggests that the organisation of political space has no relation whatsoever with these sources of legitimation; any dealings with them are only of historical value, and do not have a legitimating effect.

I will briefly dwell on the negation of this proposition, without however denying the independence of the organisation of political space. There is, so I will argue, a structural similarity between the jusnaturalistic (that includes the classical, theological and Modern version of natural law) and the non-jusnaturalistic organisation of society. Only the latter, as I will show, can be qualified a democratic organisation.

Political space in the Modern philosophical project, or civil society as it is labelled nowadays, as different from the ancient polis, belongs to the realm of construction, not to the order of what exists naturally. At its very foundation, it relies on the will of those who live in and by it. Both its existence and the order that it brings about are the outcome of human construction. This, broadly speaking, can be considered the essence of 'democracy'.

On this approach, democracy is the organisation of political space that comes into being, historically speaking, after the classical jusnaturalistic and theological forms of social organisation respectively. Despite the qualitative differences between jusnaturalistic and theological models on the one hand and the new, democratic models on the other, these models share a similar dynamics.

The core of the democratic organisation of political space is that the rules – that is, the limitations of freedom that are considered normative – can be related to the will of those submitted to them. The relation between limitation of freedom and will is the kernel of democracy, that is, it is impossible to call 'democratic' any organisation of social space where no variant of this relation can be spelled out. This is what follows from a conceptual analysis of the concept of democracy.

At its maximum, this relation will be direct in that all the members contribute immediately in the ruling activity in the so-called popular democracy that Rousseau advocates. In its minimal variant, this contribution crystallises as the designation by all of one person who will be vested with the power to limit all the others' freedom.

Within these two extreme poles, we find a variety of conceptions that can be ranged within the concept of democracy or self-legislation. Most commonly, any form of representation – upon which all designate a limited group to which they will submit, while taking these rules as imputations to themselves – will be considered democratic.

Sieyes, who turns out to have won the competition of democratic theory in the 18th century, is a fervent advocate of representative democracy, most criticised by Rousseau.[2] Whether the organisation of political space is or is not mediated by a

---

[2]   E.J. Sieyes, *Qu'est-ce que le Tiers Etat?* (Geneva, 1970).

group of representatives is not of great importance, at least from the perspective of the dynamics of the model of legitimation. The dynamics of the process of legitimation in both the popular and the representative variant of democracy starts with all the subjects. The mediation of the legitimation of the subsequent legislation by a group of representatives makes the process maybe longer than, though not essentially different from, the process established under popular democracy.

What is more important than the difference between the Rousseau and Sieyes conceptions of democracy is the dynamics of the model of legitimation that is labelled 'democratic'. A democratic legitimation model in its radical form is non-jusnaturalistic. The dynamics of the latter, though, are similar to jusnaturalistic legitimation models. What the latter models – commonly specified as classical, theological, and rational or Modern natural law – share is some form of substantive legitimation. They legitimate social order and law from the perspective of its content.

Rational natural law does so in that it legitimates the content of human ordering upon principles the content of which is discovered by Reason alone. Classical natural law is substantively legitimating in that observation of Nature provides the proper content of human ruling. In theological natural law, finally, human law's validity flows from its correspondence as regards its content, to the will of God.

These three legitimation models have, and that is their essence, a transcendent origin. They transcend, that is, human will and, consequentially, the transcendent content is not available for the latter. Their normativity consists of both their transcendence and unavailability. They will be referred to as substantive models of legitimation.

Over against this, non-jusnaturalistic or democratic legitimation models can be considered a liberation from these substantive models, just like Modern natural science can be taken to be a liberation from its medieval ecclesiastical shackles. The organisation of political space according to the Modern philosophical project is both a critique and a differentiation thereof.

According to a substantive model of legitimation, legal rules cannot contradict the transcendent norms they rely on. If they do, they lose their status of legal rules altogether. That is at least the logic inherent to this type of theories. Correspondence to the substantive transcendent content is a necessary and a sufficient condition for their validity.

According to non-substantive models this correspondence is as a matter of course, neither a necessary nor a sufficient condition for a rule's validity. There simply is no content to which a legal rule can or must correspond. This is the core of non-jusnaturalistic or democratic models of legitimation. While rules are legitimate according to substantive legitimation models, according to non-substantive models of legitimation they have to be legitimated.

The crucial difference, that is, between substantive or jusnaturalistic and non-jusnaturalistic models of legitimation, lies in the need for an active legitimation of the rules under the latter. According to the former, legitimacy as correspondence with substantive norms makes part of their very validity. Put differently, substantive legitimation models provide legitimate rules, while on non-substantive models rules must legitimated. I propose to call the non-jusnaturalistic, non-substantive or democratic models procedural models of legitimation. This difference between substantive and procedural models of legitimation is that the latter produce legitimate rules while the former calls for a legitimation of rules.

From the perspective just set out both models are prima facie opposed to each other. This opposition is what Hobbes and Rousseau were so eager to erase or to make it only apparent. Their theories were qualified as a representation-construction since, as we have seen, they spared no effort to show that they also – or better: simply – a reproduction of reality.

The erasing of the distinction between legitimacy and legitimation makes the construction look like a reproduction. This comes to what was called the process of naturalisation of hypostatisation proper to strong legalism. Under strong legalism, that is of nominalistic brand, law as a construction is moulded as a representation of reality of which it is argued to be a reproduction. Strong legalism, then, is nominalism in a realistic dress.

Apart from the opposition between substantive and procedural models, as it follows from the above articulation, and apart from the strong legalistic assimilation of both models, I suggest that there is neither complete opposition nor full assimilation. If the latter are differentiated from the former, this means that they are not necessarily opposed to it, but rather only different. According to this idea of differentiation, there must be some trace of similarity. There is at least one crucial similarity between the substantive and procedural models as described above. This similarity has to do with the direction of legitimation, that is, the dynamics of legitimation, in both models.

In a substantive model, the normative content is pre-existent to concrete legislative action. In the theological model, this normative content is given and so it precedes action.[3] Legislative action then is dependent on the accessibility of this normative content, consequential upon revelation and metaphysical reflection. Legislative action is rational insofar as the normative content is adopted as a norm. The dynamics of the legitimation chain according to a substantive model starts from the substantive content to the derived rule.

Accessibility to and knowledge of any normative content is, by very definition, not relevant in procedural legitimation models. They do no rely on any substantive content, so their resemblance to substantive legitimation models must lie elsewhere. Their specificity lies in the fact that the first step of legitimation, the identification of a specific content, revealed, or rationally discovered, is pushed out of side. Any transcendent content, natural, rational or theological, stops producing legitimacy. This content may, accidentally, show up though in the rules issued in political space. It is, though, not necessarily related to concrete rules.

Procedural models of legitimation can be said to produce legitimacy as a result of some form of active legitimation. In doing so, the legitimacy found in a substantive model is substituted for some form of active legitimation. Procedural

---

[3]   On the distinction between existent natural law and given natural law, *see* M. Weber, *The Theory of Social and Economic Organisation,* trans. A.M. Henderson, T. Parsons (ed.), (New York, 1964), p. 131.

models deal with active legitimation of the limitation of the freedom of the subject. Insofar as the subject does not himself limit his freedom to make action possible, that is, insofar as the subject is not acting on a conception of freedom, this limitation must be justified.

A procedural model, properly understood, does not provide legitimacy, like substantive models do. On the contrary, it legitimates propositional contents concerning the limitation of freedom. To use a metaphor, a procedural model is like a computer programme that processes certain data through its programme routines, and results in a certain outcome. The outcome of what you may call the 'legitimation programme' are legitimated rules, general (laws) or individual (judicial decisions or executory orders based them).

Because procedural models are disconnected from any substantive content they must legitimate both a content and the way to determine it. From that perspective, a procedural model deals with the limitation of freedom – the determination of ends and means – while substantive models basically deal with free will.

Since freedom as a whole must be dealt with in procedural models, they are a variant of what I have called a theory of freedom. Substantive models for their part, in that they are based on a substantive content that is not at our disposal, are a variant of a theory about freedom. This amounts to saying that if there is freedom, it cannot be dealt with in a completely free way, as the reflexive character of freedom would require.

The articulation of the reflexive character of freedom is the proper characteristic of a procedural model when compared with a substantive model. Just as freedom only makes sense when exercised in freedom, a procedural model of legitimation cannot refer to anything but itself or some other procedural model. Self-reference is the type of reference we find in a democratically organised political space. In the legal system embedded in it, procedural rules or meta-rules allow the change, creation, and implementation of rules within the procedurally organised system itself.

The meta-rules or programming rules of the system transform propositional contents into legitimated legal rules. This gives the following rough scheme of the chain of legitimation. According to this chain of legitimation, rules are considered legitimated on the basis of prior or higher[4] rules in the chain that can be procedural rules in the strict sense or a combination of procedural rules and primary rules of obligation.

This rudimentary sketch reflects a very classical legitimation chain operational in most western legal systems. As far as its dynamics is concerned, this legitimation chain is similar to the substantive models referred to above. The similarity is found in the unilateral character of the direction or the dynamics of the legitimation that results from it.

In a substantive model, the dynamics of the legitimation chain can be articulated as 'top-bottom', in that the chain starts from some prior/higher/existing content towards a later/lower/created limitation of freedom. What is later, lower or created gets its legitimacy from what is prior, higher or existent.

---

[4]   Most of the time, though not necessarily, prior rules are also higher rules.

Things are different in a procedural model. The subsequent steps are always thought of as legitimated by earlier stages – which is but the logic of legitimation itself. Their content though, in contrast to a substantive model, is not determined by the earlier stages. The output of an earlier stage (a legislative rule, e.g.) serves as a basis for a later stage (a judicial decision, e.g.), without completely determining the latter's content. It limits only possible contents of later stages.

Due to the unilateral character of the dynamics of both the substantive and procedural models, earlier stages can no longer be criticised in later stages of the chain. The content that is legitimate or legitimated in an earlier stage in the substantive or procedural model respectively is unavailable in later stages. The absence of the possibility of critique throws into relief the fact that in either model the legitimation chain cannot be reversed.

This is, say, the general idea. The legitimation chain, that is, cannot be reversed, except for some step expressly provided for, like judicial review, appeal and challenge of administrative acts.[5]

The unilateral dynamics of the legitimation chain, as it can by observed in both substantive and procedural models, takes earlier steps for granted. It adds to that a new content – that is yet another limitation of freedom – for which reasons are provided. These reasons are found mainly at the end of the chain, that is, after the step of legislation. So, executive orders and administrative decisions must be legally justified, as must judicial decisions. The concretisation of the more general limitation of freedom – typically, general legal rules – preceding executive orders, administrative, and judicial decisions connects this general limitation of freedom to more concrete situations. This calls for a justification. Justification in this view connects the later to the earlier, or the lower to the higher.

When it comes to freedom in the political sense, it generally goes without saying that this can be limited. This type of limitation called 'legal rules' is referred to as granted by the social contract; the latter can be further concretised in a constitution. Under this grant, elections and legislation,[6] in turn, do not require specific legitimation, since they are at the beginning of the legitimation chain. Any version of the social contract, that is, is a normative one in that their theorists provide exclusionary reasons to step into. From then on, the legitimation programme starts, and can only be corrected from within, that is, on the basis of correction mechanisms that belong to the programme itself. Reversals of the chain do not belong to that.

From this perspective, the social contract as the beginning of a procedural model can be considered a proxy. The parties to it agree to accept to the limitations of freedom imposed 'later' on. They do abide by limitations of their freedom as yet unknown to them at the 'moment' of the contract.

From the normative perspective, they also ought to do so. They enter into a programme of legitimation that is irreversible. The content of the limitation of their freedom is not available to them, just like the legitimating content of substantive

---

[5]   *See infra,* this chapter.

[6]   In popular democracy there are no elections; this does not, however, affect the argument.

models of legitimation is out of reach. Most clearly, this goes for the content of the social contract itself. Its clauses, Rousseau stresses, cannot be changed without making the contract void.[7] According to this contract, the construction of political space is set in motion. In the next paragraph, I will briefly focus on its main characteristics concerning legitimation.

The Construction of Political Space: the Proxy Model of Legitimation

The democratic organisation of political space in the Modern philosophical project purports to be more radical than its classical version. Democracy, that is, is not a natural fact nor does not follow from the nature of the polis. According to the premises of nominalism, that is proper to both Hobbes and Rousseau, it is a concept. Concepts are not natural; they are intellectual constructions. In the following pages, I will rapidly return to the analysis of the theories of Hobbes and Rousseau, from the perspective of democracy that their theories aim to set up.

Both Hobbes and Rousseau provide us with some theory of the democratic organisation of political space based on the social contract. The contract is supposed to be an act of will according to which a social group decides to submit to a sovereign (Hobbes) or to constitute itself as a sovereign (Rousseau). Theirs is a more radical version of democracy than the classical one, in that they do not refer to any external, substantive norm, at least apparently.

The social contract, so it seems, is an act of will and could mark a radically new beginning. This view has to be qualified. The social contract, most prominently in Rousseau, is a theoretical undertaking, in that it connects legitimation to truth and not to will. The irreversibility of the legitimation chain – apart from the hypothesis of giving up the contract itself – follows from this qualification.

Hobbes' theory is based on the laws of nature. They command that one should abandon one's *ius naturale*. If the subjects want to enjoy peace and the fruits of their labour, while avoiding the dangers of a *bellum omnium contra omnes*, rational reflection pushes them to abandon their natural freedom. In doing so, they submit to a sovereign power, the mortal God that is the state.

Although reason finds confirmation of this insight, as a law of nature, it is not of a purely rational nature. It is a command of God that one should seek for the best possible means available to keep one's life. As a command of God, the normative force of the laws of nature stems from his will, confirmed as it is by reason.

Hobbes' version of democracy is, in consequence, not as radical as Rousseau's. It is based on an external norm that commands the leaving of the state of nature and the acceptance of a series of other external limitations of freedom, that is, the norms of the sovereign. They are binding upon the subject as a result of an imputation based on the social contract. Subjects have in other words chosen to endure the norms of the sovereign, whatever their content may be.

---

[7]   J.-J. Rousseau, *Du contrat social*, in *Oeuvres complètes,* III, Bibliothèque de la Pléiade (Paris, 1964), I, 6, p. 360.

There is a logical and a normative reason for this. The logical reason is that on the 'moment' of the contract, they do not know what the sovereign is going to issue qua norms because there exist no civil laws yet. The normative reason is the power of the sovereign to define in an arbitrary manner the natural laws' content. In the contract they promise obedience to that which is still unknown to them. It is through the contractually expressed will that they are supposed to be authors of these norms.

Rousseau in turn conceives things differently. According to him, the normativity of law does not stem from any external moral norm. The ultimate source of the rule is the will of those submitted to it. The people having constituted itself as a sovereign, it is theirs to decide which propositions will have the force of law.

The Rousseau version of the social contract therefore turns out to be of a more radical nature than Hobbes'. We read from Rousseau:

> Chacun de nous met en commun sa personne et toute sa puissance sous la suprême direction de la volonté générale; et nous recevons en corps chaque membre comme partie indivisible du tout.[8]

In contrast to that of Hobbes, Rousseau's theory admits only one *pactum*, the *pactum unionis*. This *pactum* ties up 'each of us' with the political community. There is no need for any submission apart from this bond, that is, the bond of everyone being joined to all the others. Political space then seems finally liberated from any norm external to itself, that Hobbes felt still compelled to include. Two additional observations are to be made here.

First, the very foundation of the social contract in Rousseau's work raises a problem, at least from the perspective of the radicalism his project aims at. There are, as a matter of fact, no external or independent norms that impose the social contract, as in Hobbes. For Rousseau, both the necessity and the content of the contract result from an evolution of a pre-rational society to a rational state. Of this evolution, Rousseau's theory claims to be the last stage. It is nothing more rational than constructing political space, that finally brings in morality that was lacking in the state of nature.[9]

The conclusion of the contract follows from the access to the true principles of public law, as Rousseau discovers them.[10] It marks the end of a historical evolution, by trial and error, so to speak, of a social bond in search of its own foundations. Rousseau for his part proclaims the end of this evolution by declaring the true principles of public law, and the advent of the true structure of political space.

Consequentially, the contract is not fully the result of an act of will. It rather marks one stage, actually the final one, in the historical evolution of reason. At the very end, the true principles of public law are revealed to us.

---

[8]   Ibid., I, 6, p. 361.

[9]   Cf L. Strauss, *Natural Right and History* (Chicago, 1974), p. 274.

[10]   Rousseau, *Du contrat social*, IV, 9, p. 470.

Their content is not however submitted to the whims of history; it is, on the contrary, fixed once and for all and it cannot be changed without making the contract 'void and without any effect'.[11] What we face then is a democracy in which the demos and its will are relegated to the sidelines. While the organisation of political space aims at being a matter of will, it is in no way related to will at all. It is rather a matter of recognition of the truth of the principles that, consequently, cannot be chosen any more.

The second observation is related to the first in the following manner. If Rousseau's sovereign is going to decide on which propositions are to be law and which not, the sovereign does not have the capacity to take any initiative in these matters. The radicalism of the democratic project, that is, is seriously diminished as a consequence of this. Only the legislator can propose propositional contents that have the potential of becoming law;[12] their validation is the proper function of the sovereign. The latter though cannot amend any proposal; he can only accept or reject it.

The legislator, counsellor of the prince as he has aptly been called,[13] is a reason without will.[14] He suggests propositional contents that only the sovereign can transform into law. Rousseau shows himself as being not really confident in the intentions of those submitted to the laws, since he does not hold them capable of proposing or amending any of them. The people, as he says, do want the good, but do not always see it. Therefore, they need a guide.[15]

From these two observations follows a first conclusion. Modern democracy, that is, democracy as it is related to the Modern philosophical project, as we read from Hobbes and Rousseau, is not really radical. It is based rather on an independent, external norm for Hobbes; it results from a historical evolution that provides, according to Rousseau, the unavoidable cognitive standards. It is not an act of pure will, as would be necessary were democracy to be fully democratic.

If it were, then freedom and not reason would be the principium of democratic organisation of political space and the laws issuing from there. Freedom as a principium, as I have argued, has both the meaning of a starting point and a leitmotiv. In the democratic project resulting from Hobbes and Rousseau, it is only the former. Had it also been the latter, the philosophers would have run the risk of it not being established. As a matter of fact, a fully free will could also not will the democratic organisation of the political space.

What then both Hobbes and Rousseau are justifying is not first of all a radical version of democracy, but a proxy version of it. Their proxy version of democracy comes to the social bound giving a proxy to institutions that, in an irreversible way, as was explained above, legitimates normative contents that are limiting the subjects' freedom. Their consent does not relate to the content of these rules that is,

---

11   Ibid., I, 6, p. 360.
12   Ibid., II, 7, p. 383.
13   R. Polin, *La politique de la solitude. Essai sur J-J Rousseau* (Paris, 1971), p. 222 ff.
14   Ibid., p. 227 ff.
15   Rousseau, *Du contrat social*, II, 6, p. 380.

from the point of view of legitimation, irrelevant.

The very proxy character of their version of democracy stems from its foundation in truth. That is why their version of democracy is not radically democratic. It would be if it were based on will only, *quod non*. The truth of the foundation in Hobbes' construction stems from the truth of the laws of nature. For Rousseau, it is a matter of reason alone. The truth of the basic framework, that is, the contract, provides a stable, indeed unshakable, basis for the rules promulgated on its basis. They share in the truth of the framework.

For Hobbes, the rules of the sovereign, as they are based on the laws of nature, share in their ontological foundation. The meaning given to them by the sovereign makes them the only true expression of the will of God. Rousseau for his part claims that the social contract can only be willed as it is thought of by him, without any change, since the slightest change or amendment would make it void.

The timelessness of the social contract straightforwardly affects the character of social space. On the one hand, Rousseau is suggesting that there is only a natural man, that is, a man living without rational morality. On the other, and opposed to that, there is the citizen, that is, natural man transformed into a member of the political space as a consequence of his entering the social contract.[16] Where then, so it can be asked, is the bound of 'us' after social space is transformed into a political space? After the contractual organisation of the latter, social space is shed off as a previous phase; it lacks any relevance whatsoever from the 'moment' that political space is instituted.

The 'us' does not matter any more, nor does the subject qua subject. From the moment on that political space can be said to exist, the social bond of 'us' disappears. From then on, it is only the rules of political space that will provide the true morality lacking in the previous stages.[17] The social bound generating meanings like 'us' does not matter any more. It is replaced by a new, institutionalised setting that is substituted for their own practices within which they recognize each other as participants or 'us'.

The partners in the social contract do agree to it, because it is true. This agreement is the very heart of the Rousseau version of democracy. They do not submit to anyone, that is, the sovereign like in Hobbes. They do submit to truth.

---

[16] This double nature of man reminds us of the ancient doctrine of natural man on the one hand and spiritual man on the other. Baptism transforms natural man into a spiritual being, like the contract transforms natural man into a citizen. Both baptism and the contract operate a change in man's nature, see on the latter, Rousseau, *Du contrat social*, II, 7, p. 381: 'Celui qui ose entreprendre d'instituer un people doit se sentir en état de changer, pour ainsi dire, la nature humaine.'

[17] There are at least two stages preceding the contract. The first is the natural condition of man in the state of nature. Individuals do not know each other in that stage; they are even afraid of others, J.-J. Rousseau, *Discours sur l'origine et les fondements de l'inégalité parmi les hommes,* in *Oeuvres complètes,* III, Bibliotheque de la Pléiade (Paris, 1964), p. 136: '(...) rien n'est si timide que l'homme dans l'etat de nature (...)'. It is only after getting in touch with each other that a social bond rises. It is this social bond that calls for a transformation into a political space.

The legitimation programme that starts upon the engagement in the social contract runs like an automaton. The story Rousseau tells, then, is a discourse without a subject. Rousseau's discourse is presented from a 'view from nowhere', that is, the view of the rational philosopher. Once the programme starts, it unrolls without the subject qua subject.

This amounts to saying, first, that neither the subject nor the citizen has a right of initiative. Only the legislator is to propose contents that can become law. Secondly, others have no right to amendment. They can only approve or disapprove the contents proposed in that way. Thirdly, the citizen who approves the propositional content that is turned into a legal rule in no way expresses his own conviction. All he does is to anticipate what others will say about it, not as subjects qua subjects, but as the citizen he is.

Those who vote in favour, in case they belong to the majority, are provisionally right. Those voting against on the contrary are wrong, because they were erring as to what the majority was going to approve. Since the majority is always right, the minority has to live with the majority's decision, because its own view is wrong.[18] Put differently, since the citizen is not asked to express his own conviction, e.g., as to what is the best way to realise freedom, he is not required to abandon his conviction in case he was wrong.[19] All he has to do is to conform his external behaviour to the proposition that the majority has transformed into a legal rule. Raymond Polin expresses Rousseau's idea that citizens should be obliged to conform their will to their reason by external means.[20]

However, their reason is not necessarily identical to 'reason' altogether. First, they are not called upon to use their reason, that is, as a subject qua subject, in order to propose contents that can become law. This is the proper task of the legislator, who is not part of the 'us'.[21] Secondly, they are not called on to express what the reason for their inspiration is; they can only speak in the name of truth. Thirdly and finally, if they were to express their reason, this would amount to a form of preference or predilection which is, however, not an option. 'Their' reason therefore cannot be anything else than universal reason.

We face here a merger of the rationalist philosopher's 'view from nowhere' and the participant's perspective of the subjects. This merger shows a specific fallacy, that Pierre Bourdieu has baptised the 'scholastic fallacy'. Theories, philosophical and others, emerge from specific social conditions, as Pierre Bourdieu has pointed out.[22] The scholastic fallacy consists of leaving aside the presuppositions that are inherent to a theory. It leads to considering the agents observed or thought of as identical to the scholar himself – a philosopher or a sociologist – and presupposes that the former think in exactly the same way as the latter.

The priority and universality of reason, that is, is not a natural fact; it is a

---

[18]   Rousseau, *Du contrat social,* IV, 2, p. 441.

[19]   *See* N. Luhmann, *Legitimation durch Verfahren* (Frankfurt on Main, 1983), p. 161.

[20]   Polin, *La politique de la solitude,* p. 103.

[21]   Rousseau, *Du contrat social,* II, 7, p. 381.

[22]   P. Bourdieu, *Raisons pratiques. Sur la théorie de l'action* (Paris, 1994).

theoretical construction that is read into the head of the subject. Thinking is this respect of Descartes' *cogito ergo sum*. It suggests that all rational beings are thinking in a similar way. Hegel rightly criticises this saying that the *cogito* as *ego cogito* only applies to Descartes himself.[23] This form of *Hineininterpretierung* induces an erroneous idea of universality. It obliterates the very idea of situatedness of reason, and takes universality to be itself universal, just like rationality is held to be itself rational. What is universal is thought of as superior to what is not; this is however not due to the characteristics of universality itself, but to a value judgment that is all but universal. The privilege of the universal cannot therefore, without a fallacy, be of universal value.

As a consequence of this, what is thought of as rational, universal, etc. generates the belief of a direct access to reality. The theory resulting from this approach is presented as a theory of reality, while, at best, it is only a theory about reality.

Rousseau favours, that is, a specific conception of rationality that is supposed to be in the head of each and every subject. If citizens are to adapt their reason to 'reason' altogether, it is because the contract, the truth of which raises no doubt for Rousseau, expresses reason itself. In doing so, that is, the subject is held to be free. This approach to freedom, however, is a theory about freedom, because of the scholastic fallacy it contains.

I will dig a bit deeper under the surface of Rousseau's argument. In his interpretation of the implementation of the clauses of the contract Rousseau unduly neglects the interaction within social space, that is, the domain of meaning and not exclusively of truth. He intends to transform the latter into a political space under the auspices of truth. Social space, however, is not primarily the realm of truth; it is the realm of sense and meaning from which the subject emerges qua subject. For Rousseau, the subject's inherent natural goodness is corrupted by culture, most prominently economics, causing relations of dependence that jeopardize freedom. This is what happens in social practices, in the absence of a political space as Rousseau conceives it.

This cultural pessimism is at the root of the following alternative: the continuation of the shackles of the state of nature or the transformation of the latter into a political space. There is no real choice, since the construction of political space and its consequential institutionalisation of conflict must be chosen in the name of truth. The transformation of social space into a political space goes hand in hand with a substitution of truth for meaning.

According to this interpretation, the realm of meaning in which others are recognized as part of 'us', is set aside together with the semantic potential that is engendered by social interaction. Put differently, the only type of interaction Rousseau recognizes is interaction based on legal rules. The institutionalisation of their production within a procedural legitimation model is Rousseau's version of the legitimation of law. The demos has initially sealed propositional contents, still unknown at the moment of the contract, with its consent and so can be considered

---

[23]   G.W.F. Hegel, *Lectures on the History of Philosophy*, III, Medieval and Modern Philosophy, trans. E.S. Haldane and F.H. Simson, (London, 1995), pp. 224-225.

the author of the rules they are now to obey.

In line with this denial of meaningful interaction in social space in favour of institutionalised interaction in political space, Rousseau provides us with a rather thin version of democracy. From the moment however that the subject qua subject is taken seriously, that is, as a subject of meaning related to a social context in which both selves and meaning emerge, a wider avenue for a thicker version of democracy and the democratic legitimation of law is opened. As a subject of meaning, the subject is called to act on his conceptions of freedom, if freedom is to make sense at all. I will explore this idea in the following pages.

The Operationalisation of Political Space: Legislation

Hobbes' and Rousseau' distrust of the subjects' capacities to act on conceptions of freedom pushes them towards a theory that is helpful in avoiding the possibilities of conflict connected to the absence of any prefixed meaning. Hobbes provides us with the best starting point for discovering what the misconception of freedom and democracy consists of, as I will show in this paragraph.

Hobbes and Rousseau argue that the only way to endow social relations with true morality is to enter into the social contract. The operationalisation of political space, as we will see now, or its concrete functioning, as it follows from their theories, makes legislation necessary. Legislation consists of external limitations of freedom that are conceptions about freedom. Any external limitation, on this view, is justified by its very existence.

Freedom in its most pure understanding can only be freedom unlimited or the absence of external impediments. This is Hobbes' position.[24] According to him, freedom is embedded in the *ius naturale*, that is:

> [t]he Liberty each man hath, to use his own power, as he will himselfe, for the preservation of his own Nature; that is to say, of his own Life; and consequently, of doing any thing, which in his own Judgment, and Reason, hee shall conceive to be the aptest means thereunto.[25]

The right to all or the *ius naturale* should however be read in conjunction with the situation of man, to which the previous chapters of Leviathan were dedicated.[26]

---

[24]   T. Hobbes, *Leviathan: or, the Matter, Form, and Power of a Commonwealth, Ecclesiastical and Civil*, in *The English Works of Thomas Hobbes of Malmesbury*, III, W. Molesworth, (ed.) (Aalen, 1966, 2nd ed.), part I, XIV, p. 116: '(...) is understood, according to the proper signification of the word, the absence of externall Impediments: which Impediments, may oft take away part of a mans power to do what hee would; but cannot hinder him from using the power left him, according as his judgment and reason shall dictate to him.'

[25]   Ibid., p. 116.

[26]   Ibid., p. 117: 'And because the condition of Man, (as hath been declared in the precedent chapter) is a condition of Warre of every one against every one; in which case

Fear seems to be the determining parameter in this situation, up to defining human nature all together.

Hobbes then is correct in saying that freedom consists of the absence of any external limitations. These limitations, however, are not necessarily of a physical nature, in that gravitational force may prevent man from flying. The external limitations, that is, must also be taken in the normative sense, as the absence of normative limitations. Under the conditions of freedom unlimited, any X is free to act as he pleases, that is, to act on his own conceptions of freedom. Any Y has the same freedom to do so. Both have a right upon the *ius naturale* to act freely. There are two important aspects of this right that deserve attention.

First, Hobbes suggests that any action can give rise to conflict. I agree with this, but for another reason. In realising his freedom, X acts on a conception of freedom, the meaning of which is inherently social. X does not grasp any conception of freedom as one of its meanings in his own mind, nor does he find it 'out there' growing in the forest. The fact that meanings are social in that they emerge from interaction, is implied by their conflictual character.

Hobbes' approach suggests that any meaning, conflictual in its emergence as it is in my interpretation, can lead to a war of all against all, the latent state of war that can break out at virtually any moment. This, of course, depends on his spurious anthropological theory under which man, by his very nature, so to speak, is after the other's means and body. I do not see any compelling reason why this would be so.

When Hobbes' anthropological theory is, for a moment, severed from the overall mechanism, we get a closer look on a second aspect of the *ius naturale*. Under the definition of the *ius naturale*, it consists of freedom as the absence of external limitations (including normative limitations). Because freedom is from the very outset framed as a right, it could be expected that to any X's right corresponds any Y having a duty to respect X's right.

X having a general right, that is, a right that does not arise out of any special relationship or transaction between men[27] then, should include a corresponding duty of any Y not to interfere with it. Hohfeld has spelled out this type of relation within a legal context.[28] In a more general moral context, from the claim that X has a right it must follow that no one can interfere with it without justification. Put differently, unless it is recognized that interference with another's freedom requires a justification, the notion of right would have no place in morals.[29]

According to Hobbes' anthropological premise, man will not only strike back

---

every one is governed by his own Reason; and there is nothing he can make use of, that may not be a help unto him, in preserving his life against his enemies; It followth, that in such a condition, every man has a Right to every thing; even to one anothers body.'

[27]   *See* H.L.A. Hart, 'Are There Any Natural Rights?', in D. Lyons (ed.), *Rights* (Belmont, 1979), p. 23.

[28]   W.N. Hohfeld, *Fundamental Legal Conceptions as Applied in Judicial Reasoning* (Westport, CT, 1978).

[29]   H.L.A. Hart, 'Are There Any Natural Rights', p. 23.

when attacked, which is his justifiable right to do under the *ius naturale* thesis. If it is a justification, there must correspond some duty to the Ys not to attack X. If he does attack, X is justified in striking back. However, the anthropological thesis fully scoops out Y's duty, since everyone is preparing a possible attack. On this thesis, prevention is the better cure; because all the Ys are unreliable, X's distrust seems justified, and he will attack all the possible Ys that (he believes) threaten him.

What makes the anthropological thesis defective, however, is that it negates the *ius naturale* all together. The anthropological thesis blows up the power of the subjects to a maximum, so that it outweighs any duty of Y's to respect any X's *ius naturale*. It is only without the Hobbesian anthropological thesis that the ius naturale could make sense from a moral perspective, in that every right corresponds with a duty.

Hobbes' spurious anthropological theory results in some version of the might-is-right thesis, not to say that he adds it to his system to justify his version of the totalitarian state. From the moral perspective, because there corresponds no duty of Y to the right of X, the sovereign will be called upon to frame that duty. The absence of this duty as the main defect of Hobbes' theory from the moral perspective stems from his account of man's intrinsically bad nature. According to that premise, he will not feel limited by any duty. At least, if there is one who behaves that way, the others '(...) that otherwise would be at ease within modest bounds, should not by invasion increase their power, they would not be able, long time, standing only on their defence, to subsist. And by consequence, such augmentation of dominion over men, being necessary to a man's conservation, it ought to be allowed him'.[30]

The anthropological theory, the might-is-right thesis, and the resulting *bellum omnium contra omnes* call for some limitations. A theory of freedom, so Hobbes claims, does not work, so he turns to what was called a theory about freedom. In a rudimentary form, it is in the execution of the laws of nature that the power of the sovereign brings in the necessary limitations of the *ius naturale*.

The laws of the sovereign are semantic determinations of the laws of nature. Under Hobbes' nominalistic theory of meaning, the concepts in these laws are semantically meaningless until their meaning is constructed. The reason is that concepts or universals, including the concepts in the laws of nature, do not exist for the nominalist. They have to be created. Before they are created then, every subject is more likely to define them in the way that best fits its own interests, including his desire for power over the other.

If then Hobbes argues that man must be willing to give up his right to all, that is, his *ius naturale*, the laws of nature acquire meaning and become morally as well as legally binding. This moral duty stems, first, from the laws of nature that were binding in the state of nature. Because of the anthropological theory, however, they were far from being effective. Secondly, they are binding on the ground of the *pactum subjectionis*, that is, the promise to submit to the laws of the sovereign. To promise obedience and to withhold it afterwards is a contradiction according to

---

[30]   Hobbes, *Leviathan,* part I, XIII, p. 112.

Hobbes.[31] The promise of obedience gives rise to the sovereign's right to it.

Because and as long as no duty corresponds to the general right to be free, Hobbes theory turns into nonsense. The moral duty that is added to the *ius naturale* via the social contract makes the system complete. The price however is not a minor one. Hobbes argues that, because subjects are unable to live according to conceptions of freedom, it is better to abandon this right, and to submit to the sovereign who is going to impose his definitions of the laws of nature. The latter could have been workable in the state of nature, had men not been living in the conditions of fear that define their nature. The morality that was lacking in the state of nature, that is, the duty to respect others' right, needs a sovereign to impose it. He does so in terms of conceptions about freedom.

Remember in this respect the distinction between 'concepts' and 'conceptions' on the one side and between 'conceptions of' and 'conceptions about' on the other. What the subjects then transfer to the sovereign is their right to act on conceptions of freedom to the sovereign.

This right includes the necessity to concretise freedom in terms of conceptions. Yet, we can see more clearly that the right shows up in two versions, that is, a moral version and a political one. The political version emerges from the contract itself. However, from the reflexive character of freedom is left only the freedom to choose for or against the contract. From then on, all the choices made, that is, all the limitations of freedom in terms of conceptions, will be conceptions about freedom, since they are the sovereign's, not the subject's. This is what the contract essentially consists of.

And so, the civil laws, on Hobbes' argumentation, appear to be embedded in the laws of nature, the only true morality. Civil laws and natural laws are one and the same, as we read from Leviathan, so that truth and meaning can be presented as naturally belonging together. The truth of the matter is, however, that meaning brought in by the civil laws is imposed from the outside on the laws of nature that provide the ontological foundation for the former. Through the intervention of the civil laws, the subject finally joins an ontological definition of himself, so that his moral life is unfolding under the auspices of truth, right and duty. Moral action, that is, is confined to following the rules of the sovereign, that is, to acting on conceptions about freedom.

The Concept of Freedom and the Epistemologization of Philosophy

The distinction between conceptions of freedom and conceptions about freedom in the foregoing analysis can also be used to highlight the construction of the political space. As a reference point, I will use 'freedom unlimited', that is, the situation of freedom that exists in the absence of any external limitation.[32] Conceptually speaking, everyone is free from any external limitation in the case of freedom unlimited. The extension of freedom unlimited consists of all the possible

---

31 *See* S. Goyard-Fabre, *Le droit et la loi selon Thomas Hobbes* (Paris, 1975), p. 133.
32 Unlike in Hobbes, external limitations or laws are normative limitations.

concretisations of freedom.

Conceptions of freedom are conceptions that the subject relates to the concept of freedom. These are choices that are necessarily limitations, because all other possible conceptions are – at least temporarily – excluded. Conceptions about freedom on the contrary are also concretisations of the concept, though they are external limitations in that they do not rely on the subject's choice to operationalize the concept of freedom.

In the absence of any substantive normative datum, there are, logically speaking, no normative limitations. This is what the concept of freedom means under a conceptual analysis. The conceptual analysis of freedom necessarily leads to the conclusion that freedom means the absence of limitations. However, as I have argued, the absence of limitations in this case paradoxically entails the absence of any action whatsoever.[33] Freedom unlimited, that is, is not in itself operational. As a concept, it embraces all possible conceptions, though it does not articulate any of them.

The analysis of the social contract, as Rousseau conceives it, leaves no place for the distinction between conceptions of freedom and conceptions about freedom. This is even far less the case for Hobbes. In Hobbes' account of it, conceptions about freedom are held, upon their attribution to the subject, as conceptions of freedom. The subject is supposed to be the author of them, in that they are considered to be his choices.

As far as Hobbes is concerned, the contract is a double one. The first covenant, the *pactum unionis*, unifies the subjects who do submit, in a second covenant, the *pactum subjectionis*, to the sovereign whose choices are imputed to the subject. What are held to be conceptions of the subject are nothing but choices of the sovereign that provide meaning to the laws of nature. These laws are commands of God, and constitute the only true morality; hence they morally bind the subject. As a consequence, there is no space left for conceptions of the subject from the moment that the sovereign has defined the laws of nature. There is no limitation to the sovereign's power of definition, in that he can always forbid more than what the laws of nature do 'on their own'.[34] In the Hobbesian political space, the subject risks seeing his freedom entirely filled in with conceptions about freedom.

A similar though slightly different conclusion can be drawn from the Rousseau version of the contract. The construction of political space on the basis of the social contract is a matter of truth.[35] This is due to the universality of the clauses of the contract. They are universal in time and space, so they cannot be altered without making them void. As to the content of rules, that is, the concretisation of the concept of freedom, the subject is not asked whether these

---

[33]   L.J. Wintgens, 'Legisprudence as a New Theory of Legislation', pp. 7-8.

[34]   T. Hobbes, *Philosophical Rudiments Concerning Government and Society*, in *The English Works of Thomas Hobbes of Malmesbury*, II, W. Molesworth, (ed.) (Aalen, 1966, 2nd ed.), XIV, 3, p. 187.

[35]   This aspect of Rousseau's version of the social contract is further elaborated in L.J. Wintgens, 'The Fragile Universality of Legalism. Universality of Validity and the Contingency of Law in Rousseau', *Rechtstheorie* (2006): 1-27.

fit to his conceptions of freedom.

The subjects are only asked to express a judgment as to the correspondence of the limitations of freedom proposed by the legislator to the general will. This judgement is not a choice, far less is it a choice of their own. It is a cognitive judgment as to whether the proposed limitations do or do not correspond with the general will. If the majority holds this is the case, this judgment is held to express the general will, and so it is binding upon all.

The cognitive character of this judgment comes to the surface when Rousseau qualifies the judgment of the minority as an error. In consequence, the realm of the meaning of freedom, related as it is to the subject, disappears behind the realm of truth, related as it is to the philosopher's view from nowhere. The concretisations of freedom in terms of conceptions are not their own either, in that they would be connected one way or another to meaning as it stems from interaction in the social space. They are, on the contrary, propositional contents that stem from the legislator's initiative, without any possibility of amendment by the subject.

As a result, meaningful interaction between subjects can only take place within the political space where relations are stamped with true morality as their only possible meaning.

It could be asked, however, on what grounds meaning and truth are related in this way? How, in other words, does the philosopher know that universal truth, typically connected to the view from nowhere, as I have argued above, prevails over social meaning, unless, that is, he presupposes that truth can be known as it is? The latter suggests that theories of reality prevail over theories about reality.

Two problems arise in this respect. The first is how it can be argued that theories of reality represent the latter and thus reach truth as such, according to which theories about reality are of a 'lesser' truth value than their rivals. Under what criterion is it known that a theory represents reality? The second is even more problematic. Why would it be that, if a theory represents reality, an act of will is required for its implementation? Could not the truth of the theory suffice to compel the subject to adhere to it, that is, is truth in itself not sufficient to justify the necessity of submitting to its consequences?

The latter question points to some inconsistency in the theory of the social contract itself. If it purports to set up a democratic organisation of political space, founded on the ontological truth claim that is at its basis, and that serves as a norm for action, the theory does not fulfil its promise. My claim here is that democracy properly understood cannot be based on truth, mainly for two reasons. The first is that democracy as a legitimation procedure of the limitation of freedom must be itself, in order to be consistent, be based on a free decision. It is precisely because there is no external foundation for the organisation of political space that democracy is called upon. It is the absence of any true norm that mandates the choice of a democratic legitimation procedure. This is, as it seems to me, involved in a conceptual analysis of the concept of democracy.

The concept of democracy, like any concept, is an intellectual construction. Being itself a construction, it does not represent any reality to which it refers and that does make it, in a second step, normative. By itself, democracy is not compelling. On the contrary, the concept of democracy is related to the absence of any truth as to how freedom can be legitimately limited, apart from the conceptual need to do so, as I have argued above. It is a matter of commitment or loyalty.[36]

The connection between the democratic organisation of political space and truth, as the theorists of the social contract propose it, leads straightforwardly to strong legalism. I have shown that strong legalism, and the 'thereness' of law relies on the premise that law represents reality. The analysis of the social contract reveals how the idea of representation of reality and the truth of the social contract flow into the idea of the 'thereness' of the law. Law represents reality in that it is based on the social contract the clauses of which are universal, hence true. We face the problem of freedom as it is related to the representational view. The social contract is, so to speak, self-imposing in the name of truth.

The analysis in the foregoing pages confirms the view that the subject's freedom is limited in the name of truth. That is why he has to subscribe to the contract. The subsequent limitations of his freedom, to which the rules of the sovereign aim are then not his own conceptions of freedom. They are conceptions about freedom that are, according to Hobbes' argumentation, considered to be his own, that is, conceptions of freedom. Again, in the name of truth, the conceptions about freedom are necessarily thought of as outweighing conceptions of freedom, because Hobbes' construction precisely aims to show that subjects are not capable of living according to conceptions of freedom. A similar conclusion can be drawn from Rousseau's theory of the social contract.

In placing the organisation of political space under the auspices of truth both writers misconceive the reflexive character of freedom. The reflexive character of freedom includes the active intervention of the subject in its limitation. In Hobbes', and Rousseau's theory, the reflexive use of freedom is limited to the one shot of the social contract. From a different angle, we face here again the distinction between strong and weak legalism that essentially amounts to an articulation of the human subject.

For reasons of brevity, I do not further expose here the anthropological view that underlies legisprudence.[37] A brief summary must suffice here, taking as an example the anthropological view on the work of George Herbert Mead.[38] I argue that the position of the subject qua subject can only be properly understood if it is related to a participant's perspective. Only on that condition can be avoided the nature of the subject's identity as 'identicity', that is, the subject's substantive identity. The latter is what makes the subject identical to others. Identity under this substantive view derives from the Cartesian *cogito*, that is, the ontological anchoring of the subject in the name of truth.

'Identicity' is the theoretical or epistemological variant of the subject's identity, which is alien to, in that it misconceives, the subject qua subject.

---

[36]   *See* N. MacCormick, *Questioning Sovereignty. Law, State, and Nation in the European Commonwealth* (Oxford, 1999), p. 144 ff.

[37]   This anthropological view will be exposed in depth in L.J. Wintgens, *Legisprudence. A New Theory of Legislation* (forthcoming).

[38]   Mainly his *Mind, Self & Society from the Standpoint of a Social Behaviorist*, C.W. Morris (ed.), (Chicago, 1934).

In line with the work of Mead, an alternative view on the subject is proposed, that is, the subject of meaning and not the mere subject of truth. The subject of meaning emerges through interaction with others, through his capacity to take on the other's role. It is through the 'understanding' of the other that the subject is capable of giving meaning to himself as a self. Out of this capacity, that is, the subject's intersubjective or social character emerges.

Meaning, from this perspective, is of an essentially conflictual nature. This is a consequence of its emergent character through interaction. While disagreement or discussion might be, on the Cartesian view, a sign of the absence of truth in the participating subjects, it however is not thereby deprived of sense. Conflict, so I argue, is the source of meaning.

Both Hobbes and Rousseau consider the possibility of conflict as a jeopardy. Within Hobbes' idea of conflict we are invited to adhere to the view that the subject is inherently bad, related to the Augustinian view that man's native impulses are essentially turned to evil ends. Rousseau for his part rather tends to the Socratic view, according to which the subject is essentially good, but his life in society has corrupting effects on him. Both, that is, conclude from this the necessity of the social contract that bestows interaction with the true morality that is missing in the state of nature.

The two theorists of the social contract are in error on at least one point, that is, the historical situatedness of the subject. The necessity of the social contract flows from their denial of the time dimension, one of the main aspects of strong legalism.

They ward off the jeopardy of conflict, at its worst the *bellum omnium contra omnes*, by withdrawing the subject from his social environment and parking him in political space. This operation is justified in their opinion in the name of truth. Consistent as this may sound, the starting premise of their argument is however questionable. What justifies the truth of the premise that the subject is inherently bad (Hobbes) or unavoidably becomes corrupted (Rousseau), is a questionable anthropological fixation in the former or a spurious account of the history of culture in the latter.[39] Theirs, as I will argue in the pages to come, is a misconception of freedom in the name of truth, that is, because of an epistemologization of freedom.

I have pointed on several occasions to the idea of freedom as a principium, that is, freedom as the starting point and the guiding idea in law and politics. The distinction is an important one, and both Hobbes and Rousseau do subscribe to the first but not, or at least not sufficiently, to the second. This results in a denial of the reflexive character of freedom, and so of freedom all together.

Freedom as a starting point – that is, freedom unlimited – logically includes the absence of any limitation. It can only serve as a starting point, however, because action logically requires a limitation of the unlimited variety of possibilities to act in one way or the other. Put differently, the concept of freedom logically requires a

---

[39]   Or, as Kant argues, we have not learned from experience that man has violence as a maxim of action so that they would enter into war with each other, I. Kant, *Grundlegung der Metaphysik der Sitten*, I, *Metapysische Anfangsgründe der Rechtslehre*, in *Kant Werke*, IV, (Darmstadt, 1983, 5th ed.), § 44, p. 430.

conception, that is, a concretisation of freedom, in order for action to be possible at all.

As a concept, freedom is meaningless. It gets meaning insofar as it is concretised through a conception. Conceptions, that is, are concrete meanings of freedom. The fact that freedom as a concept is meaningless in the sense exposed above entails that it must be supplemented with a conception. Because of the reflexive character of freedom, this must be a conception of freedom.

The reflexive character of freedom at the same time refers to freedom as a guiding principle. Any limitation of freedom on the basis of a conception that denies the reflexive character of freedom, that is, a conception about freedom, is external to the subject. It is external insofar as the subject himself is not limiting freedom on the basis of a conception of freedom.

What Hobbes and Rousseau are after is precisely the limitation of freedom in terms of conceptions about freedom, preceded by a preliminary consent to that on the basis of the social contract. Their argument essentially states that the best conception of freedom is to submit to conceptions about freedom. The imputation mechanism of the social contract makes the subject the author of these limitations. This is what the proxy version of legitimation amounts to. The proxy is an a-priori limitation of freedom in that the subject does not yet know on what conceptions his freedom will be limited.[40]

What he does know, though, is that it will not be his conceptions of freedom but conceptions about freedom.

According to this idea, there is virtually no limit to the limitations of freedom. Once the subject has consented to the contract, his freedom can be limited by the Hobbesian sovereign whose rules are morally binding, whatever their content. Rousseau's sovereign for his part can transform any limitation into a binding rule insofar as the majority is favourable to it. Although to a lesser extent, the subject is surrendered to conceptions about freedom, insofar as he belongs to the minority.[41]

If any limitation sooner or later can become binding upon the subject, the reflexive character of freedom risks being destroyed. This is a consequence of the contractual argument, according to which it is a priori better that subjects act on conceptions about freedom than on conceptions of freedom. It seems to Hobbes and Rousseau that this is the only way to avoid the risk of conflict.

---

[40]   *See* N. Luhmann, *Legitimation durch Verfahren*, p. 28; Id, *Grundrechte als Institution. Ein Beitrag zur politischen Soziologie,* (Berlin, 1974, 2nd ed.), p. 141.

[41]   There are some limitations to the power of the sovereign. All the conventions on which a limitation of freedom is based must be general. And the citizen can enjoy freedom, that is, act on a conception of freedom, insofar as freedom is not limited by a conception about freedom (Rousseau, *Du contrat social,* p. 374). In other words, what is not forbidden is permitted. A similar argument is formulated by Hobbes, see Hobbes, *Leviathan,* part II, XXI, pp. 206-207, and later by Kelsen, *see* H. Kelsen, *Reine Rechtslehre* (Vienna, 1967, 2nd ed.), p. 58; Id., 'Zur Theorie der Interpretation', *Revue Internationale de Théorie du Droit* (1934): 9-17. On the incoherence of the latter view, *see* L.J. Wintgens and J.-F. Lindemans, 'Kelsen et le problème des lacunes dans l'ordre juridique' *Revue Interdisciplinaire d'Etudes Juridiques* (1986): 105-121.

Rights

The foregoing analysis of the social contract in Hobbes' and Rousseau's theory brings in the question of rights. Their theories include a version of political rights, defined as the right to participate in the ruling of the state. The common denominator of these participation rights is the social contract. By entering into the contract, they transform themselves into citizens. This makes them, via a detour, the authors of the rules they are abiding by. The detour consists of the intervention of the sovereign in Hobbes, and the legislator followed by the sovereign in Rousseau.

Decisions of the sovereign are binding upon the citizens who are supposed, under the social contract, to have consented to the procedure in the social contract. Their political right to participation is then condensed in their consent to the contract. As a consequence, every rule of the sovereign, whatever its content, will be imputed to them, as if they were its author. Their right to participation is so to speak concentrated in a proxy to the sovereign. Consequential upon that, they only abide by rules to which they have themselves consented, at least by proxy, in that they have consented to the procedure of the creation or change of the rules in the political space. Because of the proxy character of their consent in the social contract, these rules are theirs, so that they cannot be criticized afterwards for being illegitimate. No one can come up against his own action.

The proxy in both Hobbes and Rousseau is nearly complete. If for Hobbes, the *ius naturale*, or the right to everything, is to be limited for the purpose of the realisation of peace or self-defence,[42] it could be concluded that not all rights have to or even can be surrendered to the sovereign. This is correct, since if the right to one thing is given up, the *ius naturale* as a right to all does not have the same extension and so no longer exists as such. If, for example, the right to kill others is transferred to the sovereign, the *ius naturale* is affected in its overall character. The limit that is built in the transfer could result in the conclusion that after entering into the contract the subject finds himself left with a considerable volume of rights, that is, these rights that are not necessary for the realisation of peace and self-defence.

This argument is however defective, because, after the contract, when the subjects live in political space, it is up to the sovereign to define the content of their rights. He has the power to define what is 'necessary for the realisation of peace and self defence'. The consequence of the contract in the Hobbesian version is that the sovereign can define everything insofar as it serves peace and security. If this results in a totalitarian state, where the sovereign has even the right to kill subjects if this serves the purpose of the state, he is permitted to do so, even with the a-priori consent of his subjects.

There is one notorious exception to this, and that is the right to resist violence. Abandoning this right would indeed be inconsistent with the overall logic of Hobbes' construction. If the state is founded with a view to protecting life and securing peace, the subject cannot transfer his right to survival to the sovereign.

---

[42]   Hobbes, *Leviathan,* part I, XIV, p. 118.

This clause of the contract would be void because it violates the laws of nature.[43] The right to his own life is what the subject keeps in his own hands, in that he cannot promise not to defend himself when the sovereign threatens him with death. But, as I said above, this right to resist does not cancel out the sovereign's right to kill the subject if this is deemed necessary for peace and security. The sovereign's right to take someone's life outweighs what then looks as a glimpse of liberalism in Hobbes' theory.

Apart from the somewhat spurious right to resistance, the sovereign leaves the subject with no other rights than those conferred upon him.

Things are different with Rousseau. His is also a proxy version of democracy in that subjects bind themselves to all others to submit to the rules that the sovereign will promulgate. They are bound by these rules in that they bind themselves. This is a proxy, since, from the moment of the social contract on, the legitimation chain turns out to be irreversible. As in Hobbes, subjects are considered the authors of the rules. The form of the law makes any content just. Since all citizens have consented to the procedure of the social contract, i.e., the majority decision, no one can come up against his own action. Since all the citizens have participated in the contract – this is what makes them citizens – and since there is only one contract, the sovereign is not different from their personal unification with all the others. Once they enter into the contract, they are part of the sovereign.[44]

Rousseau, as it seems, is more attentive than Hobbes to political rights, in that they belong to the very status of being a citizen. Citizens have political rights that cannot be taken away, not even by the law. In order to clarify this point, consider the following hypothesis. Can a majority exclude a minority from participation rights?

Can, in other words, the majority take down the minority's citizenship rights or can this part of the citizenship right to vote itself be the object of a vote?

Let's pretend that a proposal is submitted to the sovereign. The proposal provides that the members of a minority group, say, gypsies, will be excluded from participation in the future. Call this the M(ajority) e(xcluding) m(inority) rule (Mem). From a sociological or psychological perspective the voting result is predictable. The target minority will most probably vote negatively.

Apart from that fact, however, and according to the procedure of the contract, the Mem rule will become a valid rule. But is it also a legitimate one? The answer to this question is, it seems, positive and negative.

The answer is positive, since the Mem rule is a general rule, and no general rule can be wrong as Rousseau holds.[45] Legal rules are good independently of their

---

43   Hobbes, *Leviathan,* part I, XIV, p. 127.

44   Rousseau, *Du contrat social,* III, 13, p. 427: '(...) ces mots de *sujet* et de *souverain* sont des corrélations identiques dont l'idée se réunit sous le seul mot de citoyen' (italics in original). The term *correlation* means that, *e.g.,* to be a father includes that you have a son. Inversely, being a son means having a father. So, 'father' and 'son' are correlational terms.

45   Polin, *La politique de la solitude,* p. 88, referring to J.-J. Rousseau, *Lettres écrites de la Montague* in *Oeuvres complètes,* III, Bibliothèque de la Pléiade (Paris, 1964), p. 842; J.-J.

content, by the simple fact that they are rules.

By their general character, rules organise social space and establish relations among individuals, who were solitary beings until then. Rules organise the co-ordination inside social space, and as such, it seems that they can also dispose of the right of citizenship.

This is however a border line case, that entails the negative answer to the question of legitimacy of the Mem rule.

The answer is negative in the following sense. The Mem rule is illegitimate for a more fundamental reason than why it could be considered legitimate. As a matter of fact, a consequence of the Mem rule is that no further rules can be created. When it comes to vote about a new propositional content, according to the Mem rule then in force, those excluded cannot express their vote this time. Consequential upon that, the propositional content submitted to vote could not become a valid rule, for two reasons.

First, Rousseau adds in a footnote in chapter II of book II of *Du contrat social*:

> Pour qu'une volonté soit générale il n'est pas toujours nécessaire qu'elle soit unanime, mais il est nécessaire que toutes les voix soient comptées; toute exclusion formelle rompt la généralite.[46]

The real impact then of the Mem rule is that it alters the terms of the social contract, which was, as shown above, impossible, except by a new unanimous consent. The Mem rule does not fulfil this condition, since it transforms the social contract on a mere majority basis.

Second, and in close connection to that, the Mem rule causes a rift within the sovereign. From then on, we have a class of 'haves' and 'have-nots' citizenship rights. This profoundly alters the nature of title 'sovereign', that is, of being indivisible and inalienable.[47] As a matter of definition, everyone forms part of the sovereign due to the transformation of the individual into a citizen, since subject and sovereign are 'identical correlations', as Rousseau claims.[48]

In the same way, being a citizen means belonging to the sovereign. In connection with the indivisibility of sovereignty, no citizen can be excluded from citizenship against his will. This provides Rousseau's approach with a version of political rights that rely on a stronger basis than Hobbes'[7] account of it. The theory of rights, however, is limited to that. Any other right the subject may have had in the state of nature is, by the very contract, transferred to the sovereign, of which he is himself a member. The rules, then, that are promulgated by the latter are his own work, and, consequently, the citizen is only obeying himself. The rights he has must, by very definition, stem from the authority of the sovereign. Without that, they lack the normative character of a right, since everything he had is transferred

---

Rousseau, *Emile ou de l'éducation*, in *Oeuvres complètes,* IV, Bibliothèque de la Pléiade (Paris, 1969), p. 712: '(...) aucune loi générale n'est mauvaise.'

[46]   Rousseau, *Du contrat social,* II, 2, p. 369, note.

[47]   Ibid., II, 1, p. 368 and ibid., II, 2, p. 369.

[48]   Ibid., III, 13, p. 427.

to the state.

Considering the matter from the perspective of political rights, both Hobbes and Rousseau find themselves going in the direction of a democratic legitimation of law. They consider the participation of the citizen in the construction of the limitation of freedom – that I consider the proper definition of law – essential. They satisfy this democratic requirement in that all the citizens subscribe to the contract, so that, in the end, all can be presumed to be the authors of these limitations.

The political right to equal participation is a necessary condition for their theories to be consistent. If the basic premise of their theories is freedom unlimited, that is freedom because there exist no normative limitations, the starting point of the limitations of freedom must be freedom itself. To this both Hobbes and Rousseau add a premise that affects the concept of freedom in a crucial way.

The premise they add, and on which they found the necessity of the social contract, is the possibility of war. War is not an occasional incident that causes people to limit their freedom in order to stop the war. War is an essential aspect of human nature, in that subjects are inherently bad, as Hobbes says, or dependent on each other for economic reasons, as we read from Rousseau. Both human nature and economic dependence are causes of war that must be prevented or institutionalised.

Their argument is presented as if this premise, of a purely factual nature as it is, affects the concept of freedom in a normative way. That is to say that, because of the additional premise, of which only God knows whether it is true or false, the concept of freedom is affected at its core. The core of freedom in its unlimited version is, by its very definition, equality. If everyone has an unlimited volume of freedom, it is in its 'unlimitedness' that everybody's freedom is equal. No one has an a-priori right to limit another's freedom.[49]

Hobbes and Rousseau – not unrealistically – suggest that this is barely workable. Their suggestion though is not of a normative nature. If they add it as a premise to their construction, the stable rock they claim to have discovered vanishes.

Hobbes and Rousseau aim to show that human nature is inherently bad or is good but not resistant to life in society without being corrupted, so that freedom unlimited leads to chaos. There is no a-priori *normative* reason however, as both I guess would admit, why 'freedom unlimited' or 'freedom as distance' will cause chaos. Their argument for the failure of freedom unlimited or freedom as distance is of a *factual* nature that Hobbes claims to have ontologically anchored. Rousseau rather takes it as an unavoidable effect of living in society.

If both then can be thought to be at the basis of the democratic organisation of political space, in that the latter depends on the act of will that is the social contract, the question rises as to the voluntary nature of the contract itself. It has been argued above that, according to the general thesis of the epistemologization of philosophy in the Modern philosophical project, the act of will of which the social

---

[49]   *See* J. Locke, *Two Treatises of Government*, in *The Works of John Locke*, V (Aalen, 1963), second treatise, § 4-5, pp. 339-340.

contract consists is constrained by epistemological rather than normative reasons.

Were the contract a pure act of will, the arguments would be of a normative nature. This foundation however falls apart under the weight of the factual premise concerning human nature. The subject has to act on the truth of the factual premise of the bad or corrupted human nature. The latter in turn requires the insight that the subject fails to act on his conceptions of freedom and in doing so fails to recognize the normative limits of freedom that is freedom as distance.

What then is left of freedom as a right? It turns out that the consequences for freedom are drastic, if not draconian. What the subject is required to do is to surrender to the power of the state that is supposed to be created by his own will. This power counterbalances the possibility of war, always lurking round the corner. In Hobbes as well as in Rousseau, the state determines the extent of its power, in that it can decide what limitations are necessary for peacekeeping. In the end, for both of them, this limitation can be complete, in that anything can be forbidden by the state, if this is thought useful for that purpose.

Anything can be regulated by the state. Every conception of freedom, that is, can be outweighed by a conception about freedom, and this substitution is *ipso facto* legitimated. This last qualification could allow the conclusion that Hobbes and Rousseau favour a totalitarian state. Apart from some observations in the next pages, I will not enter into this discussion here, at least not in comprehensive detail. I may be clear that if the state is capable of imposing its conception about freedom for any possible conception of freedom, the risk of destruction of the reflexive character of freedom is a serious one. And if the reflexive character of freedom is affected, the concept of freedom crumbles down.

My point here is the following. As I have argued at the beginning of this chapter, the legitimation chain that starts with the conclusion of the social contract, apart from the reasons for which it is concluded, is irreversible. According to the diagnosis of Hobbes and Rousseau, the reason why this is so can be articulated as follows. Because of the risk of war, that is, some total conflict, the breaking out of a conflict must be conjectured in advance. This risk, in their opinion, can only be outweighed by some kind of counterbalance to the totality of all power that can be invested in a conflict. The state so they believe, is strong enough to exorcise the demon of conflict. If the legitimation chain were not irreversible, then some – or even most or all – of the limitations imposed by the state could be questioned over and over again, so that conflict of the size they sketch reappears.

The irreversible legitimation chain that constitutes the democratic organisation of political space provides a straightforward justification of strong legalism, the main aspects of which were discussed elsewhere.[50]

Hobbes' and Rousseau's views of man and society claim to be true, as a representation of reality. Because of the ontological anchoring of their views, their theories are a representation-reproduction of reality. However, their qualification of human nature as the ultimate ground for their construction is, on closer inspection, an accidental aspect they claim to be essential to human nature. On that argument, their approach turns out to be a representation-construction of reality.

---

[50]   *See* Wintgens, 'Legisprudence as a New Theory of Legislation', pp. 6-11.

Politics, that is, is the source of conflict par excellence, and the aim of the construction of political space is precisely to allay these conflicts. Law as the spin-off of the construction of political space is the opposite of politics, the warrior effects of which it is called upon to banish. In switching the perspective from construction to reproduction, that is, in arguing that what is a construction of reality is a mere reproduction of it, we see the strategy of strong legalism at work.

The construction both of political space and of law is naturalised. The legitimation programme aims at preventing conflicts from showing up, and this is what happens when the legitimation chain would be reversible. Hence, it is not. In proceeding that way, they turn off the button of time. The representation of reality aims at truth, and truth is eternal.

The irreversible character of the legitimation chain fits equally well the instrumentalistic position of strong legalism. If values are to be chosen, the risk of conflict increases. The problem becomes apparent once it is clear that the realisation of freedom by the subjects relies on a conception of freedom.

Because of the conflicts these choices generate, subjects are required to transfer the capacity of choice itself, that is, their capacity to live according to conceptions of freedom, to the state. The latter is going to provide the true morality that will frame their relations. Since they do not know yet which limitations will be imposed on them at the 'moment' of the contract, the latter implies that the state's choices are simply substituted for their conceptions of freedom. Since these 'choices' are true, they will not appear as choices that, by their very nature, are contingent.

Because the organisation of political space or the state is the only purpose of the social contract, and because only the state can freely decide what limitations can be imposed, the state is to be considered the only source of law, hence, etatism.

Finally, as a consequence of their reliance on natural science as the apex of rationality, and because of the naturalisation of political space and the subsequent laws that emerge from there, law itself is considered to belong to reality and so it can be studied with the help of the method of natural science.

In the next section, I will go somewhat deeper into one further aspect of this. Naturalisation of politics and law from the epistemological perspective goes hand in hand with and is supported by the concept of sovereignty. It is this concept, so I will argue, that contributes to the irreversibility of the legitimation chain in procedural models of legitimation.

Sovereignty, or the Black Box in the Legitimation Chain

The irreversibility of the legitimation chain is sealed with the introduction of a concept, familiar in political philosophy since Bodin, who framed it in a version that was promised a career up to the 20th century. It is the concept of sovereignty. There is, I think, not too much exaggeration in saying that this concept is at the basis of at least as much confusion as it intended to resolve. Taken as it stands, the concept was known from theology, referring to the omnipotence of God. Sovereignty is an aspect of God's omnipotence, that is, to act according to his unlimited power.

The meaning of sovereignty, once it shows up in political philosophy, then is in a way difficult to grasp. One way to get a hold on this difficulty is the following. If the reality of God is taken seriously, it is impossible to bring it under a concept. Concepts are man-made, and by their very nature they fix the extension of what belongs to it and what does not. The meaning of a concept then follows from what is and what is not included, since meaning is differential.

The difficulty then lies in the secularisation of this attribute of God. Political philosophy, however, or civil philosophy as Hobbes calls it, has attempted to do so, and to frame one of its basic concepts in the image of this divine attribute, neglecting thereby a consequential internal paradox in the concept of sovereignty itself. The sovereign is so powerful that he cannot limit his own sovereignty. This paradox illustrates some of the paradoxes of the secularisation thesis advocated by Hans Blumenberg. On that thesis, secularisation is a legal process upon which the sacred is dispossessed or expropriated.[51] Carl Schmitt for his part upholds a version of the secularisation thesis in that according to him all the significant concepts of the modern doctrine of the state are secularised theological concepts.[52] This position is pretty close to Hobbes'. In assigning sovereignty to the state, Hobbes finds himself on the very track of secularisation, in calling the sovereign the 'mortal God'.[53]

The concept of sovereignty is very helpful in upholding the irreversible direction of the legitimation chain. In assigning sovereignty to the ruler, the participants engage in an irreversible chain of legitimation of his acts. With the social contract, sovereignty comes down to earth, so to speak. Its function, so it appears, is to obstruct the reversibility of the legitimation chain, if it would come to the mind to question the legitimacy of the power of the sovereign. This is simply impossible, since sovereignty has no limits, so that the power called 'sovereign' cannot be limited or questioned, not by the power holder and certainly not by those submitted to his power. Both Hobbes and Rousseau agree on that: sovereignty is inalienable and it cannot be divided.[54]

Unsurprising but decisive for this point is that the sovereign is always right. The sovereign cannot err in that his definitions of the laws of nature are true, according to Hobbes. In a similar vein, Rousseau holds that the sovereign expresses the general will that cannot err; so his laws are unquestionable as well.[55]

The consequences of this view are not hard to understand. Sovereignty, once it is built into political space, will operate as a black box. The ultimate source of

---

[51]   H. Blumenberg, *The Legitimacy of Modernity,* trans. R.M. Wallace (Cambridge, MA, 1983), p. 19 ff.

[52]   C. Schmitt, *Politische Theologie. Vier Kapitel zur Lehre der Souveränität* (Munich, 1934, 2nd ed.), p. 49.

[53]   Hobbes, *Leviathan*, part II, XVII, p. 158.

[54]   Rousseau, *Du contrat social,* II, pp. 1-2; Hobbes, *Leviathan*, part II, XVIII, pp. 167-168.

[55]   Rousseau, *Du contrat social,* II, 3, pp. 371-372; Hobbes, *Leviathan,* part II, XVIII, p. 163.

power, as Kant later claims, is unfathomable.[56] Any of its outputs is just be definition, as both Hobbes and Rousseau confirm. As a matter of logic, the magic of the black box prevents questioning of the outputs in any of its aspects. The participants cannot complain since they have created the sovereign and promised submission in Hobbes. They have created the sovereign and are part of it in Rousseau. As for Kant, they had a duty to enter into a State, so they cannot contest the subsequent duties resting on their shoulders.

Sovereignty has the propriety of lending itself to the justification of both a monarch by divine right and a totalitarian state. The monarch by divine right is the representative of God on earth, and Hobbes' sovereign is after all not far from that. Although the subjects have created him, he is called to implement the laws of nature that are the laws of God. Under the monarchy of divine right, the monarch is exercising the divine prerogatives that are included in, and of which consists, sovereignty. On this view, the sovereign does not have the power to violate the laws of God. As a matter of logic, he has no permission to do so, though he has the power to define their content according to Hobbes.

Sovereignty, on this view, also seems to support the totalitarian state to the invention of which both Hobbes and Rousseau have contributed. Hobbes' contribution can be found in his assimilation of law and morality, so that any law of the sovereign *ipso facto* entails a moral obligation to obey it, whatever its content may be. Hobbes for his part is closer to the totalitarian state, in that the subjects can directly appoint an omnipotent sovereign. In acting that way they can realise without detours Plato's paradox of democracy.[57] A majority can appoint one person who will decide about what is right or wrong, without any point of return inside political space, except the benevolence of the tyrant himself to withdraw from power.

Rousseau's contribution may be said to consist of his establishing the tyranny of the majority. In contrast to Hobbes, however, he wards off the realisation of the paradox of democracy, since the majority cannot appoint a tyrant without dividing sovereignty. At least this path to the totalitarian state is barred, since this act of appointment would be void.

On the qualification of sovereignty as a black box, we enter into the realm of absolute power that, by its very nature, cannot be legally limited, as Austin has argued.[58] Even Kant, for whom metaphysics is only legitimate within the limits of reason, does not hesitate to connect the rules of the sovereign to commands of God, in that one has to act as if the rules of the sovereign are His commands.[59]

---

[56]   Kant, *Rechtslehre*, p. 473 ff.

[57]   Plato, *The Republic*, books VI-X, trans. P. Shorey (Cambridge, MA, 1946), VIII, 562c, p. 305. This 'paradox of democracy' makes Popper plead for a limited version of sovereignty, *see* K.R. Popper, *The Open Society and its Enemies*, I, *The Spell of Plato* (London, 1966, 5th ed.), p. 123 ff.

[58]   J. Austin, *The Province of Jurisprudence Determined and the Uses of the Study of Jurisprudence*, H.L.A. Hart (ed.) (London, 1971, 4th ed.), p. 254 ff.

[59]   Kant, *Rechtslehre*, p. 438: '(A)lle Obrigkeit ist von Gott (...)', and ibid., 456: '(D)er Gesetzgeber ist heilig.' See also F. Ost and J. Lenoble, *Droit, mythe et raison. Essai*

The black box metaphor aptly illuminates another aspect of the rules that emerge from political space. That is to say, sovereignty covers all of the operations of the ruler with perfect rationality. From this perspective, the rationality of the legislator as a premise of legal interpretation, is usefully supported by the concept of sovereignty. Rationality of the legislator as a premise of the science of law and the concept of sovereignty corroborate each other.[60] Their operational force and their mutual strengthening much depends on their impenetrable character. Kant mentioned this in relation to sovereignty. The fictitious character of rationality does not resist any serious analysis, except to state it as some regulative ideal in legal interpretation that contributes to upholding the validity of legal rules.[61]

Sovereignty that is, plays a decisive role in the legitimation chain proper to strong legalism that has been analysed throughout this chapter. Apart from some weak right to resist the violence of the sovereign in Hobbes and the right not to be excluded from the sovereign in Rousseau, appealing to sovereignty can outweigh all other 'rights'. Under strong legalism, the rationality of the legislator, in that it reflects the irrefutable presumption of the perfection of his rules, is then an epistemological confirmation of sovereignty.

Consequential upon this, political philosophy, the question of rights, and the theory of law are all covered by this impenetrable concept of sovereignty. However impenetrable it is, it fixes a relation between the organisation of political space, the subsequent laws that flow from it and the rights the citizens can enforce. Following the construction of the political space the way Hobbes and Rousseau see it, and the subsequent definition of the subject as a citizen, we establish a profound transformation of the subject qua subject. It is a transformation of the subject qua subject into a subject-citizen whose identity is framed as a collection of rights and duties as constructed by the laws promulgated in political space.

What is of interest in the foregoing in relation to the theme of this book is the connection between sovereignty and the theory of law. More specifically, we should explore some of the aspects of the relation between sovereignty and the validity of law to shed some more light on the possibilities of an alternative view, that is, a view that does justice to the subject qua subject.

One way of seeing the matter is as follows. Where the power of the sovereign is unlimited, it can be observed that the content of laws is a matter of choice. Since the starting point of the construction of political space is freedom unlimited, no constraints as to the concretisation of freedom can be said to exist before that.

From the moment on that the sovereign comes into existence, any of his choices are legitimated in that they are imputed to the subjects who have consented to the contract. So, what the sovereign says – even stronger, whatever he says – becomes law. Whether this leads to totalitarianism or not is a matter of political philosophy that is not our concern here. What is of concern though is that, at best according to a few formal rules of procedure, any concretisation of freedom can

---

sur la dérive mytho-logique de la rationalité juridique (Brussels, 1980), p. 443 ff.

[60]   *See* F. Ost and M. van de Kerchove, *Jalons pour une théorie critique du droit* (Brussels, 1987), p. 100 ff.

[61]   Ibid.

acquire the form of a conception about freedom, to which the subject is supposed to have consented.

When conceptions about freedom take on the form of a law they are substituted for conceptions of freedom. This is what the mechanism of political space produces: each and every conception of freedom is transformed into a conception about freedom. When we consider this from the perspective of the subject, any of his conceptions of freedom are automatically outweighed by conceptions about freedom. Put differently, what the subject is left with are conceptions of freedom that are at large, without any normative value. They cannot be opposed to the sovereign's conceptions about freedom.[62] The subject-citizen is under constant pressure of redefinition by the sovereign, in that any of his conceptions of freedom can, without further reason, be pushed aside in favour of a conception about freedom. The main reason is, as a matter of fact, the contract and the consent to its further procedural unfolding within political space, without knowing in advance what their content will be.

Without necessarily leading to totalitarianism in the usual sense of the word, it installs into political space the embryo of the Trojan horse of the overwhelming state action we establish nowadays and call the welfare state. If it need not result in a totalitarian state that has a right of life and death over its citizens, it does not prevent the state from taking serious parts in economic life, both as a partner and – mainly – as a regulator. This can be considered yet another form of totalitarianism, that is, the fact that the sovereign regulates virtually every aspect of social life. This form of totalitarianism is founded in the belief of unlimited instrumentalism, and the possibilities of law to steer virtually every aspect of social interaction.

In conferring rights and duties on economic partners, on marriage partners, and on citizens as claimants of social security rights, in defining the content of education through subsidizing institutions that teach the 'right' contents, or by withholding recognition of degrees from institutions that in its opinion do not, to mention but a few examples, political space with it sovereign power creeps into the very definition of the subject: his rights are constructed by the sovereign, so that the former is only what he is by the grace of the latter which is, in turn, as we read from Rousseau, by the very fact of being, what it ought to be.[63]

The form of totalitarianism that is induced by strong legalism, with its stress on instrumentalism, is, of course, of a different brand to the forms of totalitarianism we have witnessed throughout history. It relies on the belief in the unlimited potential of law itself to regulate social interaction. The sovereign need not be a ruthless tyrant, as historical remnants of totalitarianism may suggest. It can also be a meddlesome mother-in-law. While respecting the spheres protected by rights on

---

[62]   This would amount to an act of resistance, which is a contradiction for Hobbes. The subject promises obedience when entering into the contract. To promise obedience and not fulfil the promise is a contradiction as Hobbes holds (*see supra*). On the impossibility of a right to resist to the rules of the sovereign and the contradiction it entails, *see also* Kant, *Rechtslehre*, p. 438.

[63]   Rousseau, *Du contrat social,* I, 7, p. 363: 'Le Souverain par cela qu'il est, est toujours ce qu'il doit être.'

which impingement is proscribed, nothing prevents the sovereign from limiting freedom in the domains where his action is permitted with such a density that the web of his regulations suffocates the subject qua subject. The subject qua subject, one remembers, is the subject that emerges from social interaction, who is embedded in interaction with others from where his self and meaning emerges. I hasten to add that this subject is also a capable subject, that is, a subject capable of acting on conceptions of freedom, and so should be held to be a responsible moral agent.

What the concept of sovereignty allows then, apart from the spheres protected by human rights or pre-state rights, is a redefinition of the subject in terms of rights and duties according to rules. As a result, the normative density of the external limitations of the sovereign, as we testify today, reaches such a degree as to deny any place for the subject qua subject, that is, a subject as a responsible moral agent capable of social interaction without a state looking over his shoulder. And without a subject looking over his back to check whether there is no state that is structuring, pre-structuring, or restructuring his actions on conceptions of freedom. As the late Pierre Bourdieu so expressively suggested, the state has taught us to think that nothing can be thought of without the state.[64]

The concept of sovereignty, for all the difficulties it contains on the level of definition, pre-empts the sovereign from any justification of his rulings. This is the logical consequence of the proxy model of the social contract. If on the one hand the participants in the contract agree to create an instance that has the ultimate power within political space that they are setting up, then there can be no argument for criticizing the outcomes of his power. If on the other hand, this power is 'defined' as having no limits, this only reinforces the idea that no justification is needed for its exercise. Hence, any proposition of the sovereign is *ipso facto* justified on the proxy the participants have previously given to him.

Here as elsewhere, the theory of social contract, from the perspective of sovereignty this time, leads to what was called 'strong legalism'. If any proposition the sovereign makes acquires the form of law, this results not only in a permanent outweighing of the conceptions of freedom of the subjects, but also in a virtually unlimited number of limitations. According to the proxy model that operates at the background of political space, the participants in the contract are ready to accept any of the limitations that are imposed by the sovereign. Any proposition that recognizably has the characteristics of a rule from the sovereign therefore is a valid law.

Apart from the legitimation problem raised by the proxy model in that it outweighs, without any reason different from the initial proxy, conceptions of freedom, there are good grounds for believing that the exponential growth of the legal system nowadays is an unintended inheritance from the Modern philosophical project. Any proposition that gets the required form is, for that reason alone, a valid limitation of freedom. Put differently, any proposition that gets the stamp of the sovereign is a valid rule. You may call this 'stamp validity'.

Stamp validity is not outweighed by rights of any sort. Rights only limit the

---

64   Bourdieu, *Raisons pratiques*, p. 101 ff.

possible content of rules, not their volume, number or normative density. So, if rights reserve domains of action where conceptions of freedom prevail, they do not prevent the overwhelming growth of limitations or conceptions about freedom in the domains covered by the proxy. The tremendous impact of strong legalism induced by the proxy version of democracy will only be strengthened as long as no counterweight is set up against its nearly perverse effects.

Reversals in the Legitimation Chain

My diagnosis may look fairly pessimistic. The overwhelming volume of external limitations of freedom that we witness nowadays, as a consequence of the political part of the Modern philosophical project, may induce the belief that self-legislation, as one of the main points on its agenda, has become a whim. The legitimation chain that is started by the social contract has been argued to be of a unilateral character. Within this chain, the limitations of freedom on the part of the sovereign, and largely of the subsequent instances executing them, are unilaterally justified.

It is the social contract that starts the legitimation chain, and so all the subsequent acts of the sovereign, the executive, and the judiciary are imputed to the will of those who subscribed to the contract.

In doing so, as I have argued throughout this chapter, the social contract absorbs *ab initio* any questioning of the external limitations of legitimacy. It can therefore be said that a legal system based on it, contains its own principle of legitimation, so we read from Weber.[65] This legitimation model I have called the proxy model from the proxy the subjects give to the sovereign.

Dworkin has recently reaffirmed this idea, in that, according to him, 'we live in and by the law' and that 'the law makes us what we are'.[66] If this view is correct, the law from the state, that is, is going to mediate the subjects' existence. The proxy model, as it was called, keeps all the promises of self-legislation, but only, as it seems, concerning the initial setting, not when it comes to the operationalisation of political space. Indeed, the limitation of freedom subsequent to the initial limitation on a conception of freedom as it results in the contract is replaced by conceptions about freedom.

Despite the overall pessimistic tone of the diagnosis, there are however also some encouraging points to be noted. The negative tone can be fine-tuned a little. Even under the proxy model of legitimation, some reversals are built into the legitimation chain. I will briefly comment on four of them. These possibilities of reversing the chain of legitimation, however limited they are, may help to overcome the idea of the new totalitarianism, that is, the overwhelming impact of the overactive sovereign on social interaction. It may help us to overcome the idea, that we only 'live in and by the law' that is unilaterally justified.

---

[65]   M. Weber, *Grundriss der Sozialökonomik*, III, *Wirtschaft und Gesellschaft* (Tubingen, 1922), p. 124.

[66]   R. Dworkin, *Law's Empire* (Cambridge, 1986), p. vii.

The reversals built into the legitimation chain give some rough idea of the potential of legisprudence. The subject can enter into the process of legitimation, in actively contributing to it, or in challenging some of its outcomes. The four reversals in the legitimation chain I will briefly comment on are: elections, referenda, constitutional review and administrative review. It goes without saying that they are only commented upon by way of illustration, without further ambitions.

Let us start with elections. Sovereignty according to Rousseau,[67] as against Sieyes and Kant,[68] cannot be divided, and so, in his view, cannot be represented without destroying freedom. Rousseau's objection to representation, and so, election by the members of the sovereign, is not wholly consistent, as it seems, since the majority binds the minority, and so represents it. If we were to push the point, we could say that the majority represents the better part of truth, since no one can know it better than the majority.[69]

Free and regular elections are considered nowadays the apex of democratic legitimation, which is a procedural model of legitimation. In accordance with the claim that they are a necessary condition of democratic legitimation,[70] what elections effectuate, apart from a representation of power, is a reversal of the legitimation chain. If elections, as a matter of logic, precede legislation, they also succeed legislation. From the latter perspective, they are a means of control of the acts of the sovereign in that they can include a critique of legislation. This confirms the position that statutory law is only temporarily valid. By voting out the majority, its legislative activity can be criticized. It can also be the other way around. By a re-election of the majority, the constituency can be considered to actively contribute to the legitimation of the former's past legislation, again via a reversal in the legitimation chain.

Elections come close to the social contract, without being able to alter it. A change in the social contract needs unanimity, and on Rousseau's version, there is not so much to change in the contract's clauses without making it void. Nevertheless, elections may be considered a form of confirmation of the contract, by voting out an existing or voting in a new set of power representatives.

A second mechanism aiming at some similar effects as elections is the referendum. It can be considered a form of election, and as a matter of fact it may turn out to be a test of popularity for the sovereign. The reluctance about making the pre- or post-legislative referendum binding, so that, as a matter of fact, 'the

---

[67] Rousseau, *Du contrat social,* III, 15, p. 430: 'Le peuple anglais pense être libre; il se trompe fort, il ne l'est que durant l'élection des membres du parlement; sitôt qu'il sont élus, il est esclave, il n'est rien'.

[68] Sieyes, *Qu'est-ce que le Tiers Etat,* pp. 177-178; Kant, *Rechtslehre,* § 52, p. 464: 'Alle wahre Republik aber ist und kann nichts anders sein als eine repräsentativen System des Volkes (...).'

[69] *See* R. Spaemann, 'Die Utopie der Herschaftsfreiheit', *Merkur. Deutsche Zeitschrift für europäisches Denken* (1972): 735-752.

[70] L.H. Tribe, *American Constitutional Law,* (Mineola, NY, 1988, 2nd ed.), p. 1097 (democracy envisions rule by successive temporary majorities).

people' and not its representatives is exercising sovereignty,[71] can be considered an eructation of strong legalism. The reluctance can indeed be taken to be a confirmation of the unilaterality of the chain of legitimation.

The referendum, however, as a matter of pre-legislative advice or consent, can be analogised to systems of policy-making, and so contribute to the legitimation of external limitations.[72] Apart from the political trouble that can be caused by a referendum, and apart from the risk of manipulation of public opinion that may come with it, the important aspect is that with the referendum we go back one step in the chain of legitimation, which amounts to its reversal.

Under the proxy model, a referendum is superfluous, since every act of the sovereign is a priori legitimated on the social contract. In reversing the legitimation chain by a referendum, the proxy is qualified in that the subjects are called in to actively contribute to the legitimation of a sovereign's legislative act.

The third and the fourth example of reversal of the chain of legitimation are of a slightly different character, in that they do not call for the subject to contribute to the legitimation of external limitations, but, on the contrary, allow him to challenge the latter's validity.

The third mechanism of reversal of the legitimation chain is constitutional review. Although it is sometimes criticized from the perspective of democracy, in that constitutional judges are not elected and have life tenure, it seems to me that neither of the arguments is convincing.[73] Even if judges were elected, the argument would go, this would enhance corruption. Life tenure, for its part, is said to give to them too much power, and yet enhance their irresponsibility. They are not responsible towards a constituency, while however exercising some prerogatives of the sovereign.

Without dwelling deeper on the problem of judicial review, I do not for my part see the point of these objections. If constitutional judges have the tremendous power they have, this is all the more a reason in favour of their election, and not against it. Arguing that it guarantees their independence can challenge the tenure argument. So, the only critique that seems to hold from this perspective is the objection to their appointment by the executive in combination with tenure. If they are elected and if their appointment is confirmed by an act of parliament, the objection does not hold.

Hobbes, Rousseau, Kant, and of course Hegel, would strongly oppose judicial review, because they all adhere in their own way to the idea of the irreversibility of the legitimation chain. Even the appointment of the constitutional judge by parliament would not find grace in their eyes, because it includes a division of

---

[71]   The Belgian Council of State's position is that a referendum is not compatible with representative democracy, Council of State, Section of Legislation, advice of May 15, 1985, *Parlementaire Stukken,* Chamber, 1983-84, 783/1; Council of State, Section of Legislation, Advice of January 21 1997, *Parlementaire Stukken* Flemish Council, 1996-97, 470/2.

[72]   Tribe, *American Constitutional Law,* p. 1096.

[73]   *See,* among many others, J. Waldron, *The Dignity of Legislation* (Cambridge, 1999).

sovereignty, which none of them would applaud.

Constitutional review reverses the legitimation chain in that the subjects can challenge an external limitation issued by the sovereign. Opponents to it, apart from the arguments they may provide to sustain their position, stick to a proxy model of legitimation in that the legislator has the first but also last word. One may wonder why a constitutional state does not, as a matter of logic, have a constitutional court, as was the case until 1989 in Belgium. What does a constitution mean in the absence of any mechanism of control, and hence, a reversal of the chain of legitimation? It simply means that the legislator is always right.

A fourth example of a reversal of the legitimation chain consists of the technique of challenging an act of the executive before an administrative jurisdiction. Although the administrative judge will not enter into the substance of the external limitation, and can only check its conformity to the power-conferring rules, the annulment of an act pushes the legitimation chain one step back. The annulment of an executive act erases the latter from the legal system, and so it cannot serve to legitimate any external limitation of a lower degree. It puts the executive back into the position where there was no external limitation, and so the chain of legitimation can be said to have been reversed.

In the foregoing, I have tried to make clear the character of the legitimation chain that operates in strong legalism. From an ideal typical perspective, strong legalism goes hand in hand with a model of legitimation that includes the irreversibility of that chain. The mechanisms described above that illustrate the possibilities of reversal are, conceptually speaking, incompatible with strong legalism.

The reason for this may be clear. Strong legalism includes a 'one shot' legitimation, in that the legitimation chain is activated at the 'moment' of the social contract. The train cannot be stopped, far less reversed, because the operation of legitimation under the proxy model is of a timeless nature. Timelessness of legitimation excludes by its very nature the possibility of the chain's reversal, because this entails a return in time, that is, back to the moment of elections, back to the moment before the enactment of a statute or an executive order, back to the moment of the social contract in the case of a referendum.

The examples should not be taken to mean more than they do, that is, an illustration of the possibility of a reversal of the legitimation chain. These reversals call in the subject on specific moments and for specific purposes, that is, to actively contribute to the legitimation of law or to challenge it

With the idea of a reversal of the legitimation chain, we are at the very heart of the dynamics of procedural legitimation models. In the next section, I propose to explore the idea of a more general reversal of this chain on the part of the sovereign. Under strong legalism, a legislator is not to give reasons for his decisions. Any of them is a priori legitimated on the general proxy. His reading of the constitution comes with the presumption that it is the best possible, since it is covered by the irrefutable presumption of rationality. A more general reversal of the chain suggests that a constitution can be read differently.

Strong Legalism and Legisprudence: Two Ways of Reading a Constitution

The representational metaphysics operational at the background of strong legalism, together with instrumentalism, etatism, and universality or timelessness are supported by the scientific approach in philosophical thinking in general and political and legal thinking in particular. This turns out, as I have argued, to be a discourse without a subject. The theorist as well as the moral agent is caught within a system of rules that represents reality. These rules are held to be ontologically true and so leave no space for responsible action by both the theorist and the subject as a moral agent.

The reversals in the legitimation chain, articulated above, show some mechanisms built into the chain that allow the subject to contribute to it in an active way in elections and referendum, or in a critical way by challenging the acts of the sovereign or his executive.

One of the consequences of the representational metaphysics for practical reason is that the latter is not held to be practical at all. On the strong legalistic view, practical matters are transformed into theoretical ones.

Under the proxy model of legitimation, the sovereign is irrefutably presumed to have followed the rules of the constitution. On this point, Lawrence Friedman's analysis of Weber's legalism is instructive. According to Friedman, legalism includes the duty for the judge to give reasons for his decision. Judges cannot avoid taking decisions; in addition to that they are expected to give reasons for it and they are confined to a – more or less – closed system of rules.[74]

Legislatures for their part do not have to articulate reasons for their decisions. Their decisions are, as Weber puts it, irrational.[75] Statutory enactment, so we read from Friedman's observations, is non-legalistic in that it cannot be deduced from any existing set of rules, like judicial ruling can and must be. This is not the same, however, as saying that there are no reasons at all for legislative enactment. What is said, is that legislative enactment does not contain the reasons in that it does not express the reasoning that lies behind its passing.

The idea that legislators, unlike judges, are not to give reasons for their decisions is, according to Friedman, the proper characteristic of legalism – strong legalism as used here. Legal systems, as he reads from Weber, contain within themselves a principle or principles of legitimacy. When the logic of derivation is a closed one, it is called legalistic. If it is, on the contrary, open, it is called non-legalistic.[76]

This characterization of legalism in my view is however unsatisfactory. It suggests that, depending on the actor in the system, the latter is either legalistic or non-legalistic. So, the system is legalistic from the perspective of the judge, and non-legalistic from the perspective of the legislator. On this view, Friedman draws a grand dividing line between legislative and judicial ruling. Judges should give

---

[74]   L.M. Friedman, 'On Legalistic Reasoning. A Footnote on Weber', *Wisconsin Law Review* (1966): 150.

[75]   Ibid., p. 154.

[76]   Ibid., pp. 158-160.

reasons for their decisions, showing that and how they are following rules. Legislators for their part are exempt from this. They are, unlike the judge, not bound to a closed set of rules.

This view easily slips into error, since it implies the suggestion that judges follow rules in that they merely deductively apply the latter. Their following rules amounts to showing how they deduce concrete decisions from general rules, and this is what judicial motivation consists of. From there it follows that legislators create rules that judges apply. The former is a matter of decision, hence a form of action, while the latter is held to be a matter of application, hence a cognitive operation.

Both positions are in need of a qualification, upon which some similarity between the activities of the legislator and the judiciary can be established. Judges, like legislators, take decisions, that is, they make norms. Judges make individual norms,[77] while legislators make general ones. Judges should make their decisions within the framework of the rules set out by the legislator. This is what the separation of powers requires. In making their decisions, they should show how they do, that is, they are required to give the reasons that support their decisions. Judges, in making their decisions, do follow the rules of the legislator; they do not merely apply them. Their following rules is to become apparent from the reasons they give to support their decisions. If they were only applying rules in a syllogistic manner, no reasons should be given because anyone could easily establish whether a decision is right or wrong, like anyone can control whether a conclusion is correctly drawn from the premises at hand.

My claim is that legislators in their turn, like judges, do follow rules. There is no doubt that legislators are bound to the rules of the constitution. This is the essence of the rule of law. It makes even less sense to hold, as with judges, that the legislator's following the rules of the constitution means that they apply these rules. They follow rules in making decisions, like judges do.

Consequential on that, the separation of powers points to different moments in the chain of legitimation. The legislator speaks before the judge, the latter cannot reverse the chain without entering into the legislator's domain, nor can the subject, unless it is specifically provided, challenge decisions – legislative or others – that were issued further up the chain.

Apart from patent differences, my claim is an articulation of the similarity of judicial and legislative ruling, in that both make decisions while following rules. On this view of the rule of law doctrine, it makes no sense to hold, as Friedman does, that judges reason within a closed set of rules, while legislative action is open-ended. This view on both positions, in my opinion, is wrong. Judges do not reason within a closed set of rules, in that they make decisions. And legislators do not decide in an open-ended way, since they are bound by rules.

On Friedman's approach, legislative enactments have some stench of decisionism. Decisionism is encouraged by the idea of sovereignty, that is, the idea of the omnipotent legislator, as it goes hand in hand with representationalism. Under the latter, the decisions of the legislator represent reality or they are said to

---

[77]   As, *e.g.,* Kelsen holds, Kelsen, *Reine Rechtslehre,* p. 20, p. 74 and p. 242 ff.

be 'just there'. What we read from Friedman, then, is an exemplary, though thinner, description of strong legalism than that proposed above.

Now, if both the judicial 'application' of rules and their legislative creation result from rule-following, we are in a position to direct our focus towards a consequence of that. This consequence is the fact that, if judges follow rules and must show that and how they do this, the legislator's following of rules requires some justification of his issuing external limitations.

This requirement of justification is yet another reversal in the legitimation chain. It challenges the idea of a general proxy that starts the unilateral dynamics of the chain.

Conclusion

In this chapter I have argued that legitimacy is the result of active legitimation. It is not simply a natural product. In line with this, I have shown some of the implication of this thesis. The legitimation chain that was supposed to be irreversible on strong legalism turns out to be reversible on a legisprudential reading. This reading starts from the distinction between jusnaturalistic and non-jusnaturalistic theories of legitimation. Legislative limitations of freedom, so it is further argued, require a justification. Justification on the principles of Legisprudence may turn out to fail. Upon this failure, the legitimation chain is reversed. Examples of these reversals already exist in legal systems, and some of them, like 'rights', 'judicial review' were briefly discussed.

Chapter 2

Lawmaking: Between Discourse and Legal Text

Wojciech Cyrul
University of Krakow, Poland

Introduction

Problems with the inflation of legal regulations, which most countries cope with, make us realise expressly today the importance of the reflection on how discourse influences lawmaking. The success of law and economic approach as well as other instrumentally oriented theories in this domain shows that lawmaking is contemporarily predominantly reduced to a process of drafting and voting statutory regulations. The shared standpoint of many lawyers and politicians is that carefully prepared and drafted legal acts can guarantee the efficiency of jurisdiction and secure the coherence of a legal system (Noll 1973, Hill 1982, Piotrowski 1988, Wróblewski 1985). Also, a comparative analysis of the principles of legal drafting and lawmaking in various countries shows in this respect some fundamental similarities: the attention to the effects of implementation of new regulations into a legal system, attention to the form and language of legal acts or a compulsory examination of the effects of the previous regulations and determination how and when they can be improved (Wronkowska and Zieliński 1993). As we can see, contemporary reflection on lawmaking to much extent is focused on the outcome of lawmaking: the quality of legal texts. Therefore, the final decision on the selection of optimal regulation depends both on the costs and effectiveness of the specific solution as well as on its compatibility with already binding legal texts.

Changes that have occurred as a result of the rising importance of constitutional review, supranational regulations and international judicial tribunals raise the question of the status of a legal text. The possibility to challenge the state before the ECJ for unconstitutional laws or for the verdicts of national courts that violate human rights put much pressure on its quality. The analysis of notions of text and discourse and their relationships in the process of lawmaking will show that the contemporary approach to lawmaking is unable to prevent these claims or may even unwillingly support them. Therefore it is necessary to analyse the inherent limitation which discourse and text put on legal text, and the consequences of contemporary expectations directed at its quality. This contribution also constitutes an attempt to present a systematic analysis of the relationship between discourse and text and its impact on the status of a legal text. On the grounds of the analysis it will be shown that instrumental and technical understanding of legal text is too narrow and should also take into consideration inherent, structural and ontological determinants of the textuality.

Discourse and Text: Some Preliminary Remarks

The contemporary theory of discourse assumes its broad interpretation. The notion of discourse is most commonly defined as a communicative event or more precisely as an oral or written usage of language in different social contexts (van Dijk 2001). In consequence, according to this standpoint discourse may be oral or written. There is also not one, unanimously accepted definition of the concept of text. In textology, well represented is the view according to which text can be defined as an oral or written expression, limited and coherent, within which the sentence or utterance order is unchangeable. As a consequence a text consists of utterances or sentences combined together by particular types of linguistic structures (Polański 1993, Dobrzyńska 1993, Wilkoń 2002). Semiology goes even further and defines text as an object or phenomenon expressed by signs within a particular culture. As we see, the contemporary reflection about the notion of text tends to assume a broad definition of text, that results in widening the scope of interest of the textological analysis and incorporating into it issues related to oral communication (Dobrzyńska 1993, Wilkoń 2002). Therefore, unsurprisingly in some contributions both discourse and text are treated as synonyms (Gleason and Ratner 2005). In order to escape the possible misunderstandings, which can occur when one uses broad definitions of text and discourse, we will take a position traditionally accepted in legal theory. Generally speaking, it follows the philological approach and limits the notion of text to linguistic expressions preserved in form of graphical signs. Respectively, discourse will be reduced to an oral usage of language.

Such a position follows from several reasons. Firstly, from a genetic viewpoint, the text is related to the notion of written communication, which is not only to the notion of performed speech but also to the notion of recorded and delimited speech (Okopień-Sławińska 2001). The notion of discourse stems from the phenomenon of live dialogue, polemics or generally speaking, from real verbal communication. Secondly, the notion of discourse covers elements that do not belong to textual categories. This in particular refers to the issue of context understood as a broad social background in which the text and the information recorded therein function. Thirdly, contrary to a text which is a finished product, recorded on a carrier and due to its autoglotic status, becomes an element of the cultural universe, a discourse both as a monologue and a dialogue has the nature of a process, is fleeting and locally related. Fourthly, the discourse takes place here and now among specific entities each of which, by performing speech acts, plays the role of a specific speaker or receiver, being a part of a real auditorium, which is not necessarily a case with text. Fifthly, the text has an autonomy of its own, is out of context, and therefore, in its semantic structure, it strives towards a possibly complete verbalisation. To the contrary, the discourse is devoid of autonomy. It is always related to a specific situation, relations among discourse participants, the pertaining circumstances, the subject of the utterances and their function. Sixthly, texts are rather products of communication behaviour than interactions. In other words, if a discourse is necessarily directed at interaction and direct transfer of information, the text is not. Obviously, it is not the goal to exclude the issues of written communication from the discourse analysis but to underline the fact that text studies mostly focus on the purely linguistic aspect, while the scope of discourse studies goes beyond the question of what was said or written. Therefore, the discourse, in its nature, is based on the notion of utterance, while the text is based on the notion of sentence.

Although the proposed position which may refer to a text of discourse only when it has been recorded on a carrier, bears a risk of simplification and remains open to discussion, however, it allows differentiation among basic legal notions as legal provision, legal rule, legal text, text of law or legal discourse. Finally, the use of the narrow definition of text will contribute to the clarity of the presentation of relationships between discourse and text in lawmaking.

Text and Discourse – Sentence and Utterance

Two major streams of reflections about the text can be identified in modern linguistics. The first approach accepts that text is a complex linguistic object consisted of at least two sentences (Bańczerowski, Pogonowski and Zgółka 1982). The second approach argues that one can speak about text on the level of single sentence or even a phrase (Dobrzyńska 1993). However, for the reason of the clarity of further presentation, I would like to adopt a moderate position. Accordingly, although the sentence constitutes the smallest element of a text, the essence of textuality emerges from relationships taking place between many following sentences. The situation is similar in a case of discourse, with the difference that the smallest entity of a discourse is an utterance. In communicative sciences the essence of the discourse is also usually understood as a metastructure that not only allow us to understand words used in an utterance, but also to perceive the chain of utterances as a meaningful and coherent whole in a particular context. Thus, the essence of the text and discourse expresses itself not so much in syntactic relations that rule the sentence or pragmatic relations that define utterance, but rather in relations between entities that are more complex than a simple sentence or a simple utterance.

Notions of a sentence and an utterance are crucial for grasping the difference between legal rule and legal provision in lawmaking. This is crucial since we can speak about legality of a rule only if we associate concept of the rule with the concept of the utterance. It is so because what makes a rule a legal one is rather the fact of it being uttered or made by an authorised institution and not its semantic content. Democracy and the rule of law assume that legal rules have to be 'sponsored'. On the other hand, binding together the concept of a legal rule with the concept of a legal text results in an autoglotic status of the former. Therefore, communicative status of legal rule becomes closer to a sentence than to an utterance.[1] The argument presented below will prove that 'problematic' communicative status of a legal rule legitimatises introduction of notional distinction between legal rule and legal provision.

The analysis of the basic elements of text and discourse reveals again the problem of the relationship between the form and the content of law. The difference between a sentence and an utterance may not be reduced just to the issue of the degree of signs' complexity of both notions. As is justly noted by A. Okopień-Sławińska, a sentence and an utterance have a different ontological and social status. The differences result in dissimilarities in the semantic status of the sign within both phenomena. The status of the sign is different within a set of potential linguistic units at the disposal of each language user and the status of the sign selected on purpose from the set and thus referred to a specific communication situation (Okopień-Sławińska 2001). In effect, an utterance, contrary to a sentence, may be assessed not only from the viewpoint of ideal models existing within a specific language system, but also from the viewpoint of language standard, which is what actually functions within a given community. A sentence is a language structure that we investigate solely with respect to its linguistic or possibly logical value. In the first instance, we focus not on a reality described by a given sentence but on the semantic and syntactic relationships occurring within its structure. In the other instance, we investigate if the sentence describes the reality as it is or not in conformity with facts (Ziembiński 1994).

Utterance is a communication structure which assumes not only the existence of the speaker of the message and a receiver, but also as a matter of principle assumes that the speaker has a specific goal in transmitting the message under the circumstances. In effect, determination of meaning within a sentence and within an utterance is different. When we analyse a sentence, we try to determine the meaning of words used therein as well as the syntactic relationships forming the sentence. In the case of an utterance, in order to determine its meaning it is not sufficient to determine the meaning of the words used therein. One has to also determine the speaker, his/her image of the receiver and their mutual relationships as well as the meaning of his/her behaviour. In the latter case, we have to determine what in fact the uttering entity does, that is if he/she is uttering a judgement, or asking a question, or is ironic, etc. Following Z. Ziembiński, we can

---

[1]   It is accepted that a legal regulation has an authoritative character mainly due to the fact that it was created by a competent body, following a specific procedure, and has not been cancelled afterwards. However, from the viewpoint of the process of determining the meaning of words, the text of legal acts is to be recognised as non-sponsored. In other words, the text of a legal act is sponsored in the pragmatic dimension as the text of law in force and non-sponsored in the semantic dimension, which is at the level of the meaning of words. However, this makes it necessary to distinguish between the binding force of the text of the source of law and the binding force of a rule in the process of interpretation and application thereof.

state that in an analysis of utterance we go beyond its descriptive layer and we also inspect its expressive, suggestive and performative aspect.

Discourse, Text and Medium of Communication

Above there is a presentation of several major differences occurring between a sentence and an utterance as well as the potential impact they can have on the lawmaking. The next step is to analyse the differences that exist between text and discourse at the level of communication medium. An issue arises how the written character of text and oral character of discourse may affect information transfer in the process of lawmaking. Is speech, based on sound and fleeting as such, a real alternative and equivalent medium of communication to writing? Writing does have a visible, durable form and additionally is related to a physical carrier on which it is recorded. Word is invisible and transient right after an utterance has been made. However, it is able to affect physically the world at large (Ong 1982). Attention should also be paid to the fact that nowadays, it is also possible to record actual discussions, dialogues or monologues, not only in writing, but also on other various carriers so that they can be replayed later a number of times. Thus, we should assume that it is not necessarily the graphic form of the sign but the fact of its recording that may change the communication status of discourse. It is also necessary to notice the fact that the process is practically irreversible. This is particularly visible in a situation of re-sounding of graphically recorded signs as is the case of recitation of literary texts or playing of musical compositions. As an effect of recording a discourse, excepting an audio-visual recording, the entire communication event is reduced to the content of the utterance and thus the object of analysis becomes restricted to a major extent. In case a text is re-sounded usually an interpreter enters between the text and the receiver and the interpretation affects the receiver's understanding.

The most obvious difference between writing and speech occurs at the level of correction of the transferred information and the impact that the correction may have on the receiver of the message (Goody 1986, Goody 1987). While a correction of an oral message usually results in impaired credibility of the speaker and quality assessment of the speech itself, corrections and changes in a written text may produce a completely different effect. This is due to the fact that the receiver of a written text, contrary to the listener of an oral expression, usually does not know how the final version of the text was generated. Therefore, the final version of the text seems to the receiver to be the original and only one. Usually the receiver is not able to perceive neither the evolution that the text has gone through before publication nor the reasons for which the author provided it with such form.

Another difference between the two media arises at the level of storage methods of the information. Oral information has to be memorised and only writing permits recording information without memorising it. Therefore, writing provides for unlimited possibilities to store all kinds of data. Memorising of information (when it cannot be recorded) not only causes that much information to be forgotten but also material data can be left out or distorted in memory by accidental events with a strong emotional angle (Memon, Vrij and Bull 2003). Thus, scepticism and a critical attitude to the presented material as well as a way of presenting arguments are not the result of a personal attitude but an effect of the extent of formalisation and access to recording of the information (Luria 1976). It is the precision and durability of written information that determines the possibility of analytical thinking and development of abstract categories. A systematic and precise recording of observations provides for a comparative analysis as well as maintaining accessibility to enable the necessary consultation.

Another major difference between text and discourse in information transfer results from the presupposition made by writing and speaking. While a discourse necessarily requires the presence of a real receiver, a text does not assume the presence of a reader (Jackson 1995). Therefore, the relation between the speaker of verbal information and the receiver of the message can be completely different from the relation between the author of a written message and its receivers. The relation between the speaker and his/her auditorium is not only direct but usually also much more personal. It is much more difficult for a speaker to remain neutral to his/her auditorium than for a writer. This is due to the fact that a text reader is usually absent when the text is written and even more frequently he/she not always is the addressee of the information message contained in the text. The text of written information may hold a sense also for persons whom the author did not take into consideration when writing the text as well as for persons who do not know either the author or the context in which the text was written. The matter is different with reference to speech. Information in a discourse as such is always 'sponsored' and it may not be abstracted from the speaker, the context of presentation or in particular from the auditorium to which it is addressed. A written text has an autoglotic nature and exists in abstraction from the author or the context of its generation. A written text, contrary to each speech act, is not sponsored by the fact that it is identifiable to a specific person performing the act. Indeed, the lack of such differentiation would prevent any formalisation.

Discourse, Text and Modes of Communication

Communication has different forms, but in the explanation of the role of modes of communication for the distinction between text and discourse, one should focus on dialogue and monologue. Monologue and dialogue are two different forms of human communicative interaction. However, while the concept of discourse gravitates toward dialogue, the concept of text has an inherently monologic characteristic. This inclination to two different modes of communication determines some important differences between discourse and text. In this contribution we will focus only on the differences at the level of immanent features of their structure, the concept of meaning they adopt, and cognitive processes that take place during the dialogue and monologue. It will be later helpful to see relationships between legal text and discourse in lawmaking.

The main feature of dialogue is a systematic exchange of communicative roles between the sender and receiver. On the structural level dialogue differs from monologue because it is two-way communication. The mutual exchange of roles of the participants of the communication results in the opportunity for all to influence the topic and the form of discourse. Moreover, it structurally determines that each participant speaks and comprehends, and therefore both sides can instantly and constantly react on what the other party is saying. In consequence, dialogue, as structurally and directly oriented at mutual understanding, does not presuppose that participants of the communicative interaction actually understand each other, as monologue does, but rather presupposes that all participants are willing to reach a common understanding. Any misunderstanding is picked out and any notion or expression can be specified and explained if necessary, as the other party hesitates as to whether he/she understood what the sender wanted to say or why he/she said so. In that way dialogue presupposes a different epistemological status of meaning (About different conception of meaning see: Ullmann 1964, Pelc 1971, Ogden and Richard 1989). In dialogue the meaning is negotiated and results from the exchange of competitive ideas and standpoints in a mutually shared communicative context. Therefore, it is not determined only at the level of semantics: dialogical communication is much more context-dependent and the meaning is negotiated or mutually constructed during the dialogue. Therefore, dialogue is inclined to accept the constructivist theory of meaning and to reject the claims of objective semantics (Goodwin 1995). It constitutes one of the reasons why dialogue is conceptually irreducible to the series of monologues or auto-deliberation. Dialogue is always a dynamic and collective process, in which the pragmatic aspect of meaning plays a key role.

Monologue, contrary to dialogue, is a one-way form of communication between the sender and receiver(s). In monologue the roles of the participants are precisely defined as sender or as receiver of the message, without the possibility of exchange. This strict attribution of roles results in the static position of participants, who either speak or comprehend, and therefore, the topic and the structure of the text of the monologue is determined and organised only by the sender. This structure implicates at least five crucial presuppositions with respect to the relations between participants and human communication. Firstly, monologue shifts the emphasis from the group onto the single sender of the message. The receivers are expected to discover the meaning as attributed to the text of monologue by the sender. Secondly, because the whole communicative interaction is subordinated to one participant, the content of monologue can be structurally and thematically closed. Thirdly, the content of monologue is teleological in its nature since it is used to promote in an authoritative fashion the ideas, values and opinions of the sender in an authoritative fashion since monologue, by definition, is not open to different or competitive standpoints. Fourthly, monologue puts on its content a series of requirements regarding its semantic formulation. This is so because the monologue, if it is to be comprehensible for the auditorium, must be explicit. It leads either to the formalisation of the language or to the creation of the model addressee. In first the case it leads to the presupposition that the semantic level of meaning is the sufficient way to convey the meaning of the content of an expression (Hoadley and Enyedy 1999). Finally, the sender in monologue, consciously or not, must presuppose a concrete vision of his/her auditorium, and the efficacy of the message depends on the correctness of that prediction. This in turn leads to idealisations, which in a hidden way usually promote the epistemological preferences of the sender.

Discourse, Text and Lawmaking

When analysing interplay between discourse and text in the course of a lawmaking process, one can easily observe that they are legally regulated in almost every aspect. Lawmaking provides them with a very particular social context of a language usage. Discourse obtains not only an institutional dimension but also becomes a particular procedure of discussing policy and rule formation. The consensus reached in the discourse shall be later on preserved in a highly technical and legally regulated way in a form of a legal text. For the clarity of following argument let us assume that the notion of lawmaking also encompasses both procedures preceding formal decisions concerning preparation of the draft of legal regulations as well as the procedures of legal drafting (Fricke and Hugger, 1979). In that way one shall be able to recognise fully the problems connected with transforming discourse into a legal text, which is the major aim of this contribution.

As already mentioned an analysis of various regulations concerning the principles of lawmaking reveals that the main stress is put on the problems of the economic and social aspects of the proposed solutions. Therefore, lawmaking authorities are required to determine possible social, economical and legal outcomes of all proposed alternatives. They are usually obliged to determine which method of intervention is most effective economically for achieving the planned results. On the other hand, to a various extent, at this stage of work, the lawmaking authorities are also obliged to request an opinion of the entities that may be interested in a particular way of regulation. Naturally, such actions are made not only to reduce the costs of law enforcement but also to put into practice the postulates of rationality, justice and the rule of law (Kustura 1994).

The process of determination of the actual state of social relations in the sphere that has to be the subject of regulation influences the meaning in the discourse. Unless it is assumed that language is able to convey fully the meaning and the intentions of the involved parties, the dialogical characteristic of the discourse in the context of lawmaking will always lead to a mutual meaning construction. It is so because the participation in the discourse forces the parties to strive for a mutual understanding so as to achieve a consensual regulation of conflicting interests. The determination of legal and extralegal measures that enable accomplishing the set political targets, motivate the participants of the discourse to analyse what solutions are optimal for them individually or as a group. It brings them to a shared understanding. This effect is also generated by the fact that the persuasive character of the discourse and a need of consensus require participants to be self-critical and reflexive. The dialogical and persuasive form of the discourse in the process of lawmaking contributes to a better understanding of differences between participants and to a development of a more comprehensive understanding between different groups of interest (Young 1993, Black 2001). Therefore, discourse in the context of lawmaking is always oriented towards the future. It is so also because the discourse aims at finding solutions acceptable for its participants combining the legal dimension with pragmatic, ethical and moral questions.

Contrary to discourse legal text has a past orientation. By definition it aims at a promotion of one already institutionalised worldview. In lawmaking the legal text is expected to 'freeze' the discourse. In consequence, the dialogical characteristic of discourse, when preserved in a graphical form of a legal text, results in an exchange of dialogical dynamics of discourse into a static monologue of the legal text. The discussions, bargaining and conflicting opinions vanish and become replaced by a monolithic and institutionalised standpoint. The interpreters of the legal text do not need to be self-critical and reflective because no consensus is required anymore. There is little place for persuasiveness because it is the legal text that matters, not anything else. While the discourse in the lawmaking functions as a kind of problem-solving procedure, the legal text is primarily expected to play an adjudicative function. Therefore, a legal text contrary to discourse must be complete and explicit.

In lawmaking the intelligibility of the discourse is replaced by the explicitness of a legal text. Although contemporarily legal texts are required to be both explicit and intelligible, paradoxically the more they are explicit the less they are intelligible. The discourse in lawmaking can simultaneously be explicit and intelligible because its context-dependency enables explicit communication with less restricted and less formal expressions. It is so because, in discourse, the linguistic level of utterances is accompanied by the whole extra linguistic context that supports their comprehensibility. Furthermore, the comprehensibility of discourse is additionally supported by its structural openness. Therefore, discourse in lawmaking is full of examples, cases, conflicting opinions and other factors, which can help to translate one language into another and in consequence, make communication accessible for all participants. The legal text is purified from all these elements. Here explicitness must usually be achieved only by purely linguistic means, which usually leads to a formalisation of the language of a legal text. The problem with intelligibility of a legal text is that it has also theoretical aspects. Firstly, intelligibility is a relative concept and therefore, always depends on the concept of an addressee. Something can be intelligible for one addressee and not for another. The subjective intelligibility or unintelligibility of the text usually results from different levels of linguistic and communicative competences of addresses. Even if a legal text were exclusively composed of the vocabulary known to the addressee, it does not imply that he/she will be able to correctly understand its meaning. As Studnicki-Gizbert rightly suggests, the linguistic competence of an addressee is a necessary but not sufficient condition for a correct understanding a legal text. Since a legal text is a product of the act of *parole,* and not of *langue,* the addressee must have a communicative competence, which goes beyond the competence to produce and understand an infinite set of the sentences of the language. He/she must also acquire the competence to reconstruct the legal rule from the provisions of legal text and to use rules of legal interpretation and legal reasoning (Studnicki-Gizbert 1986).

Both in discourse, as well as in a legal text, any message shall be communicated in a manner comprehensive to the addressees in accordance to the generally approved semantic rules and syntax of the vernacular. However, here again emerges a fundamental difference between discourse and text. In the first case it is known who the participant of the discourse is and his/her communicative competence can be tested. In the latter case, it is always a controversy who is the addressee of a legal text. It is striking that still no unified position has been taken with respect to the issue of who is the addressee of law – the judges, lawyers, ordinary people, or nobody (Binder 1911, Ross 1958, Studnicki-Gizbert 1986).

Legal text is expected to be not only intelligible and explicit but also complete and systemised. The fulfilment of both requirements will contribute to the consistency, coherence and certainty of legal regulations. However, if one takes into account differences between discourse, text and changes that occur when one tries to close discourse in the framework of text, the correctness of this implication may be questioned both on the linguistic, structural and ontological level. It is so because the legal text as a product of discourse in a lawmaking process when preserved in graphical form has to fulfil a series of requirements regarding its formulation.

The major requirement that lawmaking imposes on legal text is its very particular structure. The internal consistency, conciseness, lack of digressions and examples so characteristic for legal texts, seriously limit the possibility of any precise translation of the language of discourse into language of a legal text. The structural and communicative openness of discourse, and the different epistemological conceptions of the meaning it is based upon, result in a quite different model for linguistic practice both in the legal text and the discourse in the lawmaking process. The discourse is open to the possibility of a non-conclusive decision, whilst the legal text requires the decision to be made. The legal text, as already mentioned, contrary to discourse, is not only structurally closed but is also required to be complete. It means that the content of information concerning the duties and rights of addresses contained in the text shall be sufficient to establish how they are expected to behave. However, the fulfilment of the requirement of completeness of a legal text is questionable. The legal text is formulated in a natural language. Thus, even if one presupposes that the meaning of a legal provision is objective, the inherent imperfections of the language limit the completeness of a legal regulation (Studnicki-Gizbert 1983). On the structural level, the requirement of completeness contradicts the requirement of succinctness of a legal text. Completeness of legal text in the process of transformation of the discursive prolixity and its structural openness into a succinct and closed text would lead to constant repetition of identical, thus redundant, information in different legal texts. Therefore, the requirement of completeness of a legal regulation cannot be applicable to a single legal text but rather to a whole text of law.

The above analysis shows that the contemporary expectations directed at quality of legal text are in many respects unrealisable. Therefore, either they will have to be changed or the concept of a legal text has to be supplemented by a notion that will be able to overcome the obstacles connected with its present status. One can argue that this role may play the notion of the text of law defined as a set of all legal texts valid at a particular time in a particular country. This notion may be also useful because every day legal practice shows that often information necessary to reconstruct a complete legal rule goes beyond a single legal text. However, one should not underestimate the ontological, epistemological and structural differences between the text of law and a legal text. The internal structure of the text of law, its lack of formal beginning and end as well as its relationship with discourse differs widely from legal text. Also, its communicative and textual status has to be examined. However, these and all other issues connected with text of law must be the objects of a subsequent contribution.

References

Bańczerowski, J., Pogonowski, J. and Zgółka, T. (1982), *Wstęp do językoznawstwa,* Wrocław.

Binder, J. (1911), *Rechstsnorm und Rechtspflicht,* Erlangen.

Black, J. (2001), 'Proceduralizing Regulation: Part II', *Oxford Journal of Legal Studies,* 21, pp. 33-58.

Dobrzyńska, T. (1993), *Tekst, próba syntezy,* Warszawa.

Fricke, P. and Hugger, W. (1979), *Test von Gesetzentwürfen,* part 1: *Voraussetzungen einer testorientierten Rechtssetzungsmethodik, Speyerer Forschungsberichte,* No 11.

Gleason, J.B. and Ratner, N.B. (eds.) (2005), *Psycholingwistyka,* Gdansk.

Goodwin, Ch. (1995), 'Co-Constructing Meaning in Conversations with an Aphasic Man', *Research in Language and Social Interaction,* 28 (3), pp. 233-260.

Goody, J. (1987), *The Interface Between the Written and Oral,* Cambridge.

Goody, J. (1986), *The Logic of Writing and the Organisation of Society,* Cambridge.

Hill, H. (1982), *Einführung in die Gesetzgebungslehre,* Heidelberg.

Hoadley, C. and Enyedy, N. (1999), 'Between Information and Communication: Middle Spaces in Computer Media for Learning', *Proceedings of the Third International Conference on Computers' Support for Collaborative Learning,* Deerfield, Il., pp. 242-251.

Jackson, B.S. (1995), *Making Sense in Law,* Liverpool.

Kustura, E. (1994), *Polityczne problemy tworzenia prawa,* Toruń.

Luria, A.R. (1976), *Cognitive Development: Its Cultural and Social Foundations,* M. Cole, M. Lopez-Morillas and L. Solotaroff (eds.), Cambridge, Ma.

Memon, A., Vrij, A. and Bull, R. (2003), *Prawo i Psychologia. Wiarygodność zeznań i materiału dowodowego,* Gdańskie Wydawnictwo Psychologiczne.

Noll, P. (1973), *Gesetzgebungslehre,* Hamburg.

Ogden, Ch.K and Richard, J.P. (1989), *The Meaning of Meaning,* Orlando.

Okopień-Sławińska, A. (2001), *Semantyka wypowiedzi poetyckiej,* Kraków.

Ong, W. (1982), *Orality and Literacy*, London.

Pelc, J. (1971), *O użyciu wyrażeń*, Wrocław.

Piotrowski, R. (1988), *Spór o model tworzenia prawa,* Warszawa.

Ross, A. (1958), *On Law and Justice*, Berkeley.

Polański, K. (ed.) (1993), *Encyklopedia językoznawstwa ogólnego*, Wrocław.

Studnicki-Gizbert, T. (1986), *Język prawny z perspektywy socjolingwistycznej,* Warszawa Kraków.

Studnicki-Gilbert, T. (1983), 'Vagueness, Open Texture and Law', *Archivum Iuridicum Cracoviense*, vol. XVI.

Ullmann, S. (1964), *Semantics: An Introduction to the Science of Meaning*, Oxford.

Van Dijk, T.A. (2001), 'Badania nad dyskursem', in T.A. van Dijk (ed.), *Dyskurs jako struktura i proces*, Warszawa.

Wilkoń, A. (2002), *Spójność i struktura tekstu, wstęp do lingwistyki tekstu*, Kraków.

Wróblewski, J. (1985), *Teoria racjonalnego tworzenia prawa*, Wrocław.

Wronkowska, S. and Zieliński, M. (1993) *Problemy i zasady redagowania tekstów prawnych*, Warszawa.

Young, I. (1993), 'Justice and Communicative Democracy', in R. Gottlieb (ed.), *Radical Philosophy: Tradition, Counter-Tradition, Politics*, Philadelphia.

Ziembiński, Z. (1994), *Logika Praktyczna*, Warszawa.

Chapter 3

The Rule of Law as the Law of Legislation

Tatsuo Inoue

Graduate Schools for Law and Politics, the University of Tokyo

Introduction

In this paper I aim to redefine and reinforce the idea of the rule of law as the basic legitimacy condition of legislation. In contrast with the formal, substantive and process-oriented conceptions of the rule of law, I present a strong structural conception of the rule of law. This conception has the following features.

First, it is based on the concept of law as a project for justice. The justice-claim of law is the central component of this concept of law. It implies that law is committed to opening the institutional route for subjecting itself to incessant critical review of its justice. This commitment constitutes the core of the rule of law on this conception.

Second, it is based on the underlining common concept of justice as distinguished from specific competing conceptions of justice like libertarian or egalitarian rights-based doctrines, utilitarianism and so on. But the underlining concept of justice is not rendered into the purely formal idea of justice such as the one presented by Perelman. It is identified as the stronger moral (not just linguistic) principle of universalization that implies the requirement of reversibility and public justification.

Third, specific components of the rule of law are *extensionally* identified as those structural principles which H.L.A. Hart and Lon L. Fuller presented, but they are *intentionally* reinterpreted as protecting justice-review of law, not merely its predictability.

I argue that this strong structural conception of the rule of law can offer the basis of public legitimacy of legislation that transcends the partisan strife where rival forces with differing specific conceptions of justice compete for victory in legislative politics. It offers normative constraints upon what the political victors can do to the losers in such a way that the losers can respect the products of legislative politics as public decisions of their political society rather than as the private wills of victors.

The Problem of Legitimacy and the Rule of Law

It is often said that legislation is needed in a dynamic society that undergoes rapid and incessant changes in the conditions of life while customary law prevails in a static society. This is a half-truth. Even a dynamic society could do without legislation if there were a robust consensus among its people about how they should respond to their changing conditions. Informal coordination based on tacit shared understanding could even do a better job than formal legislation in coping with the incessant change efficiently. Legislation is needed in a dynamic society because there is no such consensus, because there are persistent moral and political disagreements among its people about the way their society should respond to the changing situations. A dynamic society needs legislation not simply because it is dynamic but because it is *pluralistic* in the sense that the value-perceptions as well as interests of its people are divided and conflicting with each other.

Legislation is the act of making a collective decision when there are moral-political disagreements on the issues that we need collective decision making to resolve. Legislation is *agonistic* by nature. There are winners and losers in the battles of legislative politics. This is the case even when a compromise is achieved in a legislative process. First, there are political outsiders excluded from the coalition of political forces that make the legislative compromise. They are losers, and as compared with them, the insiders involved in the compromise are winners. Second, more often than not, there are also winners and losers among the insiders. Losing insiders are those who have no other choice but to succumb to the pressure from the winning insiders to make greater concession than the latter.

The agonistic nature of legislation raises the issue of its *legitimacy* as distinguished from its *justifiability*. How is it possible for the losers of legislative battles, who believe that the legislative decisions are unjustifiable in the light of their own conceptions of justice, to respect them as public decisions of their political society that has a legitimate claim to their deference instead of regarding them as private wills of the winners imposed upon them? How can the egalitarian advocates of the welfare state, for example, pay deference to a libertarian tax-reform legislation that they believe to be unfair?

A quick popular answer to this question is that legislative decisions have legitimacy in the above-presented sense if and only if they are reached through *democratic* process in which those who ended up being losers were able to participate. But this answer has grave flaws. I will mention just two main ones here.

First, what counts as a genuinely democratic process fairly open to all is a highly controversial matter. To cite just a couple of examples, think of the bitter controversies about the fair election system and the proper regulation of money for political activities. How can losers in the legislative (or constitutional) battles on this matter acknowledge the legitimacy of their results? To say that the losers should do so because the results are reached through democratic process is to beg the question.

Second, the popular argument from democracy can have a convincing appeal only to those losers who have a fair antecedent chance of winning and a fair prospective chance of winning back. But it is the fact of our political life that there are structurally marginalized minorities who have no hope of winning the democratic battle even if their equal right to participate in the democratic process is fully protected and exercised. Participation in democratic process cannot offer them adequate reason to accept the legitimacy of its product.

Another prevalent answer to the question of legislative legitimacy is given by liberal constitutionalists who aim to correct the second flaw of the popular democratic argument. They hold that democratic legislation can have legitimacy for politically powerless individuals and minorities only if their fundamental rights are imposed on the democratic legislation as constitutional constraints implemented by judicial review. A stronger version of this view adds a requirement that these rights should be entrenched by immunity against constitutional amendment.

The substantive constitutional rights approach is not free from difficulty. Its stumbling block is the fact that there is a persistent controversy about what fundamental rights people have, what are the scopes and implications of the constitutional provisions of such rights and how to resolve their conflicts. This approach is under fierce attack from those who believe that democratic deliberative process of legislation is in a better position to decide those controversial issues about rights than the constitutional adjudication by the courts that exercise the power of judicial review without being democratically controlled.[1] The basic argument for this attack is something like this: the democratic deliberation in legislative process can accommodate a greater diversity of competing interests and value-perceptions than the judicial decision-making insulated from the pressures of democratic politics, so that the former is more adequate than the latter to obtain legitimacy in deciding the issues of rights in a pluralistic society.

This argument does not succeed in making a renewed defence of the legitimating force of democratic process. It turns its eyes away from the fact that the diversity shown in a pluralistic society consists not just in the differentiation of interests and value-perceptions but also in the differentiation of political resources of rival groups seeking for competing interests and values. Democratic process fails to accommodate the interests and values of minority groups whose political resources fall short of the threshold of political effectivity. The above-mentioned argument conceals this failure of democracy that liberal constitutionalism is meant to cope with.

Moreover, it fails to overcome the first flaw of the above-presented popular democratic argument. The defenders of the primacy of democratic deliberation who make this argument beg the question if they leave up to democratic deliberation the judgment on the controversial issue of what counts as genuine democratic deliberative process fairly accommodating social diversity. Ultimately they have to make their own controversial value judgment on this issue and defend it not as output of democratic process but as a precondition of its legitimacy. They

---

[1]   For a recent development of this perspective, *see* Waldron (1999a) and Waldron (1999b).

cannot accuse liberal constitutionalists of subjecting democratic practice to the constraints stipulated independently of this practice on the basis of controversial substantive value judgments. They have no other choice but to do the same thing if their standpoint is to be articulated and defended.

Although their positive argument for primacy of democratic deliberation is untenable, their critical argument against the substantive rights-based liberal constitutionalism reveals its soft spot. In a pluralistic society there is no solid consensus about the meaning and scope of constitutional rights, much less about pre-constitutional fundamental rights that constitutional rights embody and depend on for their justification. Constitutional politics,[2] where people settle the issues of rights through the process of constitutional adjudication and amendment, is as agonistic as legislative politics. There are winners and losers in the battles of constitutional politics just as there are in legislative battles.

Accordingly, the problem of legislative legitimacy that substantive constitutional rights appear to have solved reproduces itself as the problem of constitutional legitimacy. How is it possible for losers in a constitutional battle to respect its outcome as the public decision of their political society that has legitimate claim to their deference even if they believe that it is wrong? To say that they can do so because their conception of substantive rights as constraint on democracy is right whereas the losers' views are wrong is not to *resolve*, but to *dissolve*, the issue of legitimacy. It just imposes 'the victor's justice' upon the losers. The losers who believe their views are right would find no reason for deference in such an answer even if they have to acquiesce in the outcome.[3]

---

[2]   Bruce Ackerman uses the term 'constitutional politics' to refer to the political process of major constitutional paradigm transformation that he distinguishes not just from legislative politics called 'normal politics' but also from the non-revolutionary practice of judicial review that sticks to and spells out the received constitutional paradigm. *See* Ackerman (1991). I use this term to cover both the constitutional paradigm-transforming process and paradigm-sustaining judicial review practice, not to claim that the two processes are indistinguishable but to emphasize that both involve the decision-making about highly controversial matters of political morality.

[3]   Among the contemporary liberal legal and political theorists there is a perceptible tendency to accept the victor's justice in constitutional strife. Bruce Ackerman, for example, refuses to see the problem of constitutional legitimacy from the perspective of losers in constitutional strife when he holds that the United States can legitimately adopt Christianity as the state religion and impose it on non-Christians by abolishing the First Amendment to the Constitution if Christian fundamentalist forces win the battles of constitutional politics. *See* Ackerman (1991), pp. 13-15. To say that *We the People* created the constitution is not to solve the problem of constitutional legitimacy but to cover it up by hiding the irresolvable deep conflicts among the people. Ronald Dworkin distinguished the integrity of law from its conformity to the morally best conception of justice and tackled the problem of political obligation in Dworkin (1986) and emphasized the importance of the idea of legality or the rule of law for legal philosophy in Dworkin (2006), but, as far as I understand, he did not give a clear and convincing answer to the question of why and when losers in the constitutional battles about the issue of which constitutional rights people have or should be

Let me add a couple of notes here. First, this problem of constitutional legitimacy subsumes, but cannot be reduced to, the familiar problem of legitimacy of judicial review generated by its conflict with democracy. What is at issue is not just 'democracy or rights?' but also 'what rights?' The losers of a constitutional battle won by the exponents of a certain specific conception of substantive rights include not just those who believe in primacy of democracy over rights but also those who support different conceptions of substantive rights competing with the winner's one as constraint on democratic politics.

Second, to establish the legitimacy of the outcome of the constitutional battle, it is not enough for the winners to resort to the provisions of the existing positive constitutional law that confers judicial review power on the courts and stipulates the amendment procedure. The meaning, scope and even validity of these provisions can be at issue in constitutional politics.

The considerations given above lead us to confirm the following two conditions of adequacy that must be met by any account of legislative legitimacy in a pluralistic society.

(1) *Independent Normative Constraint on Democratic Politics* The issue of legitimacy of legislation cannot be settled by appealing to democratic process. An adequate account of legitimacy in a pluralistic society must show some independent normative constraints on democratic process such that all losers in democratic politics are fairly treated and can respect its outcome as worthy of their deference.

(2) *Independence from Competing Specific Conceptions of Substantive Rights* The issue of legitimacy of legislation cannot be settled by appealing to a specific controversial conception of substantive rights, either. An adequate account of legitimacy in a pluralistic society must show that the normative constraints it places on democratic process are not just independent from the outcome of democratic legislative politics but also have normative force that is independent from, and binding on, specific conceptions of substantive rights that compete for victory in constitutional politics.

What account can meet these conditions? Are the two conditions compatible? Is it possible to meet the first condition without introducing some specific controversial conception of substantive rights and thus violating the second

---

newly given should defer to winners, or to put it another way, why and when the results of the constitutional battles can enjoy the status of the institutional history that constrains competing comprehensive interpretive theories of the legal practice. He seems to take for granted the deference of constitutional losers to the settlements of constitutional politics. His conception of political obligation as a kind of associative obligation is not helpful to elucidate the problem of constitutional legitimacy. He holds that the integrity-based legal practice generates the community of principle that generates political obligation by securing equal concern for all its citizens. But the integrity-based legal practice is possible only if citizens accept the legitimacy of the living part of their institutional history the core of which is formed by constitutional settlements. The question is begged here.

condition? Is it possible, on the other hand, to meet the first condition without rendering the normative constraint on democratic politics vacuous and thus undermining the first condition? Or, are the two conditions in conjunction not a piece of counsel of perfection? Are they too over-demanding to be fulfilled, if not logically incompatible?

The idea of *the rule of law* as opposed to *the rule of Man* has been both holding a great and persistent appeal while inviting as much scepticism and criticism because this idea expresses human aspiration to establish the legitimacy of political power as something more than a 'victor's justice' by subjecting it to principles that meet the above-presented two conditions. In the following sections I would like to argue that a reconstruction of the idea of the rule of law and the concept of law it presupposes offers a basis for dealing with the challenge posed by the issue of legitimacy in such a way to meet the two conditions. Before developing my arguments on these lines, however, I would like to make some remarks to save the idea of the rule of law from the deep-seated scepticism about it and to show why we need it.

The idea of the rule of law has been charged with making an ideological disguise of the reality of the rule of Man or, more precisely, the reality of human political struggles for domination.[4] To be sure, history abundantly offers the examples of such ideological abuses of this idea. Edward Coke who drafted the Petition of Right, for instance, is idolized as one of the most sacred defenders of the idea of the rule of law in the common law tradition. He resorted to the dictum of his 13th-century predecessor, Henry de Bracton, that even the King is subservient to God and the Law. Bracton's idea of the rule of law was based on the medieval system of checks and balances between plural and multi-layered feudal powers, such as lords, churches, oligarchic ruling groups of 'free' cities and guilds, in which the King's power is embedded as one of many, if a relatively stronger one than others, and constrained by the vested interests of other privileged social orders and classes. The phrase 'God and Law' was a sanctifying symbol of these feudal privileges among which those of churches were eminent.[5] Coke's attempt to constrain the absolute monarchy by the rule of law was informed and motivated by the legacies of this feudal form of pluralistic power balances, not by the universalistic principles of justice and human rights. This is most glaringly revealed by the fact that he approved of the execution of Bartholomew Legat who was burnt alive on a charge of heresy in London in 1612. The Diocesan power of Inquisition was repealed by the King's ordinances before, but Coke defended it by resorting to precedents. Ironically enough, it was Thomas Hobbes, the advocate of

---

[4]   The current form of this charge is vehemently made by the advocates of the Critical Studies Movement. *See*, for example, Kennedy (1997), pp. 69-70.

[5]   The feudal basis of the common-law idea of rule of law is critically analysed in order to defend Kant's rejection of the right to resistance as a consequence of his commitment to radical popular sovereignty in Maus (1992). Although Maus's reinterpretation of Kant as the advocate of absolute popular sovereignty seems to be far-fetched, her critical appraisal of the common-law tradition hits the mark.

Leviathan, who scathingly criticized Coke's defence of the Inquisition as legally groundless.[6]

There is nothing paradoxical about this, however, because Hobbes held that Leviathan must be established by social contract just in order to protect the minimum human rights of individuals (the right to self-protection) not only against other individuals but, more importantly, against tyrannical powers of intermediary social groups, the most formidable of which are fanatical religious forces that caused bloody religious wars, the actual exemplification of the Hobbesian state of nature, both in England and all over the European Continent in his time. To protect individuals effectively against such powers, it is absolutely necessary to establish the stronger sovereign power that can control them. From this perspective Hobbes anticipated Bentham in debunking the deceptive, irrational and reactionary way in which the common-law preachers manipulated the idea of the rule of law to protect the privileges of feudal powers.

The Hobbesian critique includes a sobering truth. Its point can be generalized into the warning that the idea of the rule of law easily turns into an ideological device for hiding and sanctifying the social oppression by privileged social groups and organizations. But should this idea be rejected as nothing more than that? The answer is no, even for Hobbes. Social contract that establishes Leviathan or the sovereign state as a protector of individual rights against intermediary social forces does not solve but generates and continues to regenerate the problem of legitimacy that necessitates the search for the rule of law.

The fundamental reason for this is the non-dissolubility of human conflicts. The transition from the state of nature to the state of political society cannot lift the burden of conflicts from the shoulders of human beings. All that it can bring about is to turn conflicts by violence into conflicts for political power. We can reverse Clausewitz's famous dictum that war is the continuation of politics by another means.[7] Politics is the continuation of war in the state of nature by another means. The collective decision-making process of a political society is agonistic as we have seen above. The political decision-making is always subject to challenges from the political losers. To avoid returning back to the state of nature where the means of violence prevails, the political decision-making must be seen as *legitimate* in such a way that even the political losers who deem it *wrong* can pay deference to the winners. How is it possible?

Hobbes cannot solve this problem of legitimacy by resorting to the hypothesis of social contract that empowers the government or the state-apparatus. There are two reasons. First, conflicts between political losers and winners can develop into the conflicts in interpretation of the terms of the hypothesized social contract. Second, Hobbes delimits the validity of the principle of *pacta sunt servanda* as a natural law by exempting a party to a contract from contractual obligations in the absence of the guarantee of the other party's performing the counterpart obligations. Individuals in the state of nature establish the sovereign state by social

---

[6]   *See* Hobbes (1971), pp. 128-132.
[7]   *See* Clausewitz (1980).

contract to give such a guarantee, but the same logic applies to social contract itself. If there is no guarantee against the possibility that some part of the citizenry violates the terms of social contract by co-opting the sovereign or the operator of the state-apparatus into benefiting them by exploiting the rest so as to threaten the self-protection of the latter, then social contract loses its validity and becomes unavailable as a ground for demanding political losers to defer.[8] Social contract, which is constructed as a hypothetical justification for the genesis of the state, cannot by itself give such a guarantee to the participants in the lasting conflicts in the post-social-contract political world. They have to search for the rule of law in order to find such a guarantee that can solve the problem of legitimacy.

It may be objected that the all-powerful Hobbesian Leviathan has no need for the rule of law because it can repress political dissidence by force and obviate the need to meet the political losers' challenge about legitimacy. This objection fails, and it is Hobbes who should know better than anyone else that it fails. He gave a penetrating insight into the fragility of domination by sheer physical force or means of violence when he characterized what he calls the *natural equality* of human beings by saying, '[H]ow easy a matter it is, even for the weakest man to kill the strongest'.[9] A tyrannical king can be easily stabbed to death by his page while asleep. Contemporary despots can be as easily assassinated by a variety of far more sophisticated means. Power cannot be generated or sustained by violence alone because violence is vulnerable to violence.[10] Social contract is hypothesized to generate the normative tenacity of power that can overcome the factual fragility of violence. But in political battles the binding force of the original social contract itself is challenged as we have seen above. This means that political power is always in danger of losing its normative tenacity and degenerating into fragile violence. Power-holders can avoid this degeneration only if political losers who disagree with them can see them as worthy of their deference, that is, as minimally legitimate. The Hobbesian dictum that authority (*auctoritas*), not the truth (*veritas*), makes law is false if it means that law can be generated by sheer force. It can be true only if it is interpreted to mean that law cannot be generated unless law-makers have *legitimate* authority over those who deem their decisions *wrong*. The quest for the rule of law is the enterprise of establishing the conditions for the required legitimacy. Even the Hobbesian Leviathan cannot dispense with the sustained commitment to this enterprise.

---

[8]   Hobbes himself held that citizens are exempted from the duty to obey the state when they are condemned to death or sent to deadly battlefields as soldiers, for, in such cases, they are deprived of the guarantee of self-protection, which is the ultimate purpose of social contract that empowers the state. *See* Hobbes (1839), p. 119 ff., pp. 204-206. According to the Hobbesian logic of social contract, however, the dissolution of political obligation cannot be confined to these specific cases but holds generally under the condition such as shown in the text.

[9]   *See* Hobbes (1984), Ch. 1, par. 3.

[10]   For a further discussion of the distinction between power (*Macht*) and violence (*Gewalt*) and the latter's fragility, *see* Arendt (1969).

In his recent article on the rule of law Stephen Holmes, a contemporary liberal political philosopher, proclaimed, 'All justice is victor's justice.' To show that he did not abandon his hope for the rule of law, however, he hastened to add, 'But the more democratic a society becomes, the more victors there are, the larger the proportion of citizens who are strong enough to wield effectively the 'stick' of law'.[11] Here Holmes showed a realistic stance, but he is not cynical about the rule of law because he defended the idea of the rule of law as a guide for the movement to lessen the unfairness of victor's justice by increasing the number of victors and procuring checks and balances among them. The problem with his observation is that his realism stopped halfway here and thus failed to reveal the *raison d'être* of the rule of law. He failed to raise a fundamental question that must be addressed if a further realistic step is taken to criticize the optimism and hubris of victors that they can continue to repress simply by force those political losers who reject the victor's justice. The question is this. On what grounds can victors claim the deference of losers?

The strategy of avoiding this question by increasing the number of victors through democratization does not work for two reasons. First, the more democratic a society becomes, the more, not less, agonistic its politics become because a greater variety of voices come to express themselves in political process. Democratization *pluralizes* victors but it does not necessarily *increase* them. The more victors there are, the more internal conflicts there are among them, so that new losers incessantly emerge. Second, even if democratization increases victors, this strategy alienates losers and provokes their anger at the 'stick' of law wielded by victors, thereby undermining the normative tenacity of democratic power as distinguished from the 'violence of numbers'. The above-presented question about the grounds for deference by political losers is inescapable. It is the task of legal philosophers to ask this question and to look for an answer to it by investigating into the conditions of law's legitimacy as distinct from its rightness, thereby revealing the internal connection between the normativity of the rule of law and the reality of political strife. In the following I will show how this task should be tackled, by developing my arguments along the lines suggested above.

Law as a Project for Justice: Reconstructing the Concept of Law

In the preceding section I have presented the two adequacy conditions for an account of legislative legitimacy: independent normative constraint on democratic politics and independence from competing specific conceptions of substantive rights. The two conditions require us to break the dichotomy of legal positivism and natural law doctrine. On the one hand, we have to reject the natural law doctrine that unjust law cannot be law, because our account of legislative legitimacy must allow the possibility that those who believe a certain legislation is

---

[11]   *See* Holmes (2003), p. 50.

unjust in the light of their own conceptions of justice have a reason to accept its claim to deference as legitimate.

On the other hand, we are required to go beyond both the descriptive and normative positivism.[12] Descriptive positivists treat identification of law as an epistemic issue and separate it from a practical normative issue of deference to law. The normative positivists, by contrast, hold the positivist distinction between law and morality as a moral or practical, not epistemological, distinction that requires normative justification. They open the way to reunite the two issues separated by descriptive positivists, but they hold that the criteria for identifying law reunited with the conditions for deference to it should exclude moral or political standards external to the existing positive law. Descriptive positivism cannot offer any key to the issue of legitimacy. Some descriptive positivists may have some independent political theories that illuminate that issue, but their positivist view itself does not give any useful resource for constructing such theories. Normative positivists go back to sanctification of the victor's justice by regarding the positivity of positive law as a sufficient condition for legitimacy of its claim to deference.

This implies that we need a third concept of law, distinct both from natural law and positivist doctrines. The required concept of law is the one that gives us a clue for exploring the trans-positive normative constraints on positive law that constitute the conditions for our accepting its claim to deference as legitimate. As such a third concept of law I present the concept of 'law as a project for justice'.[13] This concept comprises the following key tenets:

(1) *Justice-Claim as Immanent in Law*   The natural law doctrine issues a simple but formidable challenge to legal positivists. How can we on earth distinguish law from the gunman's threat *writ large* if we exclude accordance with justice from the concept of law as positivists require? The command theory of law simply defied the challenge by holding that we cannot and need not distinguish the two. But it so grossly fails to capture the full complexity of law that it lost credibility even among positivists.

H.L.A. Hart, a leading positivist who rejects the command theory, thus attempted to meet the challenge of natural law doctrine by presenting the concept of law as the union of primary and secondary rules.[14] However, whatever merits his analysis may have in other respects, it fails to distinguish law from the system of organized coercive exploitation that can be characterized as a sophisticated gunman's threat situation, because criminal organizations such as the Mafia can have a system of primary and secondary rules to enhance the efficiency of their organized criminal activities. Hart himself admits this when he mentions 'an extreme case' of legal system where the citizens 'might be deplorably sheep-like' and 'might end in the slaughter-house'.[15]

---

[12]   For recent discussions of the relation between descriptive and normative positivism coupled with the distinction between inclusive and exclusive positivism, *see* Coleman (2001).

[13]   For a fuller exposition of this concept of law, *see* Inoue (2003).

[14]   *See* Hart (1961).

[15]   Ibid., p. 114.

The concept of law as a project for justice looks to the distinct normativity of law for a core feature that distinguishes it from the enlarged and sophisticated form of the gunman's threat situation. Normative statements are distinguished from imperatives by involving not just a demand for obedience but a claim that there are reasons that justify their demand. As a normative system law involves a claim to reason-based justifiability. The *differentia specifica* that distinguishes law from other species of norms is that the justificatory reasons it claims to have are reasons based on justice as a distinct value, distinct from love, spiritual salvation and the like. Law claims that it is in accordance with justice. This justice-claim inheres in the concept of law. The gunman's threat is not only unjust. Being a pure imperative, it does not even need to claim to be just.[16]

This difference between law and the gunman's threat situation can be clearly shown in the following fact. If a robber's victim *x* asked the robber *y* what justice-based reasons entitle *y* to require money from *x*, *x*'s question would be defied as out of place. To use the term of speech act theory, it would commit an error of illocutionary infelicity. But if a person who is required to obey a law asks the law-maker what justice-based reasons justify it, her question cannot be dismissed as out of place. It must be treated as the right kind of question to be asked about law. The questioner is entitled to be answered although the answers she actually receives may not be satisfactory for her. This difference arises from the fact that law, even unjust law, must claim to be just whereas a gunman's threat need not.

Justice-claim inheres in law because law is a project for justice. Law can make a failure in this project, which means that law may be unjust. Unjust law can still be law, but if it gives up this project itself, it is no longer law as distinct from the gunman's threat writ large. The concept of law as a project for justice has a stronger normative connotation than Lon L. Fuller's concept of law as 'the enterprise of subjecting human conduct to the governance of rules'.[17] Law is the enterprise of subjecting human conduct not just to the governance of rules but to the governance of *just* rules. The 'internal morality of law' that Fuller derived from his concept of law is tantamount to the assurance of predictability of law.[18] It can no more distinguish law from a sophisticated system of coercive exploitation than Hart's concept of law can, because clever exploiters assure the exploited of the predictability of exploitation so as to make the economy of exploitation sustainable and to maximize long-term exploitative benefits.

(2) *The Right to Justice-Review as Law's Commitment*   It may be objected that the normative hurdle of justice-claim is so low that anything can clear it because all it requires is that law must *pretend* to be just. This objection fails to capture the logic of claiming. When claiming to be something, the claimer must also claim that

---

[16]   It is possible that a gunman's threat is accompanied by justice-claim. A bank robber who is motivated by an anti-capitalist revolutionary cause may claim that her robbery is justified by an egalitarian principle of distributive justice. But robbery can be 'properly' performed without being accompanied by such a claim. Justice-claim is merely its contingent attendant circumstance.

[17]   *See* L.L. Fuller (1969), p. 96.

[18]   Ibid., chap. 2.

her claim is serious and should be taken seriously even if she pretends to be what she claims to be. She cannot do anything that betrays that she just pretends, and she must do what shows that her claim is serious and honest when she is required to do so. If she should do otherwise, she would be understood to have given up her claim. Claiming commits the actual claimer to acting just as seriously and honestly as the *ideal claimer* would do, even if the actual claimer just pretends and keeps her fingers crossed. This commitment is quite demanding.

By making a justice-claim, law commits itself to doing what the ideal justice-claimer would do. Law is committed to subject itself to constant critical review of its congruity with justice by all the people it governs. In other words, law is committed to respect and protect their right to challenge, re-examine and revise its decisions that claim to be just. This may be called the proto-right to justice-review. It is more abstract and more fundamental than the various substantive rights and democratic-process-based rights that competing conceptions of rights and democracy expound. This is a second-order ground right to re-examine and redefine the meaning, scope and relative weight of the substantive and democratic rights. Here we can find the first clue to the issue of legitimacy. If law secures the proto-right to justice-review for the people it governs, they are reasonably expected to respect its claim to deference as legitimate even if they have a critical reservation on its congruity with justice.

The mode and level of institutional guarantee given to this proto-right varies from the rights to hearing, due process, appeal to multiple instances and retrial, to the right to judicial remedies against administrative measures, to the rights to free speech, association and democratic participation, to the right to constitutional judicial review, and to the rights to conscientious objection and civil disobedience. There is no algorithm for determining what and how much institutional implementation of the proto-right is necessary and sufficient for a given alleged legal system to count as law. Specific forms of institutional implementation are themselves subject to the critical review that the proto-right entitles people to make. But an alleged legal system that closes all the institutional routes for justice-review of its prescriptions cannot be called law any more. It *is* the gunman's threat writ large. Apart from this negative pole, the legal status of a legal system cannot be decided in the all-or-nothing way. It is a matter of comparative assessment. The more effective and the more accessible are the institutional means for justice-review provided by a legal system, the higher dignity of law and the more legitimate claim to deference it has.

(3) *The Priority of the Universalistic Concept of Justice over Specific Conceptions of Justice*   Law's commitment to justice-review right implies its commitment to advance justice-based reasons for its decisions in response to critical challenge from those who are discontented with them. But justice is a very controversial idea. It is not very likely for challengers to agree to law's response. How is it possible for them to acknowledge that law is sincere in giving justice-based reasons while they hold its response is wrong?

The answer lies in the distinction between *the concept* and *conceptions* of justice. Genuine disagreement between competing conceptions of justice is possible because there is the same concept of justice of which they are competing conceptions. Controversiality of justice implies, rather than disproves, that there is a shared concept of justice such that each of the competing conception claims to be a better interpretation of it than the others. What is this underlying concept of justice?

Perelman presented the formal idea of justice as the underlying common concept of justice.[19] This formal idea is the requirement of categorization or treatment according to some rule. Specification of the rules of treatment is totally left up to competing conceptions of justice. The formal idea itself does not place any constraint on the choice of rules of treatment. The formal idea is certainly not an empty formula as some positivist critics of the idea of justice claim. It guarantees predictability by prohibiting *ad hoc* treatment. But it is normatively too weak and undiscerning to function as the regulative idea for competing conceptions of justice. It does not give any clue to moral criticism of arbitrary discrimination.

Perelman presented his formal idea of justice as an interpretation of the Justinian principle 'Treat like cases alike.' But this formula can and should be interpreted to mean a stronger principle: the requirement of universalization. This principle prohibits non-universalizable discrimination. It does not just require categorization of treatment but places constraint on the permissible justification for the use of discriminatory categories: it requires that the use of such categories must be capable of being justified without depending on non-universalizable grounds. This principle adequately captures the underlying core concept of justice because all the conceptions of justice must be committed to exclude morally arbitrary discrimination and because the arbitrariness of discrimination cannot be identified without looking not just into the mode but into the grounds of discrimination.[20]

Although the universalistic concept of justice as presented above is not committed to any specific conception of justice, it implies strong normative constraints on them that they must satisfy if they are to qualify as conceptions of *justice*. The implied constraints thus dismisses as illegitimate those conceptions that allow *free riding*, or *double standard*, or *collectivized egoism* that disguises itself as a public interest, or *vested interests* that are distinguished from rights by the lack of universalizable justification.

The moral insight underlying all these implications is the requirement of *reversibility*. Principles and their justification can meet the universalization requirement of justice if and only if they are reversible, that is to say, if and only if we would be able to accept them even if we *were* the *others* who are disadvantaged by them. The counterfactual reversion of the self and the other required by this test involves not just the situations in which people find themselves but also the perspective from which they see their situations. The test of reversibility requires us to examine whether we would be able to accept our principles and justifications for them even if we see them from the perspective of the others who are disadvantaged by them. This reinforcement of reversibility can be justified by

---

[19]   *See* Perelman (1963), pp. 6-29.

[20]   For a fuller examination of the significance, appeal and limits of the concept of justice as the universalization requirement, *see* Inoue (1986).

reduction ad absurdum. If perspectival reversibility is rejected, masochists would be allowed to torture innocent people, for example. The reinforced reversibility test is tantamount to the requirement for public justification: we must justify our judgments about justice by *public* reasons, reasons that are intelligible and acceptable for the others who do not share our *idiosyncratic* perspective, provided they subject themselves to the same discipline of public reason-giving.[21]

The primacy of the universalistic concept of justice over specific conceptions of justice as shown here offers us the second clue to the issue of legitimacy. If law takes seriously our justice-review right by responding to our challenge on the basis of reasons that meet the constraints of universalization requirement as the underlying common concept of justice, then we can respect law's justice-claim as sincere and its claim to our deference as legitimate even if we believe that our conception of justice is better than the one adopted by law. Moreover, because we would require others to defer to law under these conditions if we were the winners of legislative politics, we are also required to do so by the universalization principle that constitutes the underlying common concept of justice.[22]

I have presented and characterized the concept of law as a project for justice in terms of its three key tenets and shown the clues that it offers to the question of legislative legitimacy. In the next concluding section I would like to sketch a conception of the rule of law that is informed by this concept of law and offers the basis of legislative legitimacy.

Strong Structural Conception of the Rule of Law

The idea of the rule of law rejects the rule of Man. It aspires to establish the legitimacy condition of political power that is not reduced to a victor's justice. The democratic-process-oriented and substantive-rights-based approaches to the question of legitimacy examined in the previous section present themselves as the conceptions of the rule of law applied to the regimes of constitutional democracies. They fail to capture the aspiration of the rule of law because they end up in a victor's justice as we have seen.

Both approaches reject the formal conception of the rule of law and present themselves as better alternatives to it. They are right in rejecting it because it is too weak a constraint on political power. The formal conception has two versions. The classic version is the traditional formal idea of *Rechtsstaat* with its doctrine of reservation of law (*der Vorbehalt des Gesetzes*) which stipulates that the rights of citizens can be legitimately restricted only by the state actions that take the form of

---

[21]   For a more detailed discussion of the normative implications of the universalistic concept of justice, *see* Inoue (2003), chap. 1.

[22]   Philip Soper also looks to reciprocity of deference for a reason for deference. But his argument is not informed by the priority of the universalistic concept of justice over specific conceptions of justice and even suggests that the sincerity of law's justice-claim as a condition for the legitimacy of its claim to deference is delimited by some substantive natural-law-like conception of justice. *See* Soper (2002), chap. 6.

Gesetz, the statute law enacted by the legislature. Although this principle is of some use for controlling administrative power, it is incompetent to check legislative tyranny.[23] The modern version is a somewhat stronger idea of procedural natural law whose representative example is Fuller's theory of internal morality of law. I pointed out above that even the latter is too weak to tolerate the systematized form of gunman's threat.

But the formal conception of the rule of law has a sound insight that is worth developing. Its proponents look to the structural conditions of the rule of law that survive the vicissitudes of political strife for the source of its legitimacy. Although their interpretations of these conditions (which they call the *form* of law) are inadequate, their insight can be rescued and developed into an adequate conception of the rule of law by reconstructing it on the basis of the concept of law as a project for justice. I call this approach strong structural conception of the rule of law (hereafter referred to as SSC).

Even the reinforced version of the formal conception such as Fuller's theory interprets the structural conditions of the rule of law as guarantee of predictability of the state's actions. I call this interpretation weak structural conception of the rule of law (hereafter WSC). SSC finds concrete embodiment of the idea of the rule of law in the structural features identified by WSC. But SSC gives a stronger normative significance to these conditions by reinterpreting them as the guarantee of justice-review rights and universalizable (reversible and public) justification required by the underlying common concept of justice.

To illustrate the implications of SSC I take up ten structural conditions here and present its interpretations of them in contrast with the ones given by WSC. The first two conditions are selected from the features that Hart emphasized as what distinguishes law from orders backed by threats.[24] The subsequent eight conditions are the ones that Fuller present as constituents of internal morality of law.[25]

(1) *Reinterpretation of Hart's Conditions*   Among the several distinctive features of law analysed by Hart, the priority of power-conferring law over legislative power and the self-binding nature of legislation are the most important ones for the purpose of illuminating the rule of law. The first condition stipulates that naked human will cannot generate law unless it is empowered to do so by law.

---

[23]   This remark needs qualification. Carl Schmitt distinguishes between the two kinds of law's reservation, that is, reservation through law (*der Vorbehalt durch Gesetz*) and reservation on the ground of a law (*der Vorbehalt auf Grund eines Gesetz*). My remark applies to the former that gives a normative free hand to the legislature. The latter involves the constraint of generality requirement that Schmitt identified with the concept of justice and the idea of equality before the law and regarded as the only constraint on the majoritarian tyranny that remains after the demise of faith in natural law. This stronger idea of law's reservation has a potentiality of being developed into what I call strong conception of rule of law, but he failed to develop this potentiality because he confused this with predictability requirement. *See* Schmitt (1993), SS. 138-157.

[24]   *See* Hart (1961), chap. 4.

[25]   *See* Fuller (1969), chap. 2.

The second requires legislators to subject themselves to laws they made. Both are basic conditions that distinguish the rule of law from the rule of Man.

On WSC's interpretation, the priority of power-conferring law guarantees the predictability of legal consequences by requiring that there must be a power-conferring rule which specifies the legislative agent and legislative procedure in such a way that people can clearly know in advance by whom and in what way laws that bind them can be made. On SSC's interpretation, it sets a further requirement that the power-conferring conditions should be universalizable. Hereditary rule, for example, is acceptable for WSC. But WSC rejects it as the rule of Man that undermines the rule of law.

The self-binding character of legislation, on WSC's interpretation, just forbids legislators from upsetting people's expectations by violating the laws they made without changing them in advance according to the prescribed procedure. SSC interprets it to take a further step to prohibit legislators from using laws as a means of enriching themselves in unjust ways. It is interpreted to prohibit legislators' free ride, double-standard laws geared to the advantage of legislators. Furthermore, SSC holds that legislations can be genuinely self-binding only if legislators are subjected to the test of reversibility that requires that laws they make should be such ones that they *could* be able to obey even if they *were* in the place of those minorities who are defeated in, or alienated from, legislative politics. SSC requires that legislation should be self-binding in the same way the universalistic concept of justice requires us to be self-binding.

(2) *Reinterpretation of Fuller's Conditions*   Fuller sets eight conditions for the minimum success of what he presents as law's enterprise, that is, the enterprise of subjecting human conduct to the governance of rules. He holds them to constitute internal morality of law, morality that makes law possible. They are the following: the generality of law, promulgation (prohibition against secret laws), prohibition against retroactive laws, the clarity of laws, prohibition against contradictions in law, prohibition against laws requiring the impossible, constancy of the law through time, and congruence between official action and declared rule.

WSC, which is akin to Fuller's perspective, interprets them as conditions that enable people to predict the state's reactions to their behaviour and to adjust their behaviour in advance on the basis of that prediction. On this interpretation, the generality of law means the regular applicability of laws; the clarity of laws means the clarity of the conditions and effects of legal provisions; the consistency of law means compatibility of laws in their application; promulgation means announcement of the contents of laws, the non-retroactivity of laws means temporal antecedence of their enactment to the human conduct to be governed by them; the constancy of laws means allowance of time for people to know them and fulfil their demands; the feasibility of laws means the feasibility of conforming to legal duties (*lex non cogit ad impossibilia*); and congruence between official actions and declared laws means prohibition against illegal or trans-legal suspension of laws.

By contrast SSC interprets them as conditions that enable people to exercise their justice-review right effectively and trust that legislators and other officials are sincere in making laws for justice-based reasons and interpreting and applying them with sensitivity to such reasons. In the following I want to show how the Fuller's conditions are reinterpreted from this standpoint of SSC.

The generality of law means not regular applicability of laws but, more importantly, the universalizability of their justificatory grounds. To pass the SSC's test of generality, mere generality in formulation of laws is not enough. If a law formulated in a general language can be defended only as a protection of special vested interests, it fails to pass the test. SSC revives the idea of generality of law impregnated in Rousseau's idea of the general will that cannot seek for special interests.

The clarity of laws means not so much the clarity of conditions and effects of laws as the clarity of their justificatory grounds and their intelligibility as justice-based reasons. Even if the language of a law is not clear enough to exclude border-line cases, it passes the clarity test of SSC because we can know how to treat such cases if we clearly understand its purport, that is, the justificatory reasons for which it is enacted.   On the other hand, even if the language of a law is unambiguous, it fails this test if its justificatory ground is unintelligible as justice-based reasons.

The consistency of law means not just consistent applicability of a law and compatibility of different laws in their application but overall consistency of justificatory grounds of different laws. SSC requires this because if different parts of our legal system are based on incompatible conceptions of justice that reject each other, we cannot understand the whole of our law as a sincere project for justice.

Promulgation is not just a matter of publicity of the contents of laws. It is also required to provide publicity of their justificatory grounds. To pass this publicity test, it is not enough for a law to include a provision of its aim. It is also necessary to open to the public the deliberative process for its enactment and materials and data considered in that process.

The non-retroactivity of law means not just prospective application of new laws but it also forbids officials to discourage people from acting on their own autonomous interpretation of the laws based on a shared understanding of the justificatory grounds for these laws by upsetting the expectations people formed through such autonomous practice of interpretation.

Constancy of law is required not just because people need some time to know new laws and adjust their behaviours to them but because incessant revisions of laws are usually evidences that legislative process is dominated by competing special interests or that legislators are making double-standard changes in law to seek their own special interest opportunistically according to changing circumstances. SSC rejects this kind of legislative politics as incompatible with law as a project for justice. Furthermore SSC requires constancy of laws to enable people to make a fair critical assessment of them on a basis of adequate knowledge of its consequences for various layers of their society.

The feasibility of laws means the feasibility of something more important than conformity to legal duties although the feasibility of the latter is also necessary. For SSC, law does not just demand that people obey its order but encourages people to join in its project for justice by exercising their justice-review right that it is committed to protect. From this perspective the feasibility of laws means the feasibility of the exercise of justice-review right. This implies that law must not deceive people by disadvantaging those who seek legal remedies by enhancing the cost and risk of doing so or by refusing to help those who are helpless to resort to such remedies. This requirement may be expressed by the formula that *lex non decipit*.

Lastly, congruence between official actions and declared laws is interpreted to prohibit not only illegal suspension of laws but also incongruity between the officially declared aims of laws and the actual motives that govern their operation. Such incongruous practices are rampant in contemporary societies. Among them are the discrimination against specific groups by neutral legal language geared to target them and the special interest legislation disguised by the language of public interest.

I have illustrated how SSC reinterprets the ten major structural conditions of the rule of law. Table 3.1 recapitulates the features of SSC as presented above in contrast with WSC. This illustration is certainly not comprehensive. But I hope my discussion has at least shown that the strong structural conception of the rule of law based on the concept of law as a project for justice offers an approach to the question of legislative legitimacy that is worth the further exploration by those who want to find the basis of legitimacy that go beyond a victor's justice. I invite them to revise and expand the table below, which is certainly tentative and open-ended.

Table 3.1 Two structural conceptions of the rule of law

Structural Principles of The Rule of Law	Weak Conception: Securing Predictability	Strong Conception: Securing Justice-Review
Primacy of Empowering Law over Power	Predetermination of Legislators and Legislative Procedures	Universalizability of Empowering Conditions (Hereditary and Charismatic Rulers Rejected)
Self-Binding Force of Legislation	Legislators Bound by Legislative Product and Process	Eliminating Free Rides, Double Standards and Irreversible Discriminations from Law
Generality of Law	Regular Applicability of Law	Universalizability of Legislative Grounds
Clarity of Law	Conditions and Effects Clarified	Intelligibility of Legislative Grounds
Consistency of Law	Compatibility in Application	Overall Justificatory Coherence of Law
Promulgation	Legislative Products Promulgated	Legislative Deliberation Process Publicized

Non-Retroactivity of Law	Advance Warning Required	Respecting Popular Expectations Generated by Implications of Legislative Grounds
Durability of Law	Enabling the Citizens to Adapt Themselves to Enacted Laws	Warding off Special Interest Laws; Securing Fair Assessment of Legislative Consequences
Feasibility of Law	Practicability of Legal Duties (*lex non cogit ad impossibilia*)	Removing Disadvantages Incurred in Seeking Legal Remedies (*lex non decipit*)
Compliance of Officials	Prohibiting Illegal Suspension of Laws	Checking Unfair Political Motives Covered by Apparently Fair Legislative Grounds (Prohibiting the Rigged Discriminatory Laws and the Disguised Special Interest Laws)
Other Unenumerated Structural Principles	To Be Interpreted in the Lights of Predictability as Above	To Be Interpreted in the Lights of Justice-Review as Above

References

Ackerman, B. (1991), *We the People 1: Foundations*, Cambridge MA.

Arendt, H. (1969), 'On Violence,' in *Crises of the Republic*, New York, pp. 103-198.

Clausewitz, C. von (1980), *Vom Kriege*, Stuttgart.

Coleman, J. (ed.) (2001), *Hart's Postscript: Essays on the Postscript to 'The Concept of Law'*, Oxford.

Dworkin, R. (2006), *Justice in Robes*, Cambridge MA.

Dworkin, R. (1986), *Law's Empire*, Cambridge MA.

Fuller, L.L. (1969), *The Morality of Law*, revised ed., New Haven CT.

Hart, H.L.A. (1961), *The Concept of Law*, 1st ed., Oxford.

Hobbes, T. (1984), *De Cive: The English Version*, ed. by Howard Warrender, Oxford.

Hobbes, T. (1971), *A Dialogue Between a Philosopher and a Student of the Common Laws of England*, ed. by Joseph Cropsey, Chicago.

Hobbes, T. (1839), 'Leviathan,' in W. Molesworth (ed.), *The English Works of Thomas Hobbes*, Vol. III, Aalen.

Holmes, S. (2003), 'Lineages of the Rule of Law,' in José M. Maravall and Adam Przeworski (eds), *Democracy and the Rule of Law*, Cambridge, pp. 19-61.

Inoue, T. (2003), *Ho toiu Kuwadate [Law's Project]*, Tokyo.

Inoue, T. (1986), *Kyosei no Saho: Kaiwa toshite no Seigi* [*Decorum of Conviviality: Justice as Conversation*], Tokyo.

Kennedy, D. (1997), *A Critique of Adjudication: Fin de Siècle*, Cambridge MA.

Maus, I. (1992), *Zur Aufklärung der Demokratietheorie: Rechts- und demokratietheoretische Überlegungen im Anschluß an Kant*, Frankfurt am Main.

Perelman, C. (1963), *The Idea of Justice and the Problem of Argument*, London.

Schmitt, C. (1993), *Verfassunslehre*, 8. Auf., Berlin (first edited in 1928).

Soper, P. (2002), *The Ethics of Deference: Learning from Law's Morals*, Cambridge.

Waldron, J. (1999a), *Law and Disagreement*, Oxford.

Waldron, J. (1999b), *The Dignity of Legislation*, Cambridge.

Part II

LEGISLATION, RULES AND NORMS

Chapter 4

Legislative Techniques

Peter Wahlgren[1]
University of Stockholm, Sweden

Introduction

Legislation is presently under strain. Technical progress, internationalisation and the growth of legal information alter the presuppositions at what seems to be an ever-accelerating pace.

These developments do not merely affect the issues to be regulated. This process also challenges the concept of legislation as such. It is in several ways apparent that traditional means of solving legal problems are becoming less efficient, and that alternative solutions ought to be considered.

This article focuses on the latter. More precisely, the objective is to discuss whether there exist methods, or ways of approach, which may support lawmaking in a complicated technical environment characterised by a fast pace of change. The discussion is tentative; the ambition is merely to make an inventory of possible ways ahead. Three alternatives are addressed:

(1) The traditional approach in which legislation as we now know it is being adapted and elaborated by conventional means.
(2) The embedded approach in which rules are being physically implemented in technical mechanisms.
(3) The utopian approach in which (what is now known as legal) problems are eliminated in a proactive way before they actually occur, diminishing the need for legal rules as such.

---

[1] The article 'Legislative Techniques' was originally published in *Scandinavian Studies in Law*, 47, IT-Law, Stockholm 2004. © Peter Wahlgren 2004.

Background

Traditional, black-letter law can be adjusted in several ways. When a new problem emerges the standard procedure is no doubt to amend or alter existing provisions so that adequate solutions can be reached. In a short-term perspective there can be little doubt that this is the most efficient method. New rules can be implemented with relatively little delay and the mechanisms to produce them are readily available. From the point of view of the politicians it is also obvious that this method will always be preferred. Prompt legislative actions are not only important because they eliminate acute problems – they are also profound illustrations of vigorous leadership.

A continuous aggregation of detailed, often reformulated rules also has drawbacks, however. In a long-term perspective it is apparent that a common side effect is the accumulation of inconsistent regulations, exhibiting a poor overall structure. Equally problematic is the continuous vitiation of the legal language, following from a frequent use of *ad hoc* solutions, and the ever-increasing complexity of piecemeal legislation.[2] An additional problem is that legislation tends to become more and more voluminous. [3]

The negative effects of the traditional legislative approach often make themselves felt; in many areas there is no doubt that it is impossible for anyone not trained in law to understand the legal system. Sometimes it is difficult also for lawyers to grasp legislation, at least when it comes to issues outside their day-to-day practice. To identify, retrieve and evaluate the different components that may be relevant can simply be too complicated. Updated and detailed background knowledge about the situation at hand is in most cases a precondition for efficient work.[4] Moreover, the situation appears to be worsening as the rules become more diversified and the particularisation of solutions continues. The usual criticism, that much of current legislation is made up of short-lived provisions of dubious quality, in which contradictions and incompleteness are rife, is often valid.[5] An additional consequence of this state of affairs – as is clearly reflected in frequent debates in the media – is an increasing demand for greater transparency in the legal sector.

---

[2] *See* J. Hellner, *Lagstiftning inom förmögenhetsrätten: praktik, teori, teknik.* Juristförlaget (Stockholm, 1990); D. Westman, *Rättspolitik på IT-området – ett diskussionsunderlag,* (Stockholm, 1999) (Det IT-rättsliga observatoriets rapport 9/98), and P. Wahlgren, 'On the Future of Legal Science', *Scandinavian Studies in Law,* 40 (2000): 515-525.

[3] *See* B. Tarras-Wahlberg, *Lagstiftning till döds?* (Stockholm, 1980).

[4] H. Danelius, 'En lagrådsledamots tankar om lagstiftningen', *Svensk Juristtidning,* 1 (2004): 25-33.

[5] *See* e.g., about governmental countermeasures initiated in Sweden, Näringsdepartementet, *Reglers effekter för små företag – Hur gör man en konsekvensanalys?* and *Regeringens redogörelse för regelförenklingsarbetet med särskild inriktning på små företag,* Rskr 2003/04:8 <http://www.nnr.se/pdf/skr2003_04_8.pdf>.

The shortcomings of the traditional approach are readily apparent in the case of information and communication technology (IT) – which means in effect that the difficulties are revealing themselves in all possible situations. The reason for this is quite easy to understand. The IT sector tends to offer solutions of a complex nature and the lawmaker often encounters problems in trying to satisfy the prevailing demands. How shall, for example, poor health advice and medical prescriptions via Internet – perhaps occurring between two countries, and by the use of a drug supplier in a third country – be managed from the legal point of view? What aspects of new services should be regulated, what kind of regulation is desirable, and how can legal solutions be enforced?

To solve acute problems within a reasonable time, and simultaneously uphold a consistent structure for all parts of legislation is an overwhelming task for several reasons. Persistent complications flow from the fact that the conceptual apparatus of IT lacks in many respects equivalent counterparts in law. Yet another problem is that the meaning of legal concepts often changes, or becomes blurred when linked to new technology. In this respect a number of familiar phenomena, e.g., marketing, the signing of contracts, and forms of agreement must be looked upon in totally different ways when trading occurs via telecommunications. What is more, previously unproblematic concepts, such as e.g., documents, rules and media almost constantly require reinterpretation.

Limiting factors are also that the time allotted for preparatory investigations is continually decreasing, even as the complexity of the subject matters to be regulated increases. If one adds to the equation the necessity to continually adapt the legal language as new phenomena arise, it is clear that the objective to avoid inconsistencies is unrealistic.

Another aspect to observe is that the rapid development of communication technology and its logical consequence – internationalisation – generates previously unknown demands for standardisation and uniform solutions. This creates additional pressure on the lawmaker. A national legislature can do little on its own to solve these problems and, at our present level of development, truly effective instruments for the implementation of international legislation do not exist.

The Traditional Approach

Various strategies have been launched to cope with the accumulating difficulties. Within the traditional paradigm, several more or less efficient remedies are being advocated. At least three such approaches can be discerned, and although the terminology may appear a bit provocative, they are discussed in this context under the following labels: the quantitative strategy, the hands-off strategy and the qualitative strategy.

The Quantitative Strategy

From the citizens' point of view, a frequent explanation as to why legal problems occur is that no adequate legal rules exist, or that the available rules are not updated. From this standpoint, it can thus be argued that the most realistic counterattack against accumulating legislative problems is to radically increase the pace of *ad hoc* rule production.

To suggest that the cure for inadequate legislation lies in the production of more rules may, considering the aforementioned side effects, appear a bit whimsical. Implicit in a strategy based on an ever-increasing production of specific rules is that all the negative factors, i.e., inconsistency, lack of standardised language, incomprehensive and disparate solutions, as well as other evils, will endure and even grow worse. On the other hand, in a short-term perspective, it may be suggested that it is difficult to identify any realistic alternatives. Or, to put it a bit more cautiously, it is reasonable to claim that the alternative approaches that have been suggested still have to prove that they are practically viable. Therefore, to be sure to accomplish anything, the best thing appears to be to stick to established recipes. Concrete patchwork legislation, however poor its quality may be, is doubtlessly in many cases better than no solution at all.

The acute need for short-term problem removal is not however the only reason why *ad hoc* legislative measures must be looked upon as a pragmatic alternative. An additional argument indicating that an intensified rule production is the most logical course to follow is that such a strategy can avail itself of an established administrative mechanism. Moreover, this approach is pedagogically easy to understand, and, after all, publicly heralded legislative measures are important survival kits for politicians.

It is to be noted that a quantitative approach need not be entirely related to a worsening situation, nor does this traditional approach reflect a status quo. From the methodological point of view, the means to handle large volumes of legislation has gone through revolutionary stages of development in recent decades. To manage legal rules today is entirely different as compared to the situation thirty years ago, and despite the fragmented nature of the legislation there is no doubt that the potentialities to work efficiently have improved in recent decades. The events of digitalisation, computer-based information retrieval, and the Internet have radically changed the methods for extracting relevant information from the ever-increasing bulk of legislation. It may also be noted that explanatory information about legislation has improved considerably.

It is important to understand, however, that these changes do not reflect more efficient ways of producing updated, high-quality legislation. The advances are related to new ways of managing legislative information and in this respect it is beyond doubt that IT has been able to counterbalance many of the negative side effects of the legislative quilt approach.

On the other hand, it may be argued that the employment of IT has done little more than to postpone a possible breakdown of the traditional legislative approach by drastically improving the possibilities to locate and manage scattered information components. Following this line of thought, an even more critical argument would be to suggest that IT actually has had a negative influence on the development of the legislative method by obscuring the core problems. That is simply to say that without access to computer-based tools and modern information retrieval techniques it would probably not have been possible to accumulate such a great bulk of inconsistent material.

Arguments of the latter kind are not possible to prove, nor is it meaningful to try to isolate the factors affecting the prevailing development. What is however beyond doubt is that IT has had a considerable influence over how legislative information can be managed. It also seems uncontroversial to suggest that this development to some extent has shifted the focus; away from methods of developing legislation as such, towards research into such aspects as legal information retrieval, indexing of legal documents, and legal data-base design.

A further consequence of this is that a legislative strategy based on increased rule production appears to have little to offer in the long run. A strategy based on increased rule production means that the difficulties handling an accelerating technical development, problems of internationalisation and the growth of legal information would persist. The quantitative strategy is not a well-defined, elaborated remedy – it is a way of doing things as they always have been done, although in a more hastened way.

From this perspective, it is also clear that an increased use of IT for the management of legal information does not address the critical issue – which is to develop high-quality regulations. IT is in this respect merely a sticking plaster, used to diminish problems caused by primitive legislative techniques.

The Hands-off Strategy

For quite a long time it has been argued in various circumstances and from various standpoints that the state should intervene as little as possible and that the development of self-regulation and legal free zones is a better alternative. Quite frequently such ideas have been proposed concerning the use of the Internet, the digitalisation of music, etc.

Theories concerning self-regulation are usually underpinned by legitimate and easily understandable desires to avoid unnecessary administrative burdens and bureaucracy. At the surface level, they can therefore appear attractive, and in some situations there is no doubt that private dispute resolution and other kinds of non-authoritative agreements provide well-functioning solutions. Such approaches may also be preferred since they are comparatively cheap, can be conducted with little delay and completed without making the process public.

If one investigates this approach a little bit further, however, it is apparent that in many cases it is unrealistic to maintain a system based on self-regulation. It may even be questioned whether this approach should be recognised as a general strategy at all, and there are several reasons for this.

In an analysis of the prospects of self-regulation mechanisms it is important to keep in mind that the lawmaker usually has access to a system of sanctions, and that legislation is usually upheld and supported by a system of authoritative institutions. In an environment where self-regulation is presupposed many of these factors are absent, which is obviously a considerable complication. If the parties involved are not on an equal footing, and if mechanisms for the effectuation of legal decisions or enforceable sanctions are lacking, the incentives to follow the rules are likely to diminish.

It is important to note that large portions of the legislation seek to balance different opinions and various needs in an authoritative manner. To accomplish this is more or less impossible if the parties have unequal access to resources and no third party is involved. In many cases the objective of the law is to protect the weaker party and without access to authoritative powers it is difficult to reach acceptable solutions. In that respect, the IT sector is no exception – access to foreseeable rules and authoritative decisions are necessary prerequisites in this context as well. It is here sufficient to mention the need to vindicate consumers' rights vis-à-vis dominating software producers, and the necessity to balance privacy-infringing state control and individuals' right to be left alone.

Apart from apparent problems concerning the administration of a self-regulating system, there exist a number of substantive reasons supporting the view that substituting legislation with self-regulation is not a realistic alternative. As regards the IT sector it may well be argued that a well-functioning system of legal rules, including the means to implement them, is an indispensable prerequisite for the continued growth of the Internet and IT-related services. The presence of an authoritative legal system is not only essential for individuals engaging in business and other activities on the Internet. An adequate and reliable system of rules is also required to attract investors and companies prepared to develop new solutions – both being crucial ingredients for further advances. In this context mention may be made of issues concerning free competition, balancing of intellectual property rights, and security aspects – all examples having a poor record of functioning smoothly without intervention from the legislature.

Moreover, in any discussion about self-regulation it is to be recalled that IT and the Internet are in many ways being used in criminal and unethical activities. In this respect, there is a clear and large-scale need for mandatory legislation. Criminal activities often affect third parties, i.e., persons that have little or no influence over such activities, and to suggest that all acts performed with the assistance of IT, public networks, or telecommunications should remain unattended to by the legal system is, of course, absurd.

A further argument against various kinds of hands-off strategies is that the state and all public authorities use IT and telecommunications in their relations with the public. In this context, the need for legislative safeguards is so obvious that any hands-off strategy would for several reasons appear naïve. Constitutional principles and fundamental legislation protecting core issues such as freedom of information, privacy, and secrecy can simply not be abandoned solely because the media and the ways of communication change.

Thus, a quick overview of the so-called hands-off strategy indicates that although self-regulation may be considered in some situations, it cannot be looked upon as a *general* legislative strategy. This is not to say, however, that this approach should be ruled out altogether. Frequently, various kinds of co-operative efforts between private enterprises and the government are likely to generate better solutions as compared to what can be accomplished by the legislature alone. Obvious examples are the joint development of codes of conduct, assistance in the setting up of consumer organisations, and the authoritative backing up of self-regulation so that enforcement is guaranteed. [6]

In many cases, nevertheless, it is quite obvious that arguments about self-regulation must be looked upon as rather short-sighted and already past their time. What is more, when arguments in this direction are being put forward it is important to analyse whether there exist opposing interests, perhaps less articulated or less resourceful, that need to be protected. Instead, it may be argued, it is more likely that the development will be in the opposite direction, i.e., that the increasing number of technical components and additional activities in the IT sector will generate demands for more legislation of the traditional kind.

The Qualitative Strategy

Putting aside the primitive quantitative approach, and leaving out unrealistic arguments concerning self-regulation, a remaining question is whether the existing legislative method can be elaborated in order to better combat the problems it is facing. Historical parallels indicate that this may well be the case and that the legislation as we now know it can be relatively flexible.

Legislation has repeatedly changed its appearance. The urbanisation and development of more technically advanced societies are for instance doubtlessly reflected in the way legislation itself. One example is the abandoning of casuistic models of legislation in favour of more sophisticated solutions based on general provisions – a transfer which obviously has been closely interrelated with the industrialisation and the need for a more competent legislation.

In an attempt to improve the present legislative method, several approaches are interesting to investigate. One way of strengthening the lawmaking process, it may be suggested, is to form more or less standing committees that are able to accumulate domain-specific knowledge over longer periods of time. As compared to the usual strategy – the setting up of *ad hoc* committees which are regularly subject to restrictive time limits, and bound by short-sighted political directives – such an approach has several advantages. Most importantly, extended investigations make it possible to deepen knowledge about the preconditions in various fields, and, consequently, are more likely to produce high-quality solutions.

To try to improve legislation by providing better conditions for legislative committees is by no means a new idea. Strengthening of legislative committees is an often-suggested remedy and several kinds of 'law observatories' have been

---

[6] *See* e.g., The UK Cabinet Office, Regulatory Reform Strategy Team, *Better Policy Making: A Guide to Regulatory Impact Assessment* (London, 2003), Annex 2, Alternatives to Legislation <http://www.cabinetoffice.gov.uk/regulation/docs/ria/pdf/ria-guidance.pdf>, *and* U.S. Department of Commerce, *Privacy and Self-regulation in the Information Age*, Washington D.C. 1997 <http://www.ntia.doc.gov/reports/privacy/privacy_rpt.htm>.

established under different labels.[7] In an inventory of possible ways ahead this approach must nevertheless be mentioned. It may also be argued that the potentialities of this line of development are not yet fully understood. The need to enhance the competence of legislative committees is in many cases patent, but the possibilities to reorganise the preparatory process are seldom debated. To what extent are, for example, disparate political goals, the need to balance contradicting interests, etc., actual problems in this respect? What are the pros and cons of expanding the time frame for legislative undertakings – and how can negative effects be minimised?

In addition to potentialities that may relate to the reorganisation of legislative committees, the possibilities to develop the (written) legal language should be mentioned. The possibilities to improve the quality of legal texts have attracted a lot of attention in recent years and several projects have been initiated, both by the EU, and by national governments.[8] The assumption is that the understanding and transparency of legislation will be enhanced if the language of the law is made clearer. The focus has been placed on several aspects such as grammar and sentence structure, systematic replacement of outmoded words and phrases, means to avoid technical concepts, and the possibilities to supplement legislation with explanatory components. In this respect there is no doubt that considerable improvements have been achieved. It is also clear that a lot more will be done, as the bulk of legislation is slowly being revised from this point of view. Difficult remaining problems are however the obvious need to incorporate legal concepts of a technical and generic nature into legislation, and the fact that the background knowledge and hence also the requirements of the individuals affected by the laws varies a lot.

A less common but probably more prosperous way of enhancing the quality of legislation would be to introduce elaborated analytical tools. Broadening the horizon somewhat, it appears rather uncontroversial to suggest that legislative drafting can be supplemented by methodological rethinking of a more profound nature. At least two approaches can be envisioned; the use of knowledge representation languages (KRL) for analysis and drafting, and a more systematic utilisation of sociological methods for the evaluation of regulatory effects.

KRLs are rarely used in the jurisprudential context but they are regularly employed during the development of IT systems, in order to systematise and understand the tasks that are to be programmed.[9] A variety of KRLs exist, ranging

---

[7]   *See* e.g., *Law and Information Technology: Swedish Views. An anthology produced by the IT Law Observatory of the Swedish ICT Commission*, Stockholm 2002, (SOU 2002:112).

[8]   *See* e.g., the home page of the Swedish Government and the Government Offices, *The Plain Swedish Group – for a plain authority language* at <http://www.regeringen.se/sb/d/480/a/ 3565;jsessionid=apXn5oCi6qyh>.

[9]   *See* e.g., the American Association for Artificial Intelligence, *Languages & Structures* at <www.aaai.org/AITopics/html/struc.html> and, for a illustration of potential use in legislative drafting, *see* Tom M. van Engers and Margherita R. Boekkenoogen,

from pure logical languages to numerous graphical forms. Several tools of this kind are in fact available as interactive computer programmes.

Representation languages of a more elaborated kind are not just essential vehicles during the production of IT applications. KRLs can also be utilised in other situations and any cautious recasting of knowledge with the use of KRLs is likely to deepen the understanding of the subject matter under investigation, regardless of whether any IT application is intended. A number of positive effects can be achieved. Among other things it is apparent that KRLs make it possible to eliminate repetitions and minimize the need for cross-references when complicated matters are to be described. The use of KRLs usually also makes it easier to spot inconsistencies, the need for conceptual elaborations and voids. Moreover it is beyond doubt that KRLs lack many of the weaknesses associated with conventional texts, e.g., vagueness and excess volume.

In the legislative context this means, for example, that a collection of provisions analysed with a KRL can be more easily given a distinct logical form, and that they can also be perceived in a more holistic way. Moreover, elaborated knowledge representations can be used solely as analytical tools, i.e., the result of a KRL analysis can be easily translated back to conventional text format. It follows that, if wisely employed during analytical phases, KRLs have the potential to radically improve the quality of written legislation.

Sociological methods, in turn, include the use of statistics, observations and interviews. In addition, various forms of surveys can be employed and it is also possible to conduct experiments.[10] In this respect various components originating from the field of Law and Economics will naturally become relevant.[11] Sociological methods can be used not only to evaluate how legislation actually works; a more systematic use of sociological methods also makes it possible to accumulate knowledge of how various legislative approaches turn out, and indicate in which situations different types of provisions ought to be employed.

Sociological methods are with one exception, i.e., criminological research, much forsaken aspects of jurisprudence. Consequently, the understanding of legislative effects is poorly developed and, if one compares legislative actions with other kinds of applied sciences, it may be argued that in many cases a similar oblivious approach to the impact of initiated activities would be unthinkable, such as in the development of medicine, construction activities, technological investments, etc.

The incompleteness of knowledge in this respect is easy to illustrate. When is it for instance appropriate to select solutions based on prohibitions and sanctions? When is it more efficient to implement incentives (e.g., tax reductions, subsidies, etc.) for those who act according to the intentions of the legislature? In what

---

'Improving Legal Quality – A Knowledge Engineering Approach', *International Review of Law, Computers & Technology*, 18 (2004): 81-96.

[10] *See* e.g., for a discussion and for further references, Håkan Hyden, *Rättssociologi som rättsvetenskap* (Lund 2002).

[11] *See* e.g., R.A. Posner, *Economic Analysis of Law*, 5th ed. (New York, 1998).

situations is it appropriate to establish standards, and when should stipulated licensing, compulsory educational exams or informative actions be preferred? Does there even exist an established taxonomy over various possible legislative solutions?[12]

The shallow understanding of regulatory impact clearly indicates that a more systematic study of the outcome of various legislative actions is a fruitful approach, and that there is every reason to enhance the use of sociological methods in the further development of legislative techniques.

If one tries to summarise this brief overview of how 'classical legislation' may develop it appears indisputable that there exist several interesting options. Organisational re-thinking, a more intense focus on legal language, the employment of analytical tools such as KRLs, and a more systematic use of sociological methods are all approaches which appear to harbour considerable potentialities for the improvement of legislative quality within the traditional paradigm. A further consequence of this is that a lot can be achieved with comparatively little effort, and that legislation as we now understand it can be improved in many ways by utilising already available methods. It also seems clear that the IT-sector can play an important role in such a development, not primarily by means of providing off-the-shelf applications, but by means of illustrating how analytical investigations can be carried out in a more structured way.

The Embedded Approach

An entirely different way of increasing the efficiency of legislation would be to actively develop the means to embed regulations in the physical environment. Under such a strategy a variety of alternatives can be envisioned, depending on the ambitions and the nature of the issues to be addressed. An illustration of a more elaborated solution is road tolls with the purpose to cut congestion and predicted traffic jams, which are based on pay-as-you-drive charges. Such regulation is entirely dependent on technical systems, such as various types of satellite tracking devices and/or on microwave signals identifying tags adhering to the vehicles.

Although technical systems of this kind cannot be looked upon as alternatives to traditional legislation it is quite clear that they often provide important complements to the regulations. Illustrations of this are abundant. It is for instance obvious that modern regulations concerning verification of transactions often presuppose technical solutions. Likewise it is clear that rule-based activities within public authorities and the government rely to a large extent on technical solutions for the management of decisions, taxation, administration of elections, etc. Noticeable is also that in many situations it would be impossible to return to a 'pure', non-technical legislative strategy. Frequently, technical components are taken for granted, and they may also be essential for the effectuation of particular

---

[12]   *See* UK Cabinet Office, *Better Policy Making*, Annex 2, at <http://www.cabinet-office.gov.uk/ regulation/docs/ria/pdf/ria-guidance.pdf>.

legislation. A good example of the latter would be the Swedish Land Register Act, which in fact is a description of an IT system.

In this respect it is beyond doubt that IT provides many new potentialities and that the possibilities to integrate rule-based solutions into technical systems are constantly increasing. This development is reflected in a variety of activities. Currently under discussion are, for instance, privacy-enhancing technologies (PETs) for data protection and digital rights management systems for the administration of intellectual property rights. Potential extensions into more advanced technical solutions may include elaborated forms of e-government for virtually all kinds of administrative services, automatically supervised, dynamic road traffic regulations and, eventually, legal decision-making within the courts, perhaps based on computerised sentencing guidelines and pre-programmed procedural codes.

It should be underlined that the inclusion of regulative aspects in physical components in no way represents a new phenomenon. The need to combine legal rules with physical arrangements has always been present, and the illustrations can be quite mundane. That is simply to say that if you want to protect your home efficiently, it is seldom a good idea to depend solely on legislation concerning trespassing and burglary – locks and other tangible means are often necessary supplements to the provisions. Noticeable is also that physical means sometimes are necessary in order to communicate the content of certain legislation. This is for instance the case with road traffic legislation and for such functions there is no doubt that IT provides considerable potentialities for further developments.

Looked upon from this point of view it is quite clear that most legislation presupposes some kind of physical counterparts. From this also follows that it appears logical to utilise more sophisticated mechanisms when the technical abilities to enforce the regulations increase. In many situations such a development appears unavoidable. At present it is for instance necessary to rely on technical means in order to vindicate the regulations aiming to combat computer viruses and the situation is doubtlessly the same when it comes to upholding security for electronic communication, develop electronic payment systems, etc.

It is also to be borne in mind in this context that the legislative system fulfils the function of providing an important steering mechanism on an aggregated level. In this respect embedded solutions may bring about considerable improvements as regards efficiency. Wisely employed, IT can eliminate many of the present problems of poor legislative impact and the interest for further developments in this direction are likely to increase as understanding of the potentialities becomes more widespread.

A further consequence of this is that the prospects for traditional legislation may seem meagre. When compared to sophisticated technical solutions, do classical laws offer any realistic alternatives with respect to effectiveness, clarity and predictability? Or, to polarise a bit more, do paper laws represent anything else than a primitive form of social instrument?

In an analysis of this approach it is also relevant to discuss a number of secondary effects. Several important questions come to mind. One thing to speculate about is, for instance, whether the development of more integrated forms of legislation should be reflected in the ways in which legislative investigations are carried out. That is to say would it not be more logical to start out by means of designing technical systems when new regulations are being prepared? Likewise, if various forms of technically embedded solutions are likely to be more efficient, should not technical solutions be perceived as the primary objectives of legislative processes? And, consequently, should not black-letter legislation primarily be looked upon as a documentation of technical solutions, and, ultimately, be designed as manuals for how to operate the systems?

On the other hand, although a development of more sophisticated forms of technically dependent regulations may for several reasons seem attractive, it must be conceded that a development of this kind raises a lot of questions. A number of difficulties must be acknowledged and also noticeable is that the debate about potential negative effects has at times been intense. The contributions range from pure fiction to well-researched investigations and balanced discussions concerning the pros and cons of more technically elaborated solutions.[13]

A fundamental objection is for instance that a development of more technocratic societies puts democratic ideals in peril. This is simply because technical standards can be established without the involvement of authorities, and that actors with sufficient resources can easily alter the balance laid down in embedded legislation, by means of altering technical platforms or introducing mechanisms obstructing the systems.

A continuous development of more sophisticated systems is also likely to give rise to problems of transparency. Intricate technical solutions are often difficult to understand and they may thus be viewed as a threat. Closely related to such a scenario is the development of an Orwellian Big Brother society in which technology becomes ubiquitous and where surveillance and privacy control seriously delimits the freedom of individuals.

At a somewhat more concrete level, problems of adequate transformation of legal provisions into computer code, difficulties in upholding essential legal principles, e.g., concerning freedom of information, and unpredicted secondary effects originating from system complexity should be acknowledged. It is also obvious that the issues that need to be considered and the obstacles that have to be dealt with will vary depending on the type of issues addressed.

If one tries to summarise this approach it is clear that IT provides interesting alternatives to black-letter law in the sense that many normative aspects of legislation can be implemented in physical systems.

How this development will progress is not possible to predict in detail, however. Several of the risks related to development of a more technocratic society

---

[13] The study of legal automation (*Rechtsautomation*) has generated a comprehensive literature in the Scandinavian countries. *See* e.g., C.M. Sjöberg, *Rättsautomation. Särskilt om statsförvaltningens automatisering* (Stockholm, 1992), *and* D.W. Schartum, *Rettssikkerhet og systemutvikling i offentlig forvaltning*, Universitetsforlaget (Oslo, 1993). *See also*, for a somewhat different perspective, L. Lessig, *Code and Other Laws of Cyberspace* (New York, 1999).

are of a very serious nature. It is also beyond doubt that these aspects must be given a lot of attention. The use of embedded regulations is not unproblematic, and in many respects the development provides entirely new challenges for the legal domain.

Nevertheless, in the long-term perspective, a development of more integrated solutions appears unavoidable. Huge potentialities for increased efficiency, improved predictability for the outcome of legal decisions, and the development of more detailed specifications of legal processes will not be easily dismissed.

The Utopian Approach

Introduction

Although many of the methods that have been touched upon so far may appear well suited for the development of the legislative technique, it is quite clear that the remedies discussed in the preceding sections will not solve all of the problems legislation is likely to meet in the future.

Consequently, still additional lines of development should be taken into consideration. It may also be argued that the goal should be set even higher, i.e. the objective should not only be to improve legislation – the goal should be to *eliminate* as many legal problems as possible. Ultimately legal problems should not be solved, they should not occur at all. Hence there is a need for a utopian approach.

In the search for a more ambitious strategy it appears important to try to find new, perhaps unorthodox angles of attack. One potential strategy would thus be to first identify underlying requirements for legislation and thereafter, as an intellectual experiment, assume that conventional laws do not exist and then try to come up with ideas about how to satisfy the existing requirements by alternative means.

If this plan is followed, there are at a very general level at least three basic needs that appear to explain the existence of legislation:

(1) individuals must be able to plan ahead and society must be able to cope efficiently with changes,
(2) individuals, enterprises and society as a whole seek to avoid dangers and need to manage risks, and
(3) humans are imperfect social creatures.

If the task is defined in this way it is possible to envision several alternatives to traditional legislation. For each of the requirements identified above at least one complementary remedy can be suggested, and in the following sections three additional approaches, pattern recognition, risk analysis and biotechnology, are elaborated a bit further.

Pattern Recognition

One potential way of increasing the efficiency of legislative actions, it may be argued, would be to utilise various forms of pattern recognition.

The use of pattern recognition appears promising for several reasons, most importantly because the method can support the identification of situations in which legislative actions are likely to be requested. Noticeable in this respect is also that systematic attempts are very rarely made to identify problems that may generate demands for legislation before they actually manifest themselves. Pattern recognition can therefore be interesting to use as a planning tool and thus also, by providing means to speed up the initiation of legislative actions, facilitate the handling of changes.

Underlying these assumptions is the indisputable observation that only a few of the issues which actually could be recognised as legal issues actually establish themselves as legal problems. This is a precondition that obviously makes it interesting to try to identify factors that may have a decisive influence over the process which qualifies certain problems as legal issues.

A characteristic of pattern recognition, as compared to sociological investigations, is that the former is pursued on a general level, i.e. the focus should not primarily be set on the impact of isolated regulations. The objective is instead to pinpoint social factors and their potential interaction with the legal system. In this respect, pattern recognition represents a 'law generic' perspective, as contrasted to sociological investigations which often seek to understand the instrumental qualities of the law ('law as an instrument'). In practice, however, the two approaches are related, and pattern recognition may well be conducted by a variety of sociological means. Doubtless is also that statistics will be essential for the accumulation of knowledge of this general kind, and this is of course also a feature in common with sociological research.

In this context it would be premature to point out any factors that are likely to have a decisive influence over how certain issues become accepted as legal problems. As an illustration, nevertheless, it appears reasonable to speculate about the extent to which access to media, communication channels and lobbying activities can shift the focus of the legislature towards previously less noticed phenomena, and theories like this thus also give indications about how studies of this kind may be designed.

In a similar way it may be worthwhile to investigate the extent to which economic resources, the presence of conflicting interests, knowledge and experience of the legislature, the complexity of the problems, and the nature of the existing legislation may influence the introduction of new issues. It may also be relevant in this respect to investigate whether factors of an indirect nature, such as the need for simplification in mass media, educational activities and the pace of change can be important factors in the process of establishing problems as legal issues.

Risk Analysis

In many undertakings routines for the avoidance of mistakes are essential. The traffic pilot preparing a departure, the engineer designing a machine and the insurance company preparing to launch a new product are all likely to rely on established methods to ensure that nothing important is forgotten, and to gain an overview of the consequences of the activity initiated.

From a general point of view, efforts in this direction can be looked upon as risk analysis, and it is also quite clear that the need to avoid dangers is nearly always present in innumerable situations. Despite this it is clear that risk analysis is a rather unexplored aspect of the legislative technique. As compared to many other activities, it is quite apparent that legislation often is surprisingly reactive in its nature and that the law often reflects solutions based on prohibitions and sanctions. Efforts to avoid dangers and preventive components are rather rare. It thus appears reasonable to discuss the preconditions for amending legislation using risk analysis and various prescriptive solutions.

A scenario of this kind has been described by Richard Susskind, who under the sub-heading 'From legal problem solving to legal risk management' has suggested that

> While legal problem solving will not be eliminated in tomorrow's legal paradigm, it will nonetheless diminish markedly in significance. The emphasis will shift towards legal risk management supported by proactive facilities which will be available in the form of legal information services and products. As citizens learn to seek legal guidance more regularly and far earlier than in the past, many potential legal difficulties will dissolve before needing to be resolved. Where legal problems of today are often symptomatic of delayed legal input, earlier consultation should result in users understanding and identifying their risk and controlling them before any question of escalation.[14]

Although this vision of a proactive approach is of a general nature, i.e. it does not only focus on the design of laws, there is no doubt that a risk analysis perspective can be reflected in legislation as well. A proactive legislative approach could for instance include the use of checklists and matrices. Another alternative would be to more frequently stipulate certifications and licensing of various kinds.[15] Noticeable is also that traditional legislation could often be supplemented with customized informative activities and that the establishment of various kinds of advisory services would in many cases presumably reduce the need for control and reactive sanctions.

Likewise it can be suggested that legislation often can be supplemented by interactive instructions, codes of conduct and instructive schemes describing how

---

[14] R. Susskind, *The Future of Law* (Oxford, 1996), p. 290. *See also* pp. 23-25 on 'The paradox of reactive legal services' and 'Towards legal risk management'.

[15] *See*, for an extensive inventory of 'legal risk analysis methods', P. Wahlgren, *Juridisk riskanalys* (Stockholm, 2003).

various kinds of applications or proceedings can be completed. This would be another way of establishing a more proactive perspective, and if elaborated in the directions mentioned here there can be no doubt that legislation could be more efficient as a risk management tool.

Biotechnology

Biotechnology is presently one of the most intensive research areas and in 2002 a group of researchers stated 'that research in behavioural genetics has the potential to advance our understanding of human behaviour, and . . . the research can therefore be justified'.[16] As a final point in this study on legislative development it could therefore be discussed whether genetic information could also have significant implications for the legal sector.

That is simply to say that if factors such as sexuality, criminal behaviour and intelligence prove to be largely of genetic origin, it is likely that it will eventually be possible to alter the behaviour of individuals. That such a development will require regulation is quite obvious. The question in this context however is whether such a development can also be utilized by the lawmaker.

Although the transformation of biotechnology into a social instrument can in many respects be viewed as a controversial development, it may nevertheless be argued that it is necessary to reckon with this eventually becoming an accepted standpoint. It follows that a number of questions must be addressed. The most fundamental issue is of course whether biological remedies could be admitted as complements, or even accepted as alternatives to legislative actions.

Is it for instance reasonable to accept that the predictive use of genetic information about behaviour 'in conjunction with information about other, non-genetic influences on behaviour may be justified if the aim is to benefit the individual, and in doing so, to benefit society also'?[17] Or, to put it bluntly, being aware of the fact that humans are imperfect social creatures, and noting that this is a major cause of human suffering, should we accept that DNA manipulation, drugs and psychotherapy can be used for purposes other than addressing mental illness?

In a less polarised discussion it may be relevant to analyse whether an extension of social instrumentalism which includes biotechnology in the legal arsenal must represent a dramatic shift of perspective, or whether innovations of this kind can be utilised in a step-by-step fashion? In what ways, if any, could findings of biomedical origin be utilised in specific cases? What are the potentialities, what are the dangers, and what factors should be used to balance conflicting interests?

More concretely, what can be learned from the ongoing discussion concerning chemical castration of sexual offenders, which has (with the offender's consent) in

---

[16] Nuffield Council on Bioethics, *Genetics and Human Behaviour: The Ethical Context* (London 2002), § 11, p. 17.

[17] Ibid., p. xxxii.

several jurisdictions been advocated as an alternative to imprisonment?[18] Is the recommendation that '[w]ith regard to the sentencing of convicted *offenders*, the criminal *law* should be receptive to whatever valid psychiatric and behavioural evidence is available'[19] acceptable?

Still again, if such statements do not represent fair and balanced descriptions of the state of the matter, is it not the objective of jurisprudence to be in the forefront, pointing out obstacles and/or initiating discussions about possible ways forward?

Which Way to Choose?

The purpose of this article has been to make an inventory of possible ways of developing the legislative technique, especially in the light of challenges brought about by IT.

Ten different approaches have been possible to identify: the quantitative *ad hoc* procedure, the hands-off strategy, a potential reorganisation of the legislative preparatory process, undertakings to develop the legal language, the employment of KRLs in analytical phases, utilisation of sociological methods to learn more about legislative impact, the elaboration of means to implement laws in physical mechanisms, the introduction of pattern recognition, the development of proactive risk analysis tools and, finally, the suggestion that biotechnology may function as a social instrument.

The discussion has in parts been speculative and some of the approaches that have been mentioned doubtlessly appear provocative. In summing up it should be mentioned, however, that it is highly unlikely that the law of the future primarily will reflect one or another of the approaches outlined here. The approaches that have been discussed here should not be understood as mutually exclusive alternatives. Instead, they must be looked upon as complementary strategies. The most probable development of legislative techniques is the one of pluralism in which many kinds of methods will find suitable roles, including many which have not been observed in this tentative survey.

From such a scenario follows that an additional objective for studies of legislative technique comes into focus. Apart from further investigations into specific methodological approaches it will become important to outline a functional typology for problem areas and related legislative solutions. It may also be argued that this task should be given high priority, at present there can be no doubt that the knowledge concerning where and when various legislative solutions are best suited is poorly developed.

In what situations is it for instance appropriate to rely on short-term solutions (which would be a realisation of the quantitative approach) and when should long-term organisational reforms be initiated? And, although it may be assumed that

---

[18] *See*, for a comprehensive list of literature on the subject, <http://www.csun.edu/~psy453/ crimes_y.htm>.

[19] Nuffield Council on Bioethics, *Genetics and Human Behaviour*, § 14.32.

language reforms are of great importance when large groups are affected by legislation, as is the case, for example, when tax law reforms are to be launched, under which premises would it be more efficient to implement legislative solutions in physical components? When are meticulously formulated laws to be preferred as compared to interactive IT-systems available via Internet and vice versa?

Likewise, a current debate in Sweden concerns mandatory installation of alcohol breath-analysers in cars, the purpose being to minimise drunken driving incidents.[20] Also such an illustration raises a lot of questions. From a methodological point of view, is this a suitable solution only for certain types of problems? Must a development of this kind be propelled by technical innovations, or is it possible to detect a pattern of components that need to be satisfied when solutions of this kind are to be adopted?

---

[20] A portable breath testing machine is built into the key fob. When you use the fob to unlock your car door, you must blow into it (and pass) before the car will start. A Swedish carmaker's version, the 'Saab Alcokey', is presently being tested with the support of the Swedish National Road Administration. *See* e.g. <http://www.autoweb.com.au/cms/A_101770/newsarticle.html>.

Chapter 5

Questioning Alternatives to Legal Regulation

Philippe Thion*
University of Brussels, Belgium

Introduction

I would like to examine the issue of alternatives to legal regulation (hereafter: 'alternatives'). I want to say how I think alternatives are conceived and elucidate the context from which they have emerged.

With the downturn in world economic activity in the mid-1970s, welfare state interventionism began to lose its attractiveness and came under severe attack. Legislative interference increasingly was believed to be an hindrance to achieving the very economic and social well-being for which it was intended. Numerous authoritative reports and studies, especially those produced by international economic and financial organisations, gravely denounced unaccountable administrative discretion, lack of transparency, opaque decision processes, pursuit of narrow mission goals at any cost, and lack of attention to reviewing, updating and eliminating unnecessary or harmful legislation. Governments were said to act too often without adequate information base regarding the choices about policy instruments, about the design of a specific instrument, or about the need to change or discontinue an existing instrument.[1]

A growing number of Western countries have thus embarked in recent years on ambitious programmes to reduce regulative burdens and improve the quality and cost-effectiveness of state regulations that remain. Governments increasingly rationalised their legislative activities, especially by working out how to utilise more adequately 'alternatives', such as deregulation, self-regulation, convenants, privatisation, information campaigns, self-implementation, subsidies, labelling and experimental regulations. The most frequently advanced rationale with this

---

* I want to thank Mircea Cojanu, Bart Du Laing, René Gonzàlez de la Vega, Juliane Ottmann and Luc Wintgens for their very helpful and valuable comments on earlier versions of this text.

[1] *See* e.g. Organisation for Economic Co-operation and Development (OECD), *The OECD Report on Regulatory Reform: Synthesis* (Paris, 1997).

obviously concerned the overhaul of the Keynesian obstacles to investment, innovation and economic growth.

What makes these regulatory techniques precisely 'alternative' is that they, to induce desired change, do not merely take the shape of commands backed by the threat of strong sanctions such as a fine or a penalty. Alternatives, it is said, do not rule out or conflict with legal regulations enacted by the state. Quite the reverse, these techniques perfectly can form an integral part of legislation, this supposedly even promoting the democratic process and the 'dignity of parliament'.[2] The basic idea is that 'command and control' regulation is the very last option for the legislative body to take. To realise a particular policy goal, preference must principally be given to regulatory techniques that produce less normative density and that leave individual freedom as much as possible without hindrance. Before enacting new legislation, one should assess the self-regulating strength of society, either through scientific research or via the enhanced consultation and participation of civil society (for example by means of public hearings, polls, referenda, internet fora, complaint procedures before the ombudsman, and so on). Especially the OECD reports are written in that vein and most of its member states recently have adopted similar principles.

Alternatives, contrary to what the very word apparently suggests, occupy an highly dominant place today in the legislative arsenal. My main concern here is to map out some important conditions of possibility for the emergence and current prevalence of alternatives. Although alternatives seem rather common and natural to us today, they nevertheless constitute an historical and contingent phenomenon. I would like to introduce, in this respect, a triple distinction.[3] There is, first of all, the law itself, including legislation, which takes in the course of Western history a variety of forms. The law has shifted in different historical periods, since it is reflected upon through different rationalities or mentalities. We always are part of a legal mentality which we inherit and which does not evolve according to our rationally organised intentions. Legal practices, validity criteria, ways to identify the law and to distinguish it from non-law, that is, the very way in which the legal system is programmed, problematised and questioned, all this depends on the legal mentality in place. The second distinction is concerned with the network of power relations which delineates the field in which a legal mentality operates. Because a legal mentality postulates truth claims about legal reality, it is always preceded and supported by the particular ways in which power relations organise our conduct and our mutual interaction. Whereas the legal mentality relates to the questioning of law through the production of statements, power relations for their part deal with the form of the material environment or the visible from which these utterances arise. Both are complementary in that statements refer back to a material

---

[2]   L.J. Wintgens, 'Het wetsbegrip anders bekeken. Alternatieven voor en in wettelijke regulering. Tevens een inleiding tot de legisprudentie, een nieuwe wetgevingstheorie', in L.J. Wintgens (ed), *Het wetsbegrip*, Acta van het Centrum voor Wetgeving, Regulering en Legisprudentie, I (Bruges, 2003), p. 91.

[3]   *See also* V. Tadros, 'Between Governance and Discipline: The Law and Michel Foucault', *Oxford Journal of Legal Studies*, 18 (1998): 82.

environment, whilst the visible implies the existence of statements. Third, power relations have to be distinguished from the code by which they present themselves. It is a well-known Foucaldian theme that power relations have maintained a way of describing themselves which has little relation to their actual operations.[4] What follows, starts from this triple distinction and how these various aspects interrelate.

State Regulatory Action

The Code of Power Relations

I would like to have a closer look, first of all, at the code by which power today is presented and described. This code reveals itself very clearly in the political scheme according to which the intensified employment of alternatives is justified. Alternatives primarily are depicted as an essential means for individual freedom to be guaranteed against excessive state interference. It is said and said again that alternatives have an important part to play in finding the ideal balance between too much and too little state action. Two conflicting elements appear to be crucial in this search for a governmental equilibrium: repressive state action and unrestrained individual freedom.

Freedom is predominantly conceived as the absence of external limitations. This definition holds up a mechanical view of man and society as paradigmatically elaborated by Hobbes. Nature, for Hobbes, is reduced to motion and mankind is rooted in nature, thus mankind is equated with motion. Once the human body moves, it moves forever, unless something or someone else impedes it. Motion is characterised by its inertia.[5] Inertia, however, does not involve that human beings are left at the mere mercy of external causes.[6] The principle of inertia is a restricted version of the principle of self-movement or spontaneity.[7] Now mechanistic spontaneity is transposed on mankind and is called 'freedom', meaning the absence of external opposition or the unconstrained development of one's own natural spontaneity.[8, 9] The term 'natural spontaneity' here stands for the peculiar combination

---

[4] *See* e.g. M. Foucault, 'Two Lectures', in C. Gordon (ed), *Power/Knowledge: Selected Interviews and Other Writings 1972-1977* (Brighton, 1980).

[5] T. Hobbes, *Leviathan*, edited with an introduction by C.B. Macpherson (Middlesex, 1968), p. 87.

[6] *See* M. Bunge, *Causality. The Place of the Causal Principle in Modern Science* (Cambridge MA, 1959), pp. 108-111.

[7] According to the first axiom of Newton's *Principia*, if a body is left to itself it will not therefore cease moving, but it will continue until some force causes it to deviate or even to stop.

[8] R. Boehm, 'Vrijheid, democratie en socialisme', in R. Boehm, J. Kruithof, E. Mandel and L. Swinnen (eds), *Socialisme en Vrijheid* (Antwerp, 1990), p. 34 ff.

[9] Modern freedom clearly violates the Aristotelian concept of a hierarchically formed, ordered and harmonic cosmos, since it allows for the boundless and infinite pursuit of personal benefits. According to Aristotelian thought and the inherent teleological ontology,

of both determinism and freedom. Freedom involves the unlimited development of one's own true nature and asks that man autonomously determines what his purposes are out of his inner being. The only indication as to what man ought to do, is his doing it.[10]

This apparently simply descriptive picture of the free individual has so permeated liberal-democratic culture that its way of elaborating the world is unreflectively asserted in everyday practices and has become strongly and pervasively normative. It suffices to refer to the prevalent culture of personal authenticity and the emblematic supremacy of the market. Today, there exists a stable consensus that the free market represents a crucial catalyst of individual freedom, this ideally involving an existence without external restrictions, in which narcissistic self-fulfilment and self-analysis occupy centre stage.[11] The call for unlimited production, unlimited consumption, unlimited technological innovation, unlimited trade and unlimited mobility is made possible by adopting the modern view of freedom, upholding a picture of man whose subjective desires, if they are not hindered, preserve themselves linearly and endlessly.[12] This image of man, what is more, has been firmly anchored as the self-interest axiom of utility maximisation in rational choice theory, playing a crucial part today in scientific evaluations of legislation, given that neoclassical economics gained enormously in prestige as the leading social science.

It is this picture of the free individual as proper ontological unit that serves as point of departure to organise the political space in which alternatives are to be employed. What is characteristic of the power scheme according to which the intensified use of alternatives is vindicated today, is that it almost perfectly echoes the classical liberal matrix. Its mechanism operates as follows. The subject, conceived as an intentional actor who comes with her or his own interests, is taken to be the primary agent of social action. All legal entitlements are seen as power entitlements attaching to individuals and all questions of legal systematisation are conceived as a matter of classifying subjective rights. Public power is supposed to arise from a necessity expressed by the social actors themselves. Man is self-sufficient alone, though not entirely, since the power to secure himself against the assaults of fellow men is lacking. The conceptualisation of the gap between man's supposed autarky and man's incapacity to fully protect it, founds the authority and *raison d'être* of the public state. Its political power is thus both subsidiary and

---

to strive for an unlimited goal is meaningless and destroys the harmonious arrangement of society and nature.

[10]　T.R. Machan, 'Individualism versus Classical Liberal Political Economy', *Res Publica*, 1 (1995): 3-23.

[11]　C. Lasch, *The Culture of Narcissism. American Life in an Age of Diminishing Expectations* (New York, 1979); G. Lipovetsky, *L'ère du vide. Essais sur l'individualisme contemporain* (Paris, 1983); C. Taylor, *The Malaise of Modernity* (Ontario, 1991).

[12]　P. Koslowski, *Ethics of Capitalism and Critique of Sociobiology. Two Essays with a Comment by James M. Buchanan* (Berlin, 1996).

artificial. This involves that the state merely exists to protect particular interests,[13] and that its power originates in the explicit will of each individual member of society thus entering into the social contract.

This political stance – and this is essential – is particularly tied up with a repressive conception of power, by which are identified all kinds of state action, in the language of law, which specify limitations and restrictions of individual freedom. Power has maintained a way of describing itself as a negative instance whose function is repression. Power, in this view, is ensured both by rights and by law, and is equated with obstruction or repression exercised by the subject and by some unitary agency called the state. Politics, correspondingly, is seen as a means to protect the individual members of society, and their freedom both requires and justifies the restraint of political authority. The principle of the separation between the state and civil society encompasses both the idea of a minimum as much as a maximum state. It is at the same time conceived of as a potential enemy of freedom and as the condition of its existence.[14]

Alternatives, in this code, are said to reshape state action by confirming and intensifying the subsidiary relationship between individual freedom and the state. These techniques are depicted as explicitly posing the question of state power in terms of a distinction between legitimate and illegitimate, between justified and unjustified state coercion. Legislative action is legitimate to the extent that it is reasonably justified that its very endorsement adequately fills up the gap between man's freedom and man's incapacity to fully develop it, and no further.[15] The applied regulatory techniques have to be necessary, proportional, transparent and systematically reviewed against so-called 'principles of good regulation', this usually taking the shape of technical checklists. The legislator has to evaluate whether spontaneous social interaction has failed, and if it has, whether alternatives are sufficient, appropriate, efficient and efficacious to induce the desired policy change. Preference is in principle given to alternatives, since these techniques supposedly constitute a smaller limitation of individual freedom than the command and control type of interference does. Considered in terms of law, this model suggests that it is possible to find a loophole in the law within which social interaction fails. This would be an example of legal inadequacy. But it is also possible, conversely, to find the law overextending itself, in that the law might exercise its power to prevent a certain situation which nonetheless represents no failing social interaction.[16] The problem of alternatives thus unfolds on the basis of which regulatory acts are to be preserved and which are to be allowed.

---

[13] C. Millon-Delsol, *L'Etat subsidiaire. Ingérence et non-ingérence de l'Etat: le principe de subsidiarité aux fondements de l'histoire européenne*, (Paris, 1992), p. 83 ff.

[14] B. de Sousa Santos, *Toward a New Common Sense. Law, Science and Politics in the Paradigmatic Transition* (New York, 1995), p. 411.

[15] The most recent Flemish coalition agreement (2004), for instance, is explicitly framed in that code.

[16] Tadros, 'Between Governance and Discipline: The Law and Michel Foucault', pp. 83-84.

Legal Mentality and Alternatives

The code by which power presents itself is a constituent part, I believe, of the current legal mentality through which legal practices, such as alternatives, are reflected upon. The use and elaboration of alternatives today is an historically contingent phenomenon. Alternatives have no substance or essence that can be grasped by means of a theory. It is rather the name for an event which is constituted in our societies through a series of conceptual and practical operations as an object of certain forms of knowledge and a target of certain institutional practices. To employ an alternative is not just a regulatory label, but is encrusted with all the complex things that it means and requires to employ an alternative in a particular context at some particular point in time. This comes to say that the emergence of alternatives is not 'self-evident', but represents a singular event. It was not 'necessary' to review systematically prospective legislation in order to remedy the downturn in world economic activity in the mid-1970s. It was not 'self-evident' that the most important thing to be done with the inability of governments to resolve market failures, high unemployment and inflation, was to sophisticate the legislative process and to rationalise their set of regulatory instruments.

Alternatives, on the other hand, do not appear out of nothingness. The legislator is always free and constrained at the same time. Despite his presumed 'universal competence',[17] the legislator is constrained because the very notion of legislation only exists in the context of a set of practices that at the same time enable and limit the act of legislating. He cannot think of legislating without thinking within these established practices. This does not mean, however, that his activities are wholly determined, but that his choices depend on a prior understanding of what it means to legislate. The legislator is at the same time free because no amount of legislative practices and ideas can make his choice of one of those ways inescapable. Although the limits of what he can think to do are marked by the parameters of legislative practice he is thinking within, they do not direct to do this rather than that.[18]

Legislative judgments comply with, but are not determined by, what can be called the 'legal mentality'.[19] The legal mentality is what in a given period delineates the conditions under which participants can sustain a discourse about legal reality that is recognised to be true. Law always has comprised, at least in the Western legal experience, a critical instance in relation to legality. This traditionally was the function of natural law. Whereas 'legality' regards what the member of a social group must do and finds itself on the side of constraint, commandment and sanction,[20] 'law' on its turn regards how that person will be

---

[17]   *See*, on this notion, E. Maulin, *La théorie de l'Etat de Carré de Malberg* (Paris, 2003), p. 223.

[18]   *See also* S. Fish, *Doing What Comes Naturally: Change, Rhetoric and the Practice of Theory in Literary and Legal Studies* (Durham, 1989), p. 89 ff.

[19]   *See* P. Legrand, 'European Legal Systems are not Converging', *International and Comparative Law Quarterly*, 45 (1996): 52-81.

[20]   *See also* the next section, this chapter.

judged and questions legality by sorting out on what conditions, in a certain time and place, a legality can act as a common measure.[21] Law's critical function is neither enacted nor applied in lawmaking, adjudication or legal dogmatics, rather their respective articulation, distribution and reciprocal competence proceeds from and expresses the legal mentality, though without being reducible to it. Constantly reformulated, it never ceases to depart from itself through the judgments that express it.

This critical reflection, I believe, takes the shape of 'dominant narratives'. A double premise is applicable in this respect. My first assumption is that a certain concept of law 'inhabits' the legal participant's behavior, that is, his or her idea of law is an idea which provides internally the criteria of what is appropriate in the behavior of the member of a particular society. My second assumption is that the participant's ideas about law take their meaning from collective dominant narratives, which both limit and make sense of a certain view of law. As an accretion of cultural elements and as a modality of legal experience, law is importantly backed by collective dominant narratives, internalised unconsciously by members of the group concerned. Procedures of delimitation and order convey a kind of gradation among or hierarchy between narratives, which allows both the endless reactualisation of existing narratives and the incessant construction of new ones. Some narratives are exchanged in the ordinary course of the day, or evolve by subterranean flows and vanish as soon as they have been pronounced. Others give rise to a certain number of new narratives which take them up, transform them or speak of them. Others again are said indefinitely, they remain said and are to be said again.

It can be upheld, accordingly, that there are certain 'discursive regularities' that come into play as to the very existence of law and the mentality through which it is reflected upon. These discursive regularities authorise some to speak, some views to be taken seriously, while others are marginalised, derided, excluded and even prohibited. Every narrative thus unfolds in a characteristic *substratum* within which thought, communication and action can occur. It is in this sense that the meaning of legislative practices and concepts, their weight, their implementation and their role in society is constrained by the legal mentality. In order to grasp alternatives and to see how their appearance has been possible, they have to be tied up with the specific legal mentality in which they have emerged, and which they embody at the same time. The dominant narratives concerned with alternatives favorably fit in with today's legal mentality, while the legal mentality on its turn produces forms of visibility which reinforce alternatives. The current legal practice and its corresponding mentality can be labelled, in the wake of Ewald, as that of 'social law'.[22] That is, alternatives have to be understood as being part of the social law mentality.

---

[21] F. Ewald, 'The Law of the Law', in G. Teubner (ed), *Autopoietic Law: A New Approach to Law and Society* (Berlin, 1988), p. 48.

[22] F. Ewald, 'A Concept of Social Law', in G. Teubner (ed), *The Dilemmas of Law in the Welfare State* (Berlin, 1995), pp. 40-75; F. Ewald, *L'Etat providence* (Paris, 1986).

The notion of 'social law' here does not refer to the legal disciplines that deal with work and social security. It contains, instead, the current dominant narratives dealing with the question of the sources of law, of the relationship between fact and law, and the criterion of legality. Labor law and social security law are nonetheless typical exponents of the social law mentality, just like for instance consumer law, environmental law, insurance law, transport law, building law and medical law. What first of all characterises the social law narratives is that they no longer leave any space for natural law thinking.[23] From the second half of the nineteenth century onward, the axioms of natural law increasingly have lost the capacity to provide the fundamental basis for finding appropriate legal solutions for collective problems. Narratives dealing with natural harmony, Reason, universality and absoluteness gradually have been substituted by narratives concerned with finitude, man, society and its conflicting interests. In the social law mentality, law no longer is reflected in any reference to the harmonious finality of nature (as in classical natural law thinking), or to universal and 'evident' basic principles illuminated by Reason, such as the 'Golden Rule'[24] or the axiom *'pacta sunt servanda'* (as in rational natural law thinking). Law, instead, is reflected in society itself, that is, the organisation of society becomes fully self-referential. The legal system remains open to cognitive information, but this cognitive openness is only directed at information about the regularities and equilibria within society itself.

Society objectivised by the empirical and human sciences, especially sociology and economics, is depicted as a space in which human beings interact according to associated and opposed interests. It is a space of perpetual conflict and competing forces, that strongly recalls Hobbes' account of man and society.[25] The social law mentality has a striking anthropological character, and brings about the appearance of an historical dimension which contrasts deeply with the natural harmony, respectively, timelessness and universality of classical and rational natural law thinking. The social space is constituted, henceforth, in such manner as to accept nothing external to itself. My assertion here is that law, in the social law mentality, increasingly takes the shape of alternatives. Law does not define an order on which, despite differences, agreement might be reached, but rather seeks to be mere instrument of intervention which is to serve to compensate and correct inequalities.[26] It is a law that does not so much impose (strong) sanctions, but a law that employs rewards, incentives, (positive) discriminations and recommendations. Law is no longer enacted by a single legislator, but by a multiplicity of 'regulators' who incessantly generate technical and strategic modifications. As soon as new information about social reality is disclosed, former regulations have to be adjusted and new ones elaborated. The law programmed and problematised by the social law mentality, as a result, is a law of compromises, negotiation and argumentation,

---

[23]   Ewald, *L'Etat providence*, p. 37 ff; K. Tuori, *Critical Legal Positivism* (Aldershot, 2002), p. 57.

[24]   The Golden Rule states 'Do not to others what you do not want them to do to you'.

[25]   *See* e.g. A. Comte, *Sociologie. Textes choisis par J. Laubier* (Paris, 1957), p. 56.

[26]   Ewald, 'A Concept of Social Law'.

of weighing and balancing, requiring permanent and ever-renewed legitimation and justification. The shift from (rationalist) natural law thinking to the particularity of man and society entailed, what is more, the need to think about law without justice. This was felt very accurately by Kelsen, who elaborated for that reason the necessity to base the legality of a legal system only on its own positiveness. Legal positivism thus appeared as a means to uphold the validity and effectiveness of a legal system without having to refer to an external foundation. The appearance of so-called 'general principles of law' constitute an emblematic example of this evolution. These principles, which supposedly can be found in law itself and its very historical practice, today fulfill – at least partially – the critical function that was traditionally reserved to natural law thinking. With the emergence of the social law mentality, it became very difficult to found legality on anything external or universal, whether nature, an ideal society, a conception of justice or an 'evident' formal axiom. All universalia are but temporary and have to be adjusted whenever the actual distinctiveness of the social context is asking so. Alternatives, for this reason, do not have so much their roots in the deregulation tendency of the 1970s, but rather in the legal mentality that has emerged, at least for Western European countries, in the second half of the nineteenth century. The deregulation movement did not involve a substantial rupture in the legislative attitude. Rather, it engendered an advanced refinement, sophistication and rationalisation of the already existing regulatory matrix.

What is particularly characteristic of alternatives as part of social law, is that they tend to the normalisation and homogenisation of the social field. Alternatives operate on the basis of common standards or 'norms' which can be found in society itself. Norms do not refer to any kind of rule or obligation, but are self-referential yardsticks, provided by statistics and probability calculation, through which society judges itself by employing a criterion following from society itself. The value of an action or a practice is subsequently judged and valued in its relationship to social normality (i.e. the normal vs. the excessive, the abuse, the pathological).[27] The norm is a way for a group to provide itself with a common denominator without recourse to a point of externality. The self-referential character of the norm enables the regulation of the social field without taking into account philosophical, religious or political values. Alternatives, analogously, operate on the basis of the characteristics of the targeted population and on the play of oppositions between the normal (becoming normative) and the abnormal.[28] Social normality as reference for human behaviour, of course, has always existed, but now this criterion has become an essential instrument for governments to act on the population, to reshape their internal relationships and to delineate particular fields of intervention. The intensified employment of alternatives hence follows from a detailed examination of how the population's 'abnormality' can be tamed, of how excessive gaps of deviancy can be limited and of how excessive risks can be further reduced.

---

[27] Ibid., pp. 68-71.
[28] The norm, today, is principally conceived of in terms of risks.

Power Relations and Alternatives

The emergence of social law followed from an important shift in the network of
power relations in the course of the seventeenth and eighteenth centuries. There is
a huge gap between the depiction of both individual freedom and state action as put
forward in the predominant scheme of alternatives, on the one hand, and the reality
of power relations in our societies, on the other. Devices of power have profoundly
been analysed by Foucault, who refused to see in them the simple emanations of a
pre-existing state apparatus, analysable in terms of a repressive conception of
power. What has to be acknowledged, according to Foucault, is that power not only
weighs on us as a force that says 'no', but traverses and produces things, induces
pleasure and forms of knowledge. Power needs to be considered, in his view, as a
productive network which runs through the whole social body, much more than as
a negative instance whose function is repression. The Foucaldian account of the
current power relations, baptised 'biopower' or power over life, shows that
governmental power is involved, at least since the eighteenth century, in the
construction of the lives of individuals and is exercised on the field of life itself.[29]
The highest function of state power no longer is death and oppression, as was
symbolised by the sovereign king sanctioning legal transgression by public
executions, but the complete investment and occupation of life itself.

The productive form of power does not function through legal interdiction, but
operates in two complementary forms: discipline and the biopolitics of the
population.[30] In *Discipline and Punish*, Foucault has sketched how discipline, in
the course of the seventeenth and eighteenth centuries, became a general formula
of domination.[31] Discipline operates on particular individuals in a particular space
such as the school, the factory or the hospital. It collects information by way of
hierarchical observation and organises the optimisation of the individual's
capabilities and the increase of its usefulness and its docility. The perfect
disciplinary apparatus would make it possible for a single gaze to see everything
constantly, in order to supervise, record, control, check, judge and mould
behaviour. Discipline does not merely repress, but produces and constitutes
individuals by installing an evaluative distribution between a positive pole and a
negative pole. This allows a differentiated quantification of the 'didactic' field
through a circulation of awards and debits, and through a continuous calculation of
plus and minus points. There is no transgression in discipline, but only the
individual deviation from a norm that has to be attained. The norm individualises
and serves at the same time as the common standard that joins together the
individuals in the logic of discipline. The evaluative examination of individual
behaviour transforms each person into a source of knowledge, into a 'case'. The
examination marks the gaps, hierarchises qualities, skills and aptitudes, provides

---

[29]   M. Foucault, *The History of Sexuality. Volume I: An Introduction*, trans. R. Hurley
(New York, 1978), p. 135 ff.
[30]   Ibid., p. 139.
[31]   M. Foucault, *Discipline and Punish. The Birth of the Prison* (London, 1977), p. 135
ff.

data, while it punishes and rewards so that it is possible to normalise behaviour, to constitute individuals and to create a more homogeneous social space. The process of normalisation includes, first of all, a 'norm' or a standard that a multiplicity of individuals must reach and maintain; second, the 'normal', meaning the average or the mean, as different individuals display varying aptitudes in learning and executing the new skills; and third, the 'normative', as attaining the norm shades off into the value judgment 'good'.

Until the second half of the eighteenth century, discipline operated alongside the law, organising power relations within the spaces left by the legal framework (in the school, the workplace, the army, etc.). Discipline constituted a kind of 'infra-law' or even 'counter-law',[32] that existed in the margins of an explicit, coded and formally egalitarian juridical framework. It partitioned an area which the law had left empty and it repressed a mass of behaviour that the relative indifference of the great systems of legal punishment had allowed to escape. But by the end of the eighteenth century, the mechanisms of the state and the law themselves began to evolve. Whilst the spectacular forms of legal repression and punishment were still in place, the way in which the state operated began to be transformed. The state explicitly started acting on a large multiplicity, the 'population', in a space that was no longer enclosed but spread out and open. Political government, from the end of the eighteenth century onward, began to develop a whole cluster of practices and knowledges to act on the social body, to incite, reinforce, control, monitor, optimise and organise the forces under it. Here the norm clearly served both as a statistically determined standard of behaviour required by regulatory institutions and what is considered moral law. The particularity of the norm, with this, precisely is that it allows the passage from is to ought, from *Sein* to *Sollen*. Because the norm is merely found in society, it has the objectivity of a statistical average, while it supplies at the same time a principle of obligations that are immediately in line with what the social order requires at a given moment.[33] The primary aim of these new techniques, including measures such as large-scale campaigns and tax benefits, was not to prescribe general rules which defined a level of transgression, but was to intervene into the relationships between particular groups of people, to induce desired change and make the social body more homogeneous.

The modern view by which to judge the quality of a state regulatory act then is understood from a very different manner from its medieval equivalent, namely the unchanging *bonum commune* of scholastic doctrine, to be preserved rather than to be created.[34] Freedom, welfare and security, for the modern state, are through and through mundane, concrete matters of material happiness and as such they are to be produced by means of worldly activity, of political undertakings and of deliberate

---

[32] Ibid., pp. 222-223.

[33] Ewald, 'A Concept of Social Law', p. 70.

[34] *See* e.g. W. Ullmann, *The Individual and the Society in the Middle Ages* (London, 1967).

decisions.[35] In fact, the finality of the modern state no longer refers to a state of affairs where all the subjects without exception obey the laws and respect the established order. Instead, a whole range of specific finalities emerge, which become the objective of government as such. State action then no longer is a question of imposing law on men, but of 'disposing of things, that is, of employing tactics rather than laws, and even of using laws themselves as tactics, to arrange things in a way that, through a certain number of means, such and such ends may be achieved'.[36] The instruments of government, instead of being merely laws, thus increasingly come to be a range of multiform tactics.

At the end of the eighteenth century, a double movement converged. First, there was a dislodgement of the disciplinary mechanisms from the limited space of the enclosed institutions. The paradigmatic image of discipline no longer is the confined space of internment, but is in the style of Bentham's *Panopticon*, which is arranged in such a way that surveillance is permanent in its effects, even if the targetted individual is not constantly observed by an inspector.[37] The panopticon is a figure of political technology that is polyvalent in all its applications. Each time one is dealing with a multiplicity of individuals on whom a task or a particular form of behaviour must be imposed, the panoptical scheme may be used. Second, laws were no longer predominantly applied to prevent certain harmful transgressions, but to dispose more efficiently the relationships between members of the population. A new subjection thus emerged, one which created new subjects: the product of moral, medical, sexual, economic, social, fiscal, psychological, rather than legal, regulations. This double movement entailed that discipline escaped the world of law and right, and began to colonise the legal world, largely replacing legal principles with disciplinary principles of physical, psychological, moral, medical and social normality.

It can be upheld, accordingly, that the repressive model of state action fails to capture the specificity of contemporary technologies of power involved in the legislative practice of alternatives. The liberal scheme of the legitimate basis of state sovereignty cannot be relied upon as a means of describing the ways in which power is actually exercised under such a sovereignty. The image of power as turning on the fact that the state merely limits individual freedom by its repressive interferences – even justified, necessary and proportional ones – is no longer adequate to describe the relations of power we currently live in. Ever since the development of the modern technologies of control, citizens are ever more subject to rules, classifications, recommendations, surveys, standards, rankings, interviews,

---

[35]   This particular view, in fact, is already present in the late 16th century and early 17th century *raison d'état* thinking, but in a reversed perspective. This type of political rationality, first and foremost, aimed at securing the existence of the state and at increasing its strength. With this, the population constituted the immediate target for police measures, at least insofar as improvement of the citizens' living conditions augmented the state's capacities.

[36]   M. Foucault, 'Governmentality', in G. Burchell, C. Gordon and P. Miller (eds), *The Foucault Effect* (London, 1991), pp. 87-104.

[37]   Foucault, *Discipline and Punish*, pp. 200-201.

observations, schedules and authoritative inspections, which are not concerned with law or legal principles, nor with mere repression, but tend to normalisation and the constitution of the individual. Ever since the emergence of the modern state, and especially since the eighteenth century, the instruments of government, instead of being merely sanctioned laws, increasingly come to be a range of multiform tactics which do not differ substantially from what we call today alternatives. This range of multiform tactics goes together with 'capillary modes of power', in which people are measured, classed, examined and made the better subject to control.

Power over life, in a word, is an essential factor in the current elaboration and appliance of alternatives. There has been, through the very endorsement of alternatives, an intensification, complication and extension of the disciplinary matrix. All the micro-patterns of disciplinary power such as classification, observation, examination and normalisation are still going on today. What is more, alternatives presuppose and strengthen them, and involve that the state enlarges itself and becomes more intrusive, and that it increases the intensity of control. Alternatives are found on continuous observation and the tendency towards the keeping of records and data bases, the proliferation of concealed camera surveillance, the writing of reports, monitoring, audits and inspection. By making both the individual and the population constantly observable, alternatives exercise power with a minimum of violence and are, as a result, more difficult to resist. Alternatives define the place of each individual amongst a series of other individuals by establishing norms, which specify the goals which individuals must strive to achieve. There is no absolute difference between the space of the transgressive and the space of freedom. One does not transgress, but one deviates or underachieves. Alternatives, what is more, deploy not so much punishment, but a mix of micro-penalities and rewards, such as subsidies, accreditation, tax benefits and the assignment of labels. This escalates through graduated stages from loss of minor privileges to sanctions that mimic criminal penalities.

This peculiar mode of productive and constitutive power is what is masked in the current code by which alternatives are described and presented. There is absolutely no free space in which alternatives operate. The so-called free space is overdetermined by power over life which not only partitions its gaps, but also has colonised, not at least through the intensified employment of alternatives, the traditional repressive legal framework. The strong demand today for rational legislation and a much more balanced state activity is endorsed, not as a request for the factual withdrawal of political government, but as the consequence of a particular rationalisation of the state regulatory activity. This rationalisation has involved a political government tending to claim for itself the field that defines what an individual is and what his or her proper relation to society might be. And alternatives constitute a perfect instrument to accomplish this aspiration.

Alternatives are less prohibitive than classical legal rules and much more task-orientated. They produce and shape the behaviour and inclinations of individuals in a soft but stable way. The individuals involved must truly decide to enter into its game and logic, and this cannot be achieved by merely using permanent physical coercion or by literally taking away their freedom. Alternatives can only be productive and effective in case of 'willing players'. The legislator, in using alternatives, grasps the psychology of the human will, so as to guide it in directions that are socially useful and to encourage people to develop habits and behaviour patterns conducive to the welfare and health of the population. The structuration of behaviour, the planification of time, the presence of detailed control and regular but 'friendly' corrective intervention, all this makes it possible to speak of progress in terms of ultimate normalisation. Legislation, in this respect, no longer embodies the correspondence between government and the citizens it represents. Alternatives work below the level of the theories that privilege individual rights and the contractual consent of individuals.

From the end of the eighteenth century onward, reaching a climax with the emergence of the welfare state (which constitutes the political counterpart of social law), the population has been recognised as a domain of management, involving the development of a range of new techniques of government centred on regulating and surveying this domain. The principal objective of governmental action no longer was the criminal, nor the delinquent, nor the person who infringed the law, but each person in his everyday life, in his daily routine, in his everyday worries. Prevention became the new legislative standard and the insurance mechanism became increasingly institutionalised and compulsory. If it is true that Foucault unmistakably has distinguished repressive power from disciplinary power, both forms nonetheless are strongly tied up in our societies. The individual today is a citizen with liberties and rights, including 'social rights', in that he is part of a juridical polity. At the same time, however, he is the subject of normalisation, in that he is part of the social field targeted by a biopolitics of the population. Discourses concerned with sovereignty, individual freedom and subjective rights remain as the main justificiation of practices dealing with the management and normalisation of populations.[38] This peculiar treatment of life does not regard individual rights and liberties, but is concerned with the question of how to shape the liberty of the citizen in such a way as to ensure that he exercises his freedom responsibly and in a disciplined fashion.

A crucial point in Foucault's work is that discipline cannot be identified with any one institution or *dispositif*, precisely because it is a type of power, a technology, that traverses every kind of apparatus or institution, linking them and prolonging them. The more the mechanics of control spread and develop, that is, the more they are 'democratised', the less relevant the repressive model of state action becomes in comparison to apparatuses such as family, education, the market, the corporation, the media, morality, public assistance, medicine and social work. Each of these apparatuses exercise a power of normalisation by subjectifying individuals either as deviants or as normal. Hence, to have a strong state does not merely mean that the state is one of the locations, be it the most important, from where power is exercised. It means, instead, that all other power constellations

---

[38]   Foucault, 'Two Lectures', p. 106.

refer, directly or indirectly, to the state.[39] It appears, in this respect, that the term 'subsidiary' is highly misleading and oversimplified to characterise the current relationship between the state and the freedom of the body of peoples living within its borders.

Science and Alternatives

The relationship between the social space and state action has increasingly been mapped out through information provided by scientific knowledge. The claim I want to argue here is that alternatives rely upon and enhance the alliance between state action and science.

State action, ever since the end of the eighteenth century, has been acting directly on the population and on the lives of its members. This stance more and more called for an objective knowledge of the social praxis and how it could optimally be influenced without preventing the machine to run. From the moment that one is to manage and manipulate the population, one must necessarily reflect upon what the population is and upon the specific characteristics of society, its constants and variables. The social sciences adequately complied with this desire, providing knowledge that represented the social space in an objective, exact and accurate way. In the nineteenth century, social inquiry became scientific through the application of the new calculus of probabilities to their specific research domains. The work of Quetelet is paradigmatic in this respect. In every area, the accumulation of data was supposed to be essential for the purpose of recognising the normal distribution underneath. Almost no domain of human inquiry was left untouched by the exponential increase in the number of numbers, provided by statistics and the calculus of probability.

The social sciences thus started to provide norms, which were merely derived from the characteristics or attributes of the things, activities, facts or populations under consideration. The normative gaze operated on the sheer phenomenality of things. It supposedly remained on the level of pure facticity and is characterised by a rigorous positivism. Science thus distinguished the disengaged perspective from the ordinary political stance of engagement, in which this disengaged perspective is valued as offering a higher view of reality. This arises from the fact that, ever since modern thought, truth and knowledge have been regarded as opposite to power. The truth is arrived at by removing all constraints, by allowing the free expression of thought and unrestrained enquiry. Power, on its turn, is understood as domination and constraint, which can only operate succesfully insofar it masks itself and labels an illusion as the truth, this being merely ideology behind which lurks the real truth.

Therefore, political power, to emancipate itself and to guarantee the stability and homogeneity of the social order without appealing to anything external or

---

[39] M. Foucault, 'Deux essais sur le sujet et le pouvoir', in H. Dreyfus and P. Rabinow, *Michel Foucault: un parcours philosophique au-delà de l'objectivité et de la subjectivité* (Paris, 1984), p. 318.

universal, increasingly had to be justified by scientific knowledge of man, society and the population.[40] By the end of the nineteenth century, the violent effects of freedom were supposed to be objectively calculable, which meant that they could be anticipated and preventively insured against.[41] Insecurity, as a result, became a quantifiable risk factor and this knowledge ideally dictated the laws of the state. Law thus became transformed into an *alter ego* of science, in that it was more and more founded on the ideal of creating a social order in which legal regulations were emanations of scientific findings on social behaviour, on what was normal and abnormal.

The current demand, as part of the legitimacy process, to adequately justify and substantiate legislative decisions, likewise, is understood as a demand for a justifying argument that does not presuppose the interests of any party or the supremacy of any political goal, nor borrow its terms from the practice it would regulate. That explains why today scientific and other experts play such a crucial part in preparing and monitoring regulative decisions. Most liberal-democratic countries even have created, with this external legitimising end in view, specialised bodies in the lap of government administration that increasingly claim a monopoly over the definition of deviance and the remedies needed.[42] This tendency clearly buries the legalistic view of laws as something which is simply given or reflecting reality out there, and desecrates, what is more, the legislator-scientist as supreme and rational actor in the social field. The liberal-democratic legislative framework currently assumes that the instrumental and subsidiary relationship between freedom and state action is objectively measurable and quantifiable. Scientific legislative evaluations start from the premise that a particular regulatory technique and its produced social effects merely constitute separate factors tied up in a mechanistic causal connection.

In this wake, the governmental device called 'regulatory impact assessment' (RIA) is conceived of as an information-based analytical instrument to assess probable costs, consequences and side effects of planned policy instruments. It is also used to evaluate the real costs and consequences of policy instruments after they have been implemented. Impact assessments thus offer comparative information on foreseeable consequences of the different alternatives available to solve a given policy problem or to meet a given policy objective. Today, it can be asserted that governments increasingly acknowledge a holistic approach to the Weberian *Zweckrationalität*. Governments are not merely concerned with identifying means to the realisation of specific ends, but with the coordinated achievement of the totality of their ends. The task of regulative assessment

---

[40]   R. Foqué and A.C. 't Hart, *Instrumentaliteit en rechtsbescherming* (Arnhem, 1990), pp. 220-221. *See also* J. Habermas, *La technique et la science comme idéologie*, trans. J.-R. Ladmiral (Paris, 1984).

[41]   Ewald, *L'Etat providence*.

[42]   *See* e.g. the Office of Regulation Review in the Australian Productivity Commission, the Working Group for Proposed Regulations in the Netherlands, the Better Regulation Task Force in the United Kingdom Cabinet Office and the Office of Information and Regulatory Affairs in the United States of America.

principally is that of providing objectively sounder bases for selecting the appropriate technical means from the growing set of options science can make available to achieve individually or collectively expressed ends. These assessments display a common structure, namely considering more social facts and a wider range of impacts and interests in choosing the optimal means to fit existing ends.

The 'crisis' of the welfare state, in combination with the scientific reaffirmation that the classical rule model is not the most satisfactory instrument to realise a particular goal, seriously promoted the rational elaboration and employment of alternatives. The very idea to 'institutionalise' alternatives in the legislative process, in fact, originated in the legislative preoccupation to optimally influence the social praxis on the basis of knowledge of the regularity of its conditionalness. It has been asserted, in this view, that an excessive reliance on single instrument approaches such as command and control regulation is misguided, because none are sufficiently flexible and resilient to be able to succesfully address all social problems in all contexts. Moreover, legislative evaluations authoritatively showed that in the large majority of circumstances a mix of regulatory instruments is required, tailored to specific policy goals.[43] This assessment constituted the immediate rationale for most governments to set the rational and science-based use of alternatives at the centre of their recent regulatory reforms.

Participation

Morality

Politicians today are said to face a real paradox. On the one hand, citizens and companies want them to find solutions to the major problems confronting their societies. On the other hand, people increasingly distrust state politics or are simply not interested in them.[44] Autarkical withdrawal from society apparently contrasts with an increased and rationalised employment of alternatives, which are said to enhance participation in the legislative decision and enforcement process. Hence, the question arises how alternatives fit in with a strong tendency towards unbridled self-fulfilment and self-realisation, and to what extent effective participation by the persons involved is guaranteed by alternatives.

What is important for our purposes here is to distinguish the mechanical view of freedom from social conceptions of the properly human life. For modern freedom to have moral qualities something more, be it implicit, has to be acknowledged. This brings about the intertwined existence of two levels, particular and common. Any idea of normative order, within liberal-democratic culture, necessarily involves individual autonomy, that is, only a being that can judge between possible courses of action through voluntary commitment to some

---

[43]   N. Gunningham and D. Sinclair, 'Regulatory Pluralism: Designing Policy Mixes for Environmental Protection', *Law & Policy*, 21 (1999): 49-76.
[44]   European Commission, *White Paper on European Governance* (Brussels, 2001), p. 3.

rationally willed order, is supposed to fully grasp the concept of wrong action.[45] Accordingly, the liberal-democratic view of the properly human life at least requires that man is capable of autonomous choice, meaning not that what is right is merely a matter of inner choice, but that doing it is morally right only if it has been chosen freely by the agent.[46] The term 'free', however, cannot mean 'without constraints'. A constraint, as Fish has asserted,[47] is not something one can either embrace or throw off, because constraints are constitutive of the self and of its possible actions. Hence, being without constraints is unimaginable. At the same time, however, constraints are not fixed, but are continuously altered by the actions they make possible.

The capacity of autonomous choice is not as such given by nature, but constitutes a potential calling for a certain social and cultural context.[48] Moral value judgments, in contrast to Hobbesian freedom, appeal to capacities which do not simply belong to man in virtue of being alive. This outlook indeed carries with it the demand that one does not remain fully enmired through fear, sloth, ignorance or superstition in some code imposed by tradition or fate which tells him how he should dispose of what belongs to him.[49] Conceiving of man's freedom in terms of will to power or as acting in accordance with inborn desires, makes society or political organisation subordinate to this supposedly natural condition. But that does not hold for a liberal-democratic concept of moral autonomy, enclosing human abilities which necessitate to be properly developed.[50] The emergence and free movement of disciplinary mechanisms as the dark side of liberal-democratic societies, of course, is not foreign to this requirement. Discipline precisely aims at shaping the liberty of citizens in such a way as to ensure that they exercise liberty responsibly and in an acceptable fashion. Unless future decay of these capacities is fully acknowledged, one cannot combine such a view of the properly human condition with a Hobbesian concept of freedom promoting autarkical withdrawal from society.

Hence, affirming the value of moral autonomy necessarily involves commitment to the shape of society and culture, for it is crucial that certain social activities and institutions flourish. It is true that autonomy, contrary to compulsion, does not call for any justification,[51] but that does not alter the fact that moral autonomy has to be concerned at least with its own development and preservation, this being strongly tied up with political responsibility. Affirming moral autonomy

---

[45]   N. MacCormick, *Questioning Sovereignty. Law, State, and Nation in the European Commonwealth* (Oxford, 1999), p. 6.

[46]   Machan, 'Individualism versus Classical Liberal Political Economy'.

[47]   Fish, *Doing What Comes Naturally*, p. 27.

[48]   C. Pateman, *The Problem of Political Obligation. A Critique of Liberal Theory* (Cambridge, 1985), p. 171.

[49]   C. Taylor, *Philosophy and the Human Sciences*, II (Cambridge, 1993), p. 197.

[50]   C.C. Gould, *Rethinking Democracy. Freedom and Social Cooperation in Politics, Economy, and Society* (Cambridge, 1988), p. 37 ff.

[51]   P. Noll, 'Liberté et égalité en tant que problème législatif', *Archiv für Rechts- und Sozialphilosophie* (1967): 218.

thus implies that the sheer consideration of one's own self-fulfilment should be surpassed.[52] If one accepts that there is no reason to suppose that the authentic desires of men will spontaneously harmonise with each other, there always exists a potential conflict between individual freedom as mere self-realisation and the requirement to respect the autonomous choice of others. Consequently, the perhaps natural aspiration for unlimited and unrestricted individual freedom, as it is understood in the modern scheme, needs to be constrained from a moral point of view, and precisely this process should be, in the line of liberal-democratic logic, a major concern of common political decision-making.[53] The maximisation of profit and utility, in other words, can only be admitted as motives under constraints. What is more, if the realisation of moral autonomy partly depends on the society and culture in which one lives, then a fuller autonomy is exercised if the shape of this society and this culture is codetermined by the persons involved.[54]

Although it is in principle a matter of free choice whether someone does what he morally ought or ought not to do, if his morally wrong conduct infringes the autonomous choice of someone else, he may be obliged to do otherwise. Since autarkical withdrawal from society makes moral autonomy precarious and fragile, the perhaps natural aspiration for unlimited and unrestricted freedom needs to be constrained. The vital importance of participation in political decision-making relates to the impact of social and political institutions on the structure of human personality. A more generalised codetermination of the shape of society through participation is then fundamental, precisely because the public and private interests are linked, that is, because moral independence is intertwined with social interdependence.

Alternatives and Participation

With the emergence of modern thought, political decision-making has been limited to a specialised and sectorial practice in which participation is strictly regulated. However, the link between democracy and the state is not one of necessity but one of historical coincidence. What is more, as law becomes reduced to the state, it also becomes politicised as state law. That is, politics is merely reserved to the legal relationship between citizens and the state. This view strongly disregards the necessity of an overall participation and a global repoliticisation of the collective life, precisely because the social and cultural structure are seriously intertwined with the conditions for moral autonomy. Spheres such as the marketplace, the workingplace, medicine, public assistance and social work pertinently could be conceived as political systems, offering areas of participation additional to the state level.[55] Indeed, the confinement of the democratic ideal of collective autonomy to

---

[52] The assertion of the existence of positive duties does not oppose communitarianism to liberalism. The necessity of public support for various aspects of the culture of freedom is explicitly acknowledged by contemporary liberal theory.

[53] *See* Koslowski, *Ethics of Capitalism and Critique of Sociobiology*, p. 51.

[54] Taylor, *Philosophy and the Human Sciences*, p. 208.

[55] C. Pateman, *Participation and Democratic Theory* (Cambridge, 1970), pp. 42-43.

the public space severely limits its imaginative and creative potential, including the creation of connections in which we relate to ourselves and one another in a manner not subordinated to the 'violence' of majoritarian identity or identification. Moreover, it obscures the fact that the modern linkage between law and the state could in real terms only operate as part of a broader disciplinary configuration in which other contrasting forms of regulation and politics are included.[56] If liberal-democratic societies are characterised by a lack of participation, this is not because there is merely a lack of participation in the production of state regulation, but rather because state regulation must coexist with many other forms of medical, social, political, psychological and economic regulation in which participation is seriously lacking, sometimes completely missing.

My claim is that alternatives enhance participation, but within the well-defined borders of biopolitics and without breaching the modern participative framework. First of all, participation, as part of alternatives, essentially remains related to the realm of the public place. That is, participation is first and foremost conceived of as produced part and optimising tailpiece of state regulation, indicating its limits and its intensity. This means that the recognition of participation is in essence derivative, for it occurs principally as part and parcel of state predominance. Participation may be exercised in other power constellations than the state, but these constellations continuously remain referring to it. It can safely be asserted that the further diversification, sophistication and rationalisation of state law through alternatives reveals its adaptability to new conditions of social regulation and primarily aims at the affirmation of its own pervasiveness in social relationships and the population in general. By abandoning the very idea that state law is disembedded from all other forms of social regulation, just like the idea that command and control regulation has the capacity to steer the most diverse social fields, alternatives precisely aim at a rational restatement of the omnipresence of the state within the different regulative constellations. From the distance to which the state has so-called withdrawn, it truly tries to continue to exert disciplinary supervision on society.

Secondly, participation remains merely embedded in the instrumentality of state law and is for that reason mainly focalised on the realisation and enforcement of preconceived goals. The contemporary liberal-democratic state continues to seek its legitimacy in social and economic development of the population it saw itself promoting. Alternatives do not necessarily provide for the codetermination of the objectives that are to be realised, but their enhanced employment both follows from the 'biopolitisation' of state action and the scientific reaffirmation saying that the classical rule model is not adequate to manipulate and manage the social field. Alternatives are not concerned with the idea that politics is the continuation of the public discourse on morality. They are not concerned with how social space helps to identify, determine and interpret political concerns through a process of public opinion formation resulting in binding legal rules. Even less do they follow from

---

[56]   J. Commaille, *L'esprit sociologique des lois* (Paris, 1994), p. 227; Santos, *Toward a New Common Sense*, p. 416.

the assumption that participation is valuable in itself and that to arrive at decisions is not the only purpose of politics.

Considering the current regulatory requirement to identify the probable setbacks and advantages of each policy option, participation, in my point of view, is essentially conceived of as a way to fulfil economic and sociological standards as regards state action. Participation, in this respect, is an important way to optimise state regulation and to create a more homogeneous social space, since social changes can be detected more easily and since co-responsibility cheapens (at least for the state) and holds up the enforcement and execution of biopolitical state regulations. A greater effort through alternatives aims at accomplishing more through a lesser exertion of force and authority. Today, it seems that alternatives rather intend to open up new fields in favour of antagonistic capital valorisation, and principally operate as mechanisms for resolving conflicting claims and aggregating competing interests, rather than as a structure that allows the making of 'differences' where there are above all 'molar' identities.[57]

Conclusion

Today, liberal-democratic states, to induce desired change, explicitly favour alternatives to the command and control type of state action. The foregoing analysis as regards participation and the disciplinary underpinnings of alternatives might give us some indications as to the grounds of this preference.

Firstly, the crucial importance attached by liberal-democratic governments to foster individual freedom and the subsequent revaluation of the principle of subsidiarity currently play a significant part in the legislative discourse favouring alternatives. This discourse still seems to be found on a negative power model, in which state action is principally supposed to restrict freedom by confining the possible choices the subject naturally has. The necessity and proportionality of state intervention, in this view, has to be justified and substantiated, while alternative instruments have to be taken into consideration before and after new regulation is enacted.

However, this picture of the mutual relationship between alternatives and freedom has to be questioned. First of all, the liberal state's reason for existence, namely its basic obligation to protect individual freedom, increasingly has become an alibi to administer life from its interior and to rearticulate it through an all-embracing knowledge of the population's regularities and 'pathologies'. This stance has certainly not been restrained by the increased and rationalised enactment of alternatives. What is more, their efficiency and efficacy largely depends on a wide-ranging and comprehensive knowledge of the population's condition, this involving further observation, inspection, examination and surveillance. State subsidiarity is backed up by disciplinarian practices tending to normalisation, in which people are measured, classed, examined and made the better subject to

---

[57] *See* G. Deleuze and C. Parnet, *Dialogues*, transl. H. Tomlinson and B. Habberjam (London, 1987), p. 124 ff.

control. Alternatives continue building on these disciplinarian practices and make them even more prominent by rationally connecting the guidance of the human will and the population's inclinations with tailored state regulatory action.

Secondly, the preference for the rational employment of alternatives, furthermore, has been strongly reinforced by the firm alliance that exists between liberal-democratic states and the scientific world. Since scientifically performed legislative evaluations explicitly revealed that command and control regulation has some major regulatory disadvantages, it definitely could no longer be regarded as the key tool to shape society. This prevalent assessment brought into focus – even more than before – the steering capacities of alternatives, and intensified the mutual relationship between the state and scientific knowledge. Science, in this respect, is believed to be able to measure and quantify the conflicting relationship between freedom and state action in an objective and neutral manner.

Truth, however, is not outside power. Truth, as Foucault has argued, is produced and sustained by virtue of multiple forms of power, and power, on its turn, is induced and extended by truth.[58] As regards the present liberal-democratic regime of truth, it is clear that truth is essentially referring to so-called scientific discourse and the institutions produced by it. The actual relationship between state action and science, that is, between power and knowledge, pre-eminently represented by regulatory impact analysis practices, largely seem to underpin these Foucaldian claims. One should not be surprised then that the immense consumption of scientific discourse by the liberal-democratic state, combined with the widespread consent given by the scientific community to alternatives, especially economists and sociologists, seriously enhanced the rationalised enactment of these techniques by the state. The diversification and sophistication of state action through alternatives reveals its adaptability to new conditions of social regulation produced by and sustained in today's scientific discourse.

Thirdly, another important motive advanced by liberal-democratic states in favour of alternatives is that they intensify participation in political and legal decision-making. An increase of participation is believed to entail a proportional increase of freedom. It seems, however, that participation through the use of alternatives is in the first place conceived of as an important method to optimise state action and to homogenise the population. Participation is made subordinate to the efficacy and efficiency of state regulation and appears to be crucial to gather information about the targeted social praxis. Besides, participation largely remains limited to the enforcement and execution process, and first and foremost signifies co-responsibility, enhanced control and examination. In a word, participation via alternatives appears to be strongly tied up with both disciplinarian practices underlying freedom claims and the scientific norm underlying state legislative action.

---

[58] Foucault, 'Truth and Power', in C. Gordon (ed), *Michel Foucault. Power/Knowledge: Selected Interviews and Other Writings 1972-1977* (Brighton, 1980), pp. 131-133.

Chapter 6

The Emergence of New Types of Norms

Pauline Westerman[1]

University of Groningen, The Netherlands

Introduction

An important part of the legal theoretical literature deals with the nature of rules, in particular with mandatory rules of the prohibitive type. The exemplar of such rules is the classical 'no vehicle in the park' rule, which figures in virtually every serious work on legal interpretation (although it may be occasionally supplanted by 'no dogs allowed').[2]

It is not my intention to dismiss these examples as misleading. The deep and thoughtful analyses that are provoked by analysis of these simple rules are also helpful in understanding the more complicated legal rules that figure in lawyers' everyday life. But I want to draw attention to the fact that next to the classical mandatory rule, new kinds of norms are emerging and are produced in massive quantities by both the European and the national legislators of European countries. These new types of norms have not been analysed so far but have a quite dramatic effect on both political debate and legal decision-making.

There are two types of such norms. The first of these I shall call 'aspirational norms'. They directly prescribe the achievement of *goals*. These norms require us to ensure 'safe working conditions', to further 'the re-integration of handicapped people in the labour market' or to ensure that the emission of toxics is 'as low as reasonably achievable' (the so-called ALARA norm). The second type prescribes us to obtain *results*. I shall call them, for want of a better term, 'result-prescribing norms' (RP norms). Examples of RP norms are the detailed norms prescribing the

[1] I want to thank Bob Brouwer (Univ. of Amsterdam), Jaap Hage (University Maastricht) and Rob Schwitters (Univ. of Amsterdam) for the time and energy they spent in reading and commenting upon a first draft of this paper. They corrected numerous logical errors and came up with inspiring suggestions. I could not have written this article without the information provided by the students of the Academy for Legislation in the Hague, whom I taught philosophy but who taught me so much more than that.

[2] The latter is Schauer's favorite example. *See* F. Schauer, *Playing by the Rules: A Philosophical Examination of Rule-Based Decision-Making in Law and in Life* (Oxford, 1991). Many insights in this article are based on Schauer's lucid analysis of rules.

size and position of furniture in daycare centres, the desired length of bananas or the exact temperature at which vegetables should be stored. RP norms may also prescribe us to obtain certificates, or to produce protocols.

As I shall argue, these new types of norms belong together. Both are outcome-oriented and can be seen as the legal form of output management.[3] I shall first try to point out in which sense they deviate from the classical rule. After that, I turn to the consequences of these differences for the ways in which these rules shape both our private and public life.

Aspirational Norms

Among the many rules that are produced yearly by the national and European legislators there are quite a few norms that directly admonish the citizen to pursue aims and ends that are thought to be desirable in the eyes of the government and which are promoted in the name of general interest. These norms do not precribe specific acts to be performed, but advertise the aims in a direct manner. They urge us to maximize safety or to decrease pollution, they require us to further transparency or good corporate governance.

In order to understand the nature of such aspirational norms it is worthwhile to recall the distinction, made by Schauer in his treatment of the paradigmatic mandatory rule, between a rule and its underlying aim or aims.[4] The rule prescribes or prohibits a specified act in the expectation that general adoption of that rule will lead to the achievement of the desired aim. Schauer calls these rules 'instantiations' of the underlying aims. Instantiations refer to concrete actions by means of which the desired aims are thought to be achieved.

There may be different instantiations of the same aim. The aim 'silence' can be instantiated by the rule prohibiting dogs, but also by a prohibition of mobile telephones. More importantly: there may also be different aims underlying the same rule/instantiation. Dogs may be banned because they are thought to be noisy *and* unhygienic. Silence and hygiene then both figure as underlying aims. We call these aims justificatory because they can be mentioned as justifications of the rule.

Whereas the classical paradigmatic rule can be seen as an instantiation of one or more justificatory aims, this is not possible with the aspirational norm. These norms do not indicate a concrete manner by means of which one can arrive at the desired

---

[3]   Output management as described in C. Pollitt, *The Essential Public Manager* (Maidenhead, 2003).

[4]   Schauer, par. 4.1. I find Schauer's distinction more suitable to understand these new norms than the distinction between formal and substantive reasons as employed by Summers and Raz. *See* e.g. R.S. Summers, 'Form and Substance in Legal Reasoning', in: *Essays on the Nature of Law and Legal Reasoning* (Berlin, 1992); P.S. Atiyah and R.S. Summers, *Form and Substance in Anglo-American Law: A Comparative Study of Legal Reasoning, Legal Theory and Legal Institutions* (Oxford, 1987); J. Raz, *Practical Reason and Norms,* (London, 1975); J. Raz, *The Authority of Law: Essays on Law and Morality* (Oxford, 1979).

aim but *directly* prescribe us to achieve that desired aim. Whereas in the case of the classical rule there is always a certain distance between instantiation and justification, such a distance is absent with aspirational norms. Here instantiations and aims coincide to such a point that the distinction can no longer be made. The rule is its own justification. It therefore refers to only one aim.

In practice this means that the norm-addressee is obliged to fulfil the prescribed aim but can decide for himself *how* he can arrive at that aim. He is not obliged to follow a certain prescribed path; he is obliged to reach the destination and is free to follow the paths he may find.

Aspirational norms should not be identified with standards or general clauses. Standards and general clauses leave the rule intact and also the distance between rule and underlying justificatory aim. They merely allow or require a careful consideration of the underlying justificatory aims. The rule that only 'reasonable and fair contracts' are valid requires the judge to do more than merely applying specified formal criteria: he is asked to use his own judgement as well. That means that he is supposed to jump between the level of rules-as-instantiations and the level of justificatory aims. He is required to judge whether it would not be reasonable (in the light of the underlying justificatory aims) to allow the quiet dog or to ban the noisy cat. Obviously, this cannot be done in the case of aspirational norms, for they directly prescribe the underlying aim.

It is difficult to operationalize aspirational norms. This is not because of the vagueness of terms. Many rules contain terms that are evaluative or normative and even those terms that at first sight seem to be clear and unproblematic can move towards the problematic fringes of a rule as a result of technical, social or normative developments, unforeseen by the legislator. All these problems are well-known and we speak of interpretation rather than application in order to refer to these 'inevitable' problems.

The problems posed by aspirational norms run deeper than that and have to do with the fact that the aims prescribed in the aspirational norms can be realized to a *larger* or to a *lesser* extent. The answer to the question whether someone complies with an aspirational norm cannot be phrased in a simple yes or no, but requires a gradual answer. That means that there is no fixed criterion that enables one to judge whether the norm was complied with or not. Neither is there any criterion for violation of the norm. There simply is no zero-line, below which conduct can be punished. This is apparent for instance in the case of the so-called ALARA norm, the norm that the emission of toxics should be As Low As Reasonably Achievable. Judges struggled to operationalize this norm into a criterion that could guide them in sentencing the firms who had violated the norm. So another aspirational norm was added, which was that the Best Available Techniques had to be used. But again, nobody could tell what those techniques were (did 'available' imply that they should be available to firms with a low budget as well?). Finally, judges themselves developed a kind of minimum norm as a zero-line which enabled them to do their job. They abandoned the aspirational norm and replaced it with a more concrete rule in order to make it possible to punish the firms who violated environmental norms.[5]

Result-prescribing Norms

Aspirational norms, therefore, always tend to be translated into more precise rules. Sometimes, these concretisations are worked out by the national legislator, sometimes the aspirational norm is codified in national legislation, while it is concretized by lower organs, by the judiciary or by (groups of) norm-addressees into more precise rules.

The fact that aspirational norms should be made more concrete in order to be workable does not mean that they are necessarily turned into rules of the classical paradigmatic type. These classical rules usually prescribe or prohibit acts. The rules that are designed as concretisations of aspirational norms are often (though not always) of a different type. They prescribe us to obtain *results* that can be conceived as concrete elements of those goals.

In the case of the ALARA-norm we see that the aspirational norm is translated into rules requiring specific technical devices to be installed. In the case of 'reintegration of handicapped people in the labour market', the rules typically demand a 'protocol' for application procedures, or additional facilities that make the working-place accessible to handicapped people. These rules require the norm-addressee to make visible to what extent the norm-addressee has realized the aim as expressed by the underlying aspirational norm. The prescribed objects are not *acts*, but *results* as measurable and controllable units by means of which one's commitment to the underlying aims can be constantly assessed. That is why I call the norms that require them Result-Prescribing (RP) norms.

Many of these required results are couched in numbers.[6] Judges should pronounce a certain amount of verdicts, policemen should solve a fixed amount of cases and orthopaedists should carry out a fixed amount of knee operations (not less, but certainly not more).

The required results may also consist of other visible signs: one should think of the detailed RP regulation concerning municipal playgrounds (which prescribe the rubber tiles to measure 60x60 cm) or the prescribed format of municipal reports (requiring the subject dividing sheets to be placed before the subject and not after).[7]

---

[5] For the Dutch history of the norm: Rob van Gestel and Jonathan Verschuuren, 'Alara: minimumregel of beginsel met aspiraties?', in P.C.Gilhuis and A.H.J. van der Biesen (eds.), *Beginselen in het milieurecht* (Deventer, 2001).

[6] *See also* Th. M. Porter, *Trust in Numbers: The Pursuit of Objectivity in Science and Public Life* (Princeton, 1995). Porter remarks that many institutions themselves insist on this form of standardizability (sometimes against their own better professional judgement) in an attempt to limit their vulnerability to criticism from outsiders, p. 96.

[7] Last year, the Dutch municipality of Culemborg incurred a substantial fine for having violated this rule (oral communication).

A special variety of RP norms requires *rules* as a sign that the norm-addressees take the aspirational norms seriously: they demand protocols or codes to be produced. The care in Dutch nursing homes has recently be found defective by a governmental committee. The most serious allegation was not that staff are underpaid and undereducated, but that they could not produce a 'care plan'. Nor did they have a 'protocol' for dealing with dying inhabitants. In these cases the RP norm can be regarded as a kind of meta-rule. It demands that a set of rules is drafted and presented as a visible sign that to a certain extent one complies with an aspirational norm.

There is probably no logical ground for a special distinction between the classical paradigmatic rule that prescribes acts and RP norms. RP norms also and necessarily refer to acts and persons. The production of results is an act carried out by (groups of) people who can be held accountable for failing to obtain the required results.[8] It might be possible, therefore, to reformulate these RP norms into rules that look like classical rules: 'There should be a protocol within a year after the establishment of the institution' can be translated into 'The board should see to it that there is a protocol within a year after the establishment of the institution' or: 'The director is obliged to bring about a protocol within a year after the establishment of the institution'.

But what is important here is that such translations do not normally occur. Whereas many act norms are in the process of being translated into RP norms, one rarely comes across translations of RP norms into act norms. There is a tendency to focus on the required results and to suppress references to actors and acts.[9]

The suppression of elements in norms is not unusual. Many norms addressed to citizens suppress the extra conditions in the antecedent that are addressed to officials and many norms which are explicitly directed to officials are supposed to be understood as it were 'by implication' by the citizens as well, although the implied norm is directed to another category of norm-addressees and although it expresses a different kind of obligation than the explicit norm. As the Swedish

---

[8]   One may be tempted to regard RP norms as a variety of ought-to-be norms, in the sense coined by G.H. Von Wright, *Norm and Action: A Logical Enquiry* (London, 1963). However, I share Jaap Hage's analysis of these norms as either describing an ideal state of affairs (in which case they do not guide human behaviour) or as guiding human behaviour (in which case they cannot be distinguished from ought-to-do norms). RP norms tacitly refer to actors or supervisors and not only describe what is ideally the case. *See* Jaap Hage, 'Contrary to Duty Obligations: A Study in Legal Ontology', in B. Verheij *et al.* (eds.), *Legal Knowledge and Information Systems* (Amsterdam, 2001), The Fourteenth Annual Conference, pp. 89-102.

[9]   The emphasis on results is so strong that one tends to forget that results are prescribed by rules – an oversight that was exemplified by the Dutch Minister of Justice, who ended his bi-annual lecture to the 500 legislative jurists who were assembled with the exclamation: 'What counts are results, not rules!'

theoretician Frändberg remarked, there is a legal system in a 'concentrated version' and a legal system in a 'spelled-out version'.[10]

The choice of the specific formulation (or the choice of suppressed elements) is often inspired by practical considerations. The choice to formulate many penal laws as duties imposed on the judge to apply a sanction is inspired by the wish to emphasize that sanction. The choice to formulate rules as only directed to citizens can be inspired by the wish to communicate that the intervention of authorities is not always needed.[11]

If we construe a spelled-out version of RP norms there seem to be only two verbs that can be added: 'to bring about' and 'to see to it that'. The first formulation is directed to those who are obliged to produce the results, the second is directed to the many supervisory boards and controlling agencies. The concentrated version of RP norms in which results are emphasized are meant to convey two messages at the same time. The first is that persons and/or institutions should produce the prescribed results; the second is that these results should be controlled and assessed.

Although 'to produce' is an act, it is a special kind of act. The citizens who are required to produce results, are not addressed as *actors*, but as *producers*. They are not responsible for the consequences of their acts, but for their products. Those who fail to comply with RP norms have the kind of product liability of manufacturers. In other words, the emphasis on the production of results entails a shift towards strict liability. The actor is not liable for having failed to act in the prescribed way, but for not having obtained the result. Whether that failure can be attributed to his own fault or someone else's does not legally matter.[12]

Common Features

One may be inclined to think that there is a vast difference between the abstract aspirational norm and the concrete RP norm. Whereas the former leaves the citizen free to decide by himself how to arrive at the required end, RP norms regulate in the minutest detail how these aims can be reached. The literature on legislative techniques is for a large part devoted to the choice between detailed regulation and aspirational norms and the wish to reduce overregulation tends to favour the latter.[13]

---

[10]   Ä. Frändberg, 'The Legal Philosophical Addressee Problem', in *Rättsordningens idé: En antologi i allmän rättslära*, Iustus Förlag (Uppsala, 2005). It is not necessary to solve here the problem of priority. The question whether citizen-directed norms are deduced from official-directed norms (Kelsen) or vice versa (Hart) is only relevant to an inquiry into the grounds for legal obligation. This issue falls outside the scope of this article.

[11]   Frändberg, 'The Legal Philosophical Addressee Problem'.

[12]   Correspondence with Jaap Hage.

[13]   Actually, in the Netherlands, legislative jurists are now instructed to reduce the amount of legislation with 25 per cent. This typical RP norm naturally leads to the

Nevertheless, RP norms and aspirational norms have some features in common. The most conspicuous of these is that both types of norms are *outcome-oriented*. They convey the message that it is the outcome that counts. The legislator is not interested in the actions of the norm-addressee, as long as the desired effects are brought about. Whether these effects are phrased in abstract or in concrete terms is a matter of legislative policy, and depends on whether the legislator is capable of regulating a certain field. In areas which are technically complex (environmental law) or technically and morally complex (medical ethical questions) there will be the tendency to leave it to the social field of norm-addressees to fill in the details, whereas areas that are more easily surveyed (daycare centres) the level of concreteness will increase. And for obvious social and political reasons employers are addressed in much more 'aspirational' terms than the unemployed who seek social assistance and who are confronted with a host of detailed RP norms. But in both cases obligations refer to desirable end-states.

The second feature they have in common and which is closely linked to their outcome-orientedness, is that they are positive. By 'positive', I do not merely imply that they are phrased in positive terms in the sense that the (positive) order to keep the window open is a mere reformulation of the negative prohibition to close the window. Whether one uses a negative or positive formulation may be a matter of indifference and is dependent on the legislative technique which is currently in use. By positive norms I refer to those norms that can only be obeyed by doing something, not by refraining from doing something.[14] Aspirational norms and RP norms do not prohibit courses of action, but they positively require us to achieve aims and to obtain results. As directed to (groups of) citizens, these norms require to bring about desirable end-products such as favourable working conditions and clean or safe environments or to produce commodities in fixed quantities. As directed to controllers and supervisors, such individuals are obliged to see to it that these end-products are realized and achieved.

The third feature these norms share, and which is closely linked to their positive nature, is their lack of generality. Norms can be general in the sense that they can be addressed to a more or less general class of *norm-addressees* or in the sense that they prescribe a more or less general category of *acts*.[15] Obviously, the generality of norm-addressees is not affected. It is possible to require certain results or end-states from all members of a certain class.[16] But we run into problems when we try

---

formulation of aspirational norms, despite their problems of operationalisation at a later stage (but with which the hard-pressed legislative jurists are not concerned).

[14] P.W. Brouwer, *Samenhang in recht: Een analytische studie*, Rechtswetenschappelijke Reeks (Groningen, 1990), p. 171.

[15] *See* Brouwer, Ch. V. I include the other two aspects of generality he mentions (time and place) in the description of acts.

[16] But this is probably not the most important aspect of generality. Austin thought it was wholly insignificant: the difference between incidental commands and general law is according to him entirely dependent on the generality of the required *acts*. *See* J. Austin, *The Province of Jurisprudence Determined*, Lect. 1, 1832.

to imagine general acts to be prescribed by an RP norm or aspirational norm. Whereas negative rules usually prohibit *all* acts of a certain kind (e.g. theft), positive rules have to be more specific: they prescribe the performance of *an* act of a certain kind.[17] Negative rules can be universally quantified without leaving any doubt on what is required. 'Do not kill' means simply that there should be zero instances of killing of whatever variety. But as soon as positive requirements are universally quantified ('save lives'), one is in the dark as to whether one is supposed to save one life or thousands, or in which circumstances or where and when. Negative prescriptions can be general and yet informative (there is no doubt what counts as zero), whereas the generalisation of positive prescriptions immediately turns them into vague and uninformative norms. Everything more than zero requires additional specification.

This is the reason why aspirational norms immediately tend to proliferate into a host of detailed concrete norms. I have already remarked that they have to be made more concrete because they are gradual and can only be obeyed to a greater or a lesser degree: there is need of a kind of critical zero-line, which makes it necessary for them to be supplemented with concrete norms. Here we see that there is another reason as well. The mere fact that they do not prohibit but prescribe make them vulnerable to unclarity if they are generalized. Since they are meant to be generally applicable, the only way to make them clear is by specifying them into concrete rules.

It is therefore only for analytical purposes that one differentiates between aspirational norms and RP norms. The two belong together. As soon as aspirational norms appear on the scene we will find them proliferating and splitting up into a host of concrete RP rules. But we should be cautious not to overemphasize organic metaphors of cell division. That would imply that there is only a tendency of divergence. We should keep in mind that there is convergence as well. The formulation of aspirational norms is also a reaction to overregulation and the desire to bring the enormous amount of RP rules together in the comprehensive framework of a more abstract norm. That that abstract framework is bound to disintegrate[18] is not sufficiently recognized and may be an important reason why attempts to reduce the amount of rules fail.

Two Meanings of 'Concrete'

These similarities between aspirational norms and RP norms reveal that they only differ in the degree of abstraction. RP norms are formulated in a more concrete way than aspirational norms. But what do we mean by 'concrete' here? It is important to distinguish two senses in which rules can serve as 'concrete instantiations' of underlying justificatory aims.

---

[17] *See* Brouwer, *Samenhang in recht: Een analytische studie*, p. 172.
[18] Because of its positive and gradual nature.

The classical rule of the 'no dogs allowed' type is concrete in the sense that it specifies how the underlying aims (silence, hygiene) can be *brought about*. Such a rule refers to a concrete course of action that should be followed or avoided in order to arrive at the desired aim. The course of action prescribed is a means to an end. The RP rule, on the other hand, is concrete in the sense that it tells us what the aim *consists in*. 'Reintegration of the handicapped' is concretized in RP norms requiring special toilet facilities, application procedures, adapted furniture and the like. The RP norm positively identifies and specifies the component parts of the underlying aim. The relationship of an RP norm to its underlying aim is not that of a means to an end but that of *a part to the whole*.

The differences between parts-whole and means-ends relationships are crucial. If we deal with means-ends relationships, we may discover that alternative means can be devised for arriving at the same end. We may argue from rules to underlying aims and arrive at the conclusion that the intended aim is not served by that rule in this particular case, but that another rule (intended to serve that same aim) covers the case in a more appropriate way. We may also argue the other way round and come to the conclusion that although the rule at hand cannot be justified by the aim for which the rule was originally issued, it can nevertheless be regarded as a fitting means to a different aim, not contemplated by the legislator. In this case the rule leads to the consideration of new aims, which may function as rival or better justifications of that same rule. These new aims may be used to interpret the rule in a new light.

The relationship between parts and whole is less flexible. The more concrete rule merely identifies and specifies the ingredient parts of the whole. Once the legislator defines an aim such as 'security' as consisting of surveillance cameras, identification procedures and an x amount of police arrests, there is virtually no room for asking whether these means are appropriate to bring about the desired end of security. Security '*is*' no more than these component parts. The problem is defined away from the start. In a parts-whole relationship it is hard to conceive of alternative component parts.

It is also difficult to think of alternative aims. Confronted with rules that prescribe component parts, the choice between alternative aims is a restricted one. It might be possible to regard surveillance cameras as a component part of 'totalitarian control' rather than 'security', but we only need to think of the rubber tiles in municipal playgrounds or the furniture in daycare centres to see that the array of possible aims is a rather limited one.

So far I assumed that there are only two levels at stake: the level of rules and the level of underlying aims. This picture is too simple. As Schauer noted, each justificatory aim can be regarded as the instantiation of an aim that figures at a deeper level.[19] That means that each aim can in turn be seen as the instantiation of a further aim. The distinction between rules and aims is therefore not an absolute but a gradual one. One might for instance view the prohibition of dogs in the restaurant

---

[19]   Schauer, *Playing by the Rules*, p. 73.

as a concrete instantiation of 'silence'. 'Silence' in turn may be formulated as a rule: 'keep silent' and the justification underlying that rule may be 'enjoyment of visitors'. It should be noted that the construction of such hierarchies may be an artificial affair. It depends on one's point of view whether one regards 'enjoyment of visitors' as an underlying aim or as a competing aim which figures at the same level. I tend to think that most hierarchies are not constructed along one straight line, but can equally be pictured as trees as soon as the line branches off in various directions. This happens as soon as multiple aims can be discerned that operate at the same level.[20]

In the case of RP norms and their underlying aims, we have to keep in mind that the instantiation does not consist in a concrete course of action as a means to further the underlying aim, but as a component part of that aim. That means that the aims are not translated in act rules ('keep silent') but in enumerative lists of component parts. 'Re-integration of handicapped people' is split up in facilities and protocols, facilities are further divided in wheelchair facilities, toilet facilities and so on.

This kind of relation between rules and aims can be pictured as a kind of Russian matrioshka doll, in which each concrete RP norm is nested in a wider and more abstract aim. The matrioshka doll does not allow for branching of aims. But it does allow for the possibility that the doll contains two or more 'children'. In fact, the tendency of RP norms to proliferate into more concrete RP norms suggests that such multiple pregnancies are frequent.

These metaphors should not lead us to think that there are two essentially different hierarchies, a doll-like and a tree-like one. We should keep in mind that it is all a matter of perspective. In the first place, it is dependent on how we select the elements of a rule we want to emphasize or to suppress (acts or desired end-states). Second, whether the relations between rules and aims are to be pictured as trees or as dolls is also dependent on one's starting point. If one starts with a formulation of end-states, the movement is towards more concretisation in sub-ends or parts of those ends. If we start by focussing on concrete acts, we may end up by unravelling and discovering a multitude of values or aims.[21] Whereas in the classical model there is a proliferation at the more abstract levels of the hierarchy (leading to a *plurality of values and aims*), the new model leads to a proliferation at the more concrete level (i.e. to a *plurality of concrete results* to be obtained).

---

[20]   A possibility which is overlooked by Schauer, who squeezes all aims into a straight hierarchical relationship.

[21]   The emergence of new aims is reason for Schauer to remark that Raz's focus on the exclusionary character of rules is one-sided. Rules also seem to give rise to new considerations; it can also serve as an inclusionary reason. Schauer, *Playing by the Rules*, p. 92.

Control Versus Debate

This metaphorical talk about trees and matrioshka dolls should not obscure what is at stake here. Once people start thinking of aims as end-states or 'things' to be concretized into more concrete 'things', a dramatic change takes place. An enormous amount of detailed RP norms are produced, regulating all spheres of life, whereas the scope for inquiry into the possible aims that are served by the co-ordination of our actions has become restricted. The dominant tendency to formulate and codify desirable end-states is responsible for the emergence of three problems, which are closely connected to each other.

The first is the problem of overregulation. The problem is deplored in all quarters, but no remedy seems to be successful as yet. As I noted earlier, the attempt to replace the numerous RP norms by aspirational norms only enhances the problem since aspirational norms are uninformative, hard to operationalize and call for an immediate 'concretization' which sets the process of further proliferation in motion. Sometimes, the legislator deliberately leaves it to the social fields to concretize the aspirational norms. In these cases the process of proliferation may be hidden from the view of the ordinary citizen, but it is still there and only too tangible for the citizens involved who are confronted with an enormous amount of regulation issued by either their own managers or by the numerous public, private or semi-private supervisory boards erected to see to it that the targets are reached.[22]

The second problem is that of inconsistency. RP norms are usually concretisations of only one aim. It is difficult to think of concrete and visible results which are component parts of several aims at the same time. The Ministry of Health issues directives that prescribe results conducive to health; the Ministry of Labour obliges us to obtain results that are component parts of safe working conditions. The former may issue the rule that kitchen floors of restaurants should be smooth in order to safeguard hygiene; the latter may prescribe floors that are not slippery. The problem of inconsistency is not merely a result of the organization in departments: in fact, regular inter-departmental meetings are organized in order to prevent these inconsistencies. That these meetings do not really help has to do with the fact that the chosen form of RP norms is not a suitable tool in harmonizing different or conflicting aims at the same time.

---

[22] I disagree here with N. Luhmann, who attributes the problem of overregulation to the typical form of legal reasoning which proceeds from conditions to acts. According to Luhmann such a 'Konditionalprogramm' involves the impossibly complex task of enumerating all possible conditions and hence to overregulation. This complexity could be resolved by turning to a 'Zweckprogramm' in which reasoning proceeds from the establishment of aims to acts. I would rather argue the other way round. Exactly those Zweckprogramme, borrowed from economical discourse, are to my view responsible for overregulation. *See* N. Luhmann, *Zweckbegriff und Systemrationalität: Über die Funktion von Zwecken in sozialen Systemen* (Tübingen, 1968), p. 66.

The third problem which is generated by the matrioshka doll relation between aims and their component parts is that it changes the discussion about those rules. Because they offer no room for a consideration of aims they stifle political debate. It is a common complaint that in parliamentary discussions there is a tendency to focus on administrative affairs, often very detailed ones. Matters of implementation rather than political choices seem to dictate the political agenda. I think that this tendency can be understood as the effect of the formulation and codification of desirable end-states. There is little to discuss on the desirability of these end-states. Everybody agrees on the importance of a clean environment or re-integration of handicapped on the labour market. The real debate is usually on the hierarchy of aims; the question *which* of all these noble aims should gain priority.

The peculiar relation of aspirational aims and RP rules and the fact that the abstract aims are taken as a starting point, makes it hard to initiate such a debate. The attention shifts from a plurality of aims to a plurality of means-as-component-parts. This turns the political debate into a technical affair. It does not address the question what the relation should be between clean environment and safe working conditions, but it focuses entirely on the technical requirements to be met in order to arrive at that clean environment. This is the reason why (scientific) experts are constantly called upon to give their advice and why most members of parliament feel drowned in a sea of technical complexities.

In view of these problems, which are acutely felt (although usually not linked together), one may wonder why legislators persist in the formulation and codification of desirable end-states. The reason is, I think, that the greatest disadvantage is at the same time its greatest advantage. The formulation of aspirational norms and their concrete offspring, the RP norms, minimizes the risk of unintended side-effects.

Such unintended effects can be brought about by either the courts or the social fields of norm-addressees. I was told that in legislative circles there was a genuine fear for undesired consequences brought about by judicial decision-making on the basis of a simple anti-discrimination rule. Judges might decide, for instance, that all municipal buses should be adapted to the transport of handicapped persons. The formulation of more or less explicit goals in this area was deliberately meant to avert that expensive danger. The formulation of aspirational norms thus channels judicial inquiry into the preordained goals and the component parts of these goals enlisted in the RP norms.

But also in relation to (groups of) norm-addressees the risk of side-effects is diminished. Classical act rules, rules that prescribe a concrete manner of achieving a certain aim, are issued on the basis of the assumption that general adoption of that rule will lead to the desired aim. This assumption may turn out to be unwarranted. In fact, the relation between direct effects of a rule (rule-following by norm-addressees) and its indirect effects (the desired aims for which the rule was instituted) is quite problematic.[23] One never knows beforehand whether the

---

[23]   *See* J. Griffiths, 'The Social Working of Anti-Discrimination Law', in T. Loenen et

adoption of the rule will lead to the intended result. Empirical research and so-called 'evaluations of law' are needed to gauge its effects. The success of the rule therefore depends on adequate empirical knowledge. Moreover, even if a rule seems to lead to the desired aim, one still does not know whether the achievement of the aim is really brought about by rule-following. Other factors may play a role.

Obviously, neither aspirational norms nor RP norms suffer from this problem. They directly admonish people to achieve the desired aim or to obtain such and such results. As such they are appropriate to regulate groups which are hard to control because they have a strong tradition of autonomy, in the sense that they have a high degree of internal cohesion and their own set of norms and standards. The norms that prevail in such a semi-autonomous social field[24] (for instance professional associations) may collide with the official rules issued by the legislator, or may at least colour their interpretation to such an extent that compliance is diminished.

The introduction of norms prescribing end-states or results can bring such groups and institutions within the sphere of governmental regulation. It can be left to the discretion of these fields *how* they reach the prescribed aims or results, as long as they make sure *that* they achieve these aims. By obliging the members of these fields to come up with results and to achieve aims, it is no longer necessary to supplant the internal norms of these fields by a set of governmental decrees. The 'indigenous' rules can simply be mobilized and turned into means of achieving the desired governmental goals. There is no need to see to it that the official rules are followed as long as the goals and targets are reached.

However, the efficiency of this arrangement should be balanced against the above-mentioned problems, especially the lack of substantial debate in the legislature and its apparent inability to co-ordinate the various interests.

One way of solving this dilemma is to downplay the importance of the legislature as the *locus deliberandi*. In many books and treatises on so-called 'deliberative' democracy,[25] it is claimed that we should no longer confine democratic debate to parliament. Instead, the institutions of 'civil society' are regarded as the proper places for debate; it is there that the participating citizen should weigh the various conflicting aims and values. But although these theories serve as a useful reminder that democracy should be more than parliamentary procedure, we should be realistic about the potentials of civil society. Probably, most groups and institutions will select the most suitable aspirational norms as the ones guiding their enterprise without taking into account the competing ones. And rightly so. The discussion about harmonisation and co-ordination of different perspectives, different interests and different aims can only take place in a public

---

al. (eds.), *Non-Discrimination Law: Comparative Perspectives* (Den Haag, 1999), pp. 313-330.

[24] In the sense coined by S.F. Moore, 'The Semi-autonomous Social Field as an Appropriate Subject of Study', *Law and Society Review*, 7 (1973): 719-746.

[25] A term which rhetorically suggests that other forms of democracy are not deliberative and amount to mere vote-counting.

space, where *all* involved parties are present.[26] That was the reason why legislative assemblies were invented in the first place, and that is why we should not allow these public spaces to degenerate into another branch of the executive.

Freedom Curtailed

The decision on the part of the legislator to codify desirable end-states instead of rules that prescribe acts to be done or refrained from is usually defended by reference to the mature citizen. The formulation of aspirational norms is defended by the argument that the legislator should make use of the creative powers of citizens. The enlightened citizen should be allowed to follow his own way in order to reach the desired aims. Citizens should no longer stick to the rules against their better judgement, but should make the most of that better judgement. The formulation of aspirational norms is advocated as a strategy that belongs to responsive government in dealing with responsible citizens. In a recent memorandum by one of the members of the Dutch Cabinet,[27] the citizen is admonished to 'take full responsibility'. He should no longer confine himself to perform the required minimum by living to the letter of the law, but is exhorted to do *his utmost* to fulfil governmental aspirations.

In a sense, these assertions should not be discarded as mere rhetoric. It is true that the emphasis on ends and outcomes leaves the citizen free in deciding how he wants to reach these goals. In this sense, the new regime of aspirational norms liberates the citizen from the pressure of constant monitoring in which each and every act is exposed to the governmental gaze. The regime of aspirational norms is the opposite of the regime sketched by Foucault[28] in which 'exercise' and 'discipline' figure as keywords. Foucault's paradigm model is furnished by the pupil or the military cadet, who should be taught the right way of doing things and whose every act and posture is subject to scrutiny, standardisation and training.

Under the regime that has been established during the last decades, only the outcomes count. The paradigm-model has evolved into that of the employee or, more appropriately, into that of the so-called 'tele-worker' who works from his home, is free in choosing working hours, and is only responsible for the output. Such a tele-worker can be required to do his 'utmost' in an unspecified way, like the scientist who is admonished just to be 'excellent'. Or he can be asked to come up with results that are specified in advance, like the data-typist. It is important to note that neither scientist nor tele-worker is subjected to constant monitoring. They

---

[26] 'In practice, we prefer a form of representation in law-making that matches the plurality of the represented with a plurality of representatives', Jeremy Waldron, *Law and Disagreement* (Oxford, 1999), p.54.

[27] 'Verkenning burgerschap en andere overheid', memorandum for Second Chamber. 4/ 2005, no. 29361.

[28] M. Foucault, *Surveiller et punir: Naissance de la prison* (Paris, 1975).

may carry out their jobs in pyjamas or in the sunshine, as long as they produce the right results. Only their products are controlled at regular and fixed intervals.

We should be cautious not to be overly enthusiastic about the freedom generated by this new arrangement. The classical worker who fulfils his 9 to 5 hrs job is under strict control during working time, but after 5, he enjoys genuine leisure. The modern tele-worker experiences fluid boundaries: in space (workspace and private space intersect) as well as in time. He is not under strict control, but at the same time he never enjoys leisure. The more unspecified the outcome is, the less it is possible to fix the boundaries between work and leisure.

The new regime of norms that prescribe us to obtain results and to achieve ends is a regime in which all citizens experience the fate of the tele-worker. The move towards the formulation of aspirational norms or general duties of care obliges the citizen to do his *utmost*. He can never point at loopholes in the law in order to excuse himself. The above-mentioned memorandum makes this very clear. Speaking about the aspirational norm to 'take care of good working conditions', it asserts that the modern employer 'can no longer claim not to be obliged to make provisions on the sole ground that it was not exactly prescribed by law'. And it adds ominously: 'In a sense, the roles will be reversed. The employer who is unable to show that he has taken his duty seriously (...) has not fulfilled his obligation (..)'

Indeed, the roles are reversed, and in a double sense. In the first place, because it shifts the burden of proof to the citizen. It is no longer to the government or administration to prove that the citizen did something wrong, but it is now to the citizen to prove that he did his utmost to comply with the aspirational norms. But also in a second sense the roles are reversed. One used to think that where there was no law, one was to be considered free. Now we are made to think that what is left undetermined is still covered by law. Kelsen could still write: 'By imposing obligations on human beings to behave in particular ways, the legal system guarantees them liberty outside those obligations' and 'where one is not obligated to do or to forbear from doing, there one is free'.[29] But to the modern and mature citizen this kind of freedom is denied: he is supposed to be under an obligation in all spheres of life regulated by the aspirational norms. Since there are no boundaries to the aspirational norms, there are neither gaps nor loopholes. There is no *place* to be free.

When we add to this that most aspirational norms are vague, this all-pervasive obligation becomes unbearable. The uncertainty of aspirational norms may be intended as an invitation to use one's own creativity, but when one is under an obligation to be creative all the time without exactly knowing what is required, this advantage turns into a major drawback. In this sense, it is not coincidental that the same Kelsen emphasized the importance of certainty. That people should be able to understand and follow the law and to anticipate its application and enforcement are not merely principles of order; they are at the same time indispensable for freedom.

---

[29] H. Kelsen, *Introduction to the Problems of Legal Theory*, trans. B.L. Paulson and S.L. Paulson (Oxford, 2002, orig. 1934), pp. 94-5.

Just as the classical worker can enjoy leisure as a result of his strict working hours, citizens can frame their lives according to their own choice when they know when they will be free from governmental interference.[30] If I know that I will not be punished if I refrain from stealing, murdering or entering by vehicle, I can choose either to follow these rules and be free, or not to follow these rules, in which case I know that I will probably not be able for a specific period of time at least to plan my life as I see fit. If I am, on the other hand, constantly asked to reach targets, to obtain results or to achieve aims, there is no opportunity to organize matters according to one's own wishes. There is no *time* to be free.

Conclusion

We have seen how an almost imperceptible shift in norm-formulation can have a massive impact on both our public and individual life. The emphasis on results to be obtained and ends to be achieved may be only one step removed from the classical emphasis on acts to be performed, but sets a chain of intended and unintended effects in motion.

No doubt, one important and intended effect of the new legislative strategy is to make the most of the internal norms of social groups and to mobilize these norms to the advantage of governmental aims and objectives. Another such intended effect is that by means of aspirational or RP norms, areas can be regulated which are highly technical or subject to rapid change. The formulation of desirable end-states or outcomes is meant to exercize maximum control with a minimum of effort, and this is particularly clear in those cases where the formulation of concrete RP norms is left to the field of norm-addressees.

This way of governing by 'sketching the outlines' furthermore ensures that officials as well as citizens stick to these main lines and confine themselves to the task of making them 'more concrete'. There is little room for coming up with alternative aims, or for a careful balancing of the various aims at stake. That is why the political process of decision-making on ends tends to degenerate into technical discussion on means. The attempt on the part of the legislator to minimize the risk of undesired side-effects seem to paralyse political decision-making as a whole or to delegate it to areas which are not capable of co-ordinating the various conflicting values at stake. In other words, the new regime of control by fixing outcomes may leave the citizen free to decide on means, but limits the freedom of choice of ends.

Finally, the all-pervasive setting of ends and targets tends to blur the boundaries between obligation and freedom. There is no longer a prevailing presumption of freedom (unless otherwise regulated) but a presumption of perpetual obligation to act in conformity with the aims dictated by general interest.

---

[30] For this well-known argument, *see also* e.g. H.L.A. Hart, *Punishment and Responsibility, Essays in the Philosophy of Law* (Oxford, 1968), p. 23.

The conclusion seems to be justified that the benefits of this new empire of ends are mainly enjoyed by the legislator, at the expense of the citizen. Politicians nowadays tend to compare the nation to a company. They frequently refer to 'The Netherlands Inc.' One may be tempted to think that the phrase is more accurate than they seem to be aware of themselves. It indeed reflects a situation in which the citizen is essentially a productive employee, required to reach the targets set by the board of directors of his firm. That that firm is about to merge into 'Europe Inc.' does not change that situation.

Chapter 7

A Peacekeeping Mission as a New Category of War? An Institutional Analysis

Hanneke van Schooten
Tilburg University, The Netherlands

Introduction

In their introduction to *An Institutional Theory of Law,*[1] MacCormick and Weinberger state that radical critique to any normative theory of knowledge is: there is *no matter of fact to be known.*[2] The realm of the legal 'ought' is sheer mystery.[3] The only reality to be studied here is the reality *behind* the mystification talk of 'norms', 'oughts', 'obligations' and the like. The admitted fact that people do talk and write about 'norms' and 'oughts' is open for study, along with the other facts of the case. There has to be some *realistic* (which is usually taken to imply *materialist*) accounting both for what happens and for the fact the people deludedly and delusively talk in normative terms about 'law'.[4]

The facts of reality and the fiction of the law are central in Institutional Legal Theory (ILT). ILT aims at the foundation for two equally valid and mutually complementary disciplines: legal dogmatics and the sociology of law. ILT tries to avoid the traps of idealism to which realists and materialists have always rightly objected but which, on the other hand, avoid the pitfalls of reductionism to which realist theories have always tended. 'If law exists at all, it exists not on the level of brute creation along with shoes and ships and sealing wax (...), but rather along with kings and other paid officers of state on the plane of institutional fact'.[5] The

---

[1]   N. MacCormick and O. Weinberger, *An Institutional Theory of Law* (Dordrecht, 1986), p. 2.

[2]   MacCormick and Weinberger, *An Institutional Theory of Law*, p. 2.

[3]   MacCormick and Weinberger point at the earlier writings of the 'Scandinavian Realists' Hägerström, Lundstedt and Olivecrona, who represented this view. *See* Ibid., p. 2.

[4]   Ibid., p. 3.

[5]   Ibid., p. 49.

notion of a legal institution is explained by means of an example: a contract.[6] For every busload of passengers, there exists, in addition to the solid, physical bus and the stolid, palpable passengers, as many contracts of carriage as there are passengers. The existence of a contract between each passenger and the bus corporation is obviously not a matter of physical fact. Possibly some people on any bus know or believe that they have made a contract on entering and paying their fare to the driver, almost certainly some do not realize this at all. Getting on a bus and paying a fare becomes a centrally significant fact that brings the contract into existence.[7] The law ascribes certain rights and duties to individuals conditionally upon the existence of a contract, for instance, in the case of a crash in which people are injured and property is damaged.[8] In this example, the legal institution of 'contract' involves social realities, as well as ideal objects: ILT's interesting endeavour to narrow the gap between norm and fact, as propounded by Kelsen's pure theory of law. As a development of a normative theory, ILT offers to the sociology of law an ontology which the authors claim to be essential for any realistic analysis of the legal sphere. At the same time, however, ILT's ontology theses also lead to a suitable theory of knowledge for legal dogmatics, black-letter law.

Regardless of the concept of law that is adopted – either the viewpoint that law is '[t]he prophecies of what the courts do in fact ...',[9] or the viewpoint that law is a system of norms, a separate universe of normativity, apart from the factual effects in the real world[10] – enacting legislation is generally recognized as an act of communication. Even in the latter legal-positivist view, the working of the law (the effectiveness of the law) cannot be completely set aside. Kelsen's basic assumption is that the relationship between norm and fact, between rule and conduct, is logically irreducible in character. From the fact that something *is*, it cannot be concluded that it *ought* to exist. The same goes for the opposite: if something *ought* to be, it cannot be concluded that it *is*.[11] This conclusion is the basis of the concept of law as a hierarchical system of *norms*, separate from factual considerations, i.e. *conduct*. However, the gap between norm and fact is not quite unproblematic, as Kelsen indicates. He states that the validly enacted norm needs to have a minimum degree of effect in the real world in order to be a legitimate norm.[12] This implies that the conduct prescribed in the legal rule has to be realistic. The legal rule enacted in Tsarist Russia, which prescribed that every female

---

[6]   Ibid., p. 52. Next to contract, the authors also use marriages, rights of ownership, corporations, etc., as examples of legal institutions.

[7]   MacCormick distinguishes three rules that contracts (legal institutions in general) have in common: institutive rules (bring the contract into being), consequential rules (regulate further legal consequences, such as rights, duties, and liabilities), and terminative rules (regulate the termination of the contract at some point in time). Ibid., pp. 52-53.

[8]   Ibid., p. 51.

[9]   O.W. Holmes, 'The Path of the Law', *Harvard Law Review*, 457 (1897): 461.

[10] H. Kelsen, *Reine Rechtslehre* (Vienna, 1992), p. 5.

[11] Ibid., pp. 5-6.

[12] Ibid., pp. 10-14, pp. 215-221.

prisoner had to give birth to a child of the male sex every year, is, in this sense, not a legitimate legal norm. The interdependence of the legitimate rule and its social effect illustrates the problematic character of strict separation.

For a long time, the processes in the relationship between a rule and its materialization took place, to some extent, in a black box; rules entered on one side and norm-conforming conduct came out, or was expected to come out, on the other. Lack of insight into these processes resulted in the creation of several models of legal communication.[13] Although the legal effects differ, most models are in essence based upon linear causality of goal-oriented legislation. The legal 'message' is 'transported' in a one-sided flow model of information, that is, from 'lawgiver' to 'lawtaker', from sender to receiver. This metaphor presupposes the possibility of transmittable legal information: the words obviously express a meaningful 'message'. This raises the question of what this 'message' is and how it is communicated.

Institutional Legal Theory has adopted a concept of law through which a reciprocal element can be added to the one-sided models of legal communication, i.e., by defining the meaning of legal information in a semiotic-pragmatic way. In the next section, I will analyse ILT, its concept of law, the metaphors used, and the consequences for the ideas about meaning transmission and sense construction. In particular Ruiter's tripartite conceptual model will be scrutinized: the interplay between rule, rule application, and social practices. Then, a case study on the shifts in the concept of war is described. New war terminology and new categories of war can be observed, originating from social and political practice instead of the legitimate legislature. New war terminology, e.g., armed conflict, peacekeeping mission, operation, etc., is not unproblematic. The legal consequences of the new war terminology are uncertain since their legal status is unclear. The problematic character can be expressed by the question: what rules apply in a situation which is neither war nor peace? A classic example in this light is the Eric O. trial. The case study will then be analysed by means of the institutional model in the following section. What can be learnt from the analysis with respect to the classical concept of law as an instrument[14] to create one-sided patterns of behaviour in society? In the final section, conclusions concerning the concept of law will be drawn.

---

[13]   For an elaboration and description of several models of legal communication, *see* my chapter on 'Instrumental Legislation and Communication Theories', in H. van Schooten (ed.), *Semiotics and Legislation: Jurisprudential, Institutional and Sociological Perspectives* (Liverpool, 1999), pp. 183-211.

[14]   Known as 'social engineering'. *See* R. Pound, 'Contemporary Justice Theory', in D. Lloyd (ed.), *Introduction to Jurisprudence* (London, 1965).

Institutional Legal Theory: Reciprocal Dimensions?

Legal Language

What has been described as the 'linguistic turn' in science, at the beginning of the 20th century, has pushed the question of language and communication processes more and more to the centre of theorizing; it emphasized the centrality of symbols and meaning to social life. A dichotomy frequently referred to in this context is the dual character of language. On the one hand, descriptive language is a representation of the real, factual world – the real world constitutes the touchstone, the test, for the truth or untruth of the spoken or written words. If the words constitute untruth, the *words* have to be adapted to the brute facts of the real world. On the other hand, with the use of language, 'speech acts' can be performed.[15] An example of a classic speech act can be found in the Bible. In Genesis, the words of God took effect according to their literal sense: 'Let there be light, and there was light'.[16] The light came into being because He so commanded and everything else on earth was created in the same way: by commands of God. In this example, the effects of the commands (or imperatives) were physical. The almighty Creator was supposed to be capable of bringing about brute facts: light, herbs, animals, etc., through His words. However, the effects of the imperatives in legal language are not physical: they bring about 'legal effects': rights, duties, and legal qualities. In legal language, the legal norm is the touchstone, the test for the correctness or incorrectness of the actual or factual behaviour. The legal rule expresses reality or part thereof in words. The words of the legal rule cast realizations ahead: they determine behaviour before it has taken place; they express future behaviour and events. The latter function of language provides the opposite image of the former: the real world has to be adapted to the words, not the reverse. Legal language aims at creating a new world. Here, implicitly, the view is adopted of a unilateral transmission of rule information: conduct caused by norms.

This brings us to the second characteristic of legal language, i.e., the observation that its terminology has no physical counterpart or reference in the world of fact, while terms like 'gun', 'truck', and 'tin hat' do. The terms 'right', 'duty', and 'legal quality' cannot be pointed out as 'facts'. Herbert Hart called this phenomenon 'the anomaly of legal language'.[17]

Nevertheless, legal terminology plays an important role in social life. Often without a proper understanding of the phenomenon, 'property' is obtained, 'contracts' are signed, 'states' are created, 'rights' are granted, 'borders' are fixed, and 'marriages' are performed. Relatively uniform ideas of ownership, states, and all kinds of rights and their corresponding duties and legal qualities are disseminated among the general public. The regular use of these terms, if correctly applied, is connected to uniform ideas about corresponding behaviour. Here, we

---

[15] J.R. Searle, *Speech Acts: An Essay in the Philosophy of Language* (Cambridge, 1970).

[16] Genesis 1:3-4.

[17] H.L.A. Hart, *Essays in Jurisprudence and Philosophy* (Oxford, 1983), pp. 22-23.

recognize the opposite of 'brute facts': 'institutional facts', i.e., facts that exist by virtue of rules, like playing chess which exists by virtue of the rules of chess. Two fundamental insights are offered by ILT in relation to this range of issues. Unlike Kelsen, for whom legal dynamics is a process internal to normative systems, and hence isolated as far as possible from observable social processes, ILT emphasizes the *interplay* of socially existent norms and observable features of social life. It takes the basis of legal dynamics to lie in this very interplay.[18] Secondly, Kelsen regards the *Grundnorm* as constitutive of legal systems as a whole. A *Grundnorm* is a hypothetical postulate, a kind of axiomatic stipulation, which constitutes a final level of justification just as axioms do in logic or mathematics.[19] In ILT, however, the existence of law is regarded as an institutional fact, a matter of what is actually existent in social reality, even when norms are considered as ideal entities available not to direct observation but only to the understanding. ILT emphasizes that the precondition for the existence of a legal system is the *interplay* of a normative system with organizations and social proceedings which have an observable side, too.[20]

What is the importance of these observations? This question is analysed in the next section.

Legal Rules as 'Thought Objects'

The observation that legal language refers to 'supersensible'[21] mental entities is considered to be one of the essential elements of law. Law as a linguistic phenomenon and its relationship with social practices can be divided into three subsystems:

(1)   The legitimate legal rule (the formal dimension), which comprises a message (the material dimension);
(2)   The acts of the application of the rule by an official, and, in the case of a conflict, a judge;
(3)   A degree of rule-conforming patterns of behaviour in social practice.[22]

Given the relationship between words and reality described above, it has been concluded that, within these three categories, only subsystems (2) and (3) are *discernible*:[23] in other words, the acts of the official applying the rule are *perceptible* (and, in the case of a conflict, the decision of the judge, both testing factual behaviour against fictitious law (see 2)) and the rule-conforming patterns of

---

[18]   MacCormick and Weinberger, *An Institutional Theory of Law*, p. 19.
[19]   *See also* Kurt Gödel's incompleteness theorems. K. Gödel, *On Formally Undecidable Propositions of Principia Mathematica and Related Systems*, (New York, 1931/1992).
[20]   MacCormick and Weinberger, *An Institutional Theory of Law*, p. 20.
[21]   This terminology is used by Karl Olivecrona in *Law as Fact* (London, 1971), p. 223.
[22]   D.W.P. Ruiter, *Legal Institutions* (Dordrecht, 2001), pp. 24-25.
[23]   Among others, Ibid., p. 25.

behaviour are *observable* in social practice (see 3). The legal rule itself is an indiscernible construct; it is *thought* to be the basis of the two other subsystems. The words of the legal rule project an image that is aimed at actualization in the real world.[24] This means that the substantive message of the legal rule is a mental construct (a thought object): an ideal entity to be distinguished from physical things.[25] The message of the fictitious rule projects an imaginary reality; people should *think* of it as being real. In the words of Jeremy Bentham: '(...) we are under the necessity of talking about them [fictions] in terms which pre-suppose their existence'.[26] And '(...) the existence of a fictitious entity is feigned by the imagination' and 'is spoken of as a real one'.[27]

The imaginary reality of the rule's message can only be distinguished in its perceptible application by officials (or, in the case of a conflict, by the judge), on the one hand, and in observable social practice, on the other. In this view, the message of legal language can only be observed through *acts*. Only *by acting* does the written legal message obtain its meaning. Wittgenstein's frequently quoted 'the meaning is in the use' also seems to be relevant in this context.

Unlike the Institutional Legal Theory (ILT) developed by MacCormick and Weinberger – which starts from the viewpoint that law consists of *two dimensions*, i.e., normative institutions (a set of rules) and real institutions (a set of patterns of behaviour)[28] – Ruiter creates *three dimensions*: (1) a set of rules, (2) the acts of application of the rules by officials, and, in the case of a conflict, the acts of the judiciary, and (3) patterns of behaviour in social practice.[29]

With respect to the relationship between the legal rule and its materialization, the following categories can be submitted:

(1) *Ideally*, the projected image of a legitimate legal rule is entirely materialized in corresponding patterns of social behaviour.
(2) An imaginary reality that is projected by a legitimate legal rule, but is not the object of a common belief underlying the legal practice, is *ineffective*.
(3) An imaginary reality that is the object of a common belief underlying a legal practice but is not projected by a legitimate legal rule is '*illegal*'.

In the second category, the substantive sense of the projected legal picture partly fails to materialize. In the third category, an imaginary reality emerges from observable social practice without the existence of any legal rule. In both categories, *common belief* or *shared beliefs* in the existence of the imaginary

---

[24]   Olivecrona suggests that the original explanation of the sense of a legal command may have been magical; Olivecrona, *Law as Fact*, p. 98, p. 226 and p. 231.

[25]   Olivecrona states that the notion of legal rules should be viewed as a reality only as an idea in people's mind, a 'fantasy'; Ibid., p. 223.

[26]   C.K. Ogden, *Bentham's Theory of Fictions* (New York, 1942), p. iii.

[27]   Ibid., p. iii.

[28]   MacCormick and Weinberger, *An Institutional Theory of Law*, pp. 1-27.

[29]   Ruiter, *Legal Institutions*, pp. 24-25.

reality of the legal message are (partially) absent.[30] The phenomena called mutual or shared beliefs, and common belief or common knowledge, are not well established. These terms are used in different senses, for example, in the sense that images of legal rules are objects of mutual beliefs causing patterns of behaviour in conformity with these beliefs.[31] This point of view differs from the sense that a variety of observable patterns of social conduct can be *interpreted* as resting on shared beliefs. The latter definition takes the observable patterns of social conduct as a basis. These patterns of conduct *suggest* the existence of particular common beliefs in society, *regardless* of what the members of society *really and actually believe*.[32] Patterns of social conduct, interpreted as resting on a common belief in an imaginary reality of a legal rule, show the existence of *reciprocity* in the relationship between the fictitious rule and factual conduct. In categories b and c, the partial absence of such a common belief in the imaginary reality can be recognized,[33] expressed by observable behaviour in social reality.

Unlike MacCormick and Weinberger's ILT, that emphasizes the interplay of socially existent norms and observable features of social life, Ruiter's ILT extends the observable features of social life with another dichotomy: the observable patterns of social conduct, as an expression of indiscernible common belief.

A Tripartite Conceptual Framework

From this viewpoint, the relationship between rule and conduct has reciprocal elements. The idea of the existence of linear causality between rule and social practices is partly put into perspective. On the one hand, observable social practices express the existence of a particular common belief in the projected image of the legal rule, on the other, social practice – actions – determine the meaning of the corresponding words of the legal rule. This interplay is not exclusively restricted to the relationship between normative and real institutions, as developed by MacCormick and Weinberger,[34] but takes place twice. Firstly, it takes place when the rule is applied by officials, for instance, the police officer stopping a cycling woman in a park by saying 'Vehicles are not allowed in the park' and imposing a fine on her for riding a bike in an area which is not open to vehicular traffic. When a conflict arises about the application of the legal rule, the Court has the competence to take a final decision. Both police officer and judge test the factual conduct against the fictitious rule. In this observable process of testing, the imaginary picture of the legal rule is reconstructed and legitimately established in every new case. Secondly, in social behaviour, substantive legal rules can partly or wholly be realized, but patterns of behaviour may also be observed without the existence of any legal rule: the 'illegal' practices. Illegal

---

[30]   E. Lagerspetz, *The Opposite Mirrors: An Essay on the Conventionalist Theory of Institutions* (Dordrecht, 1995), p. 14.

[31]   Ruiter, *Legal Institutions*, p. 9.

[32]   Ibid., pp. 22-23.

[33]   For a definition of Ruiter's 'common belief', *see* Ibid., pp. 21-24.

[34]   MacCormick and Weinberger, *An Institutional Theory of Law*.

practices indicate that particular behaviour is subject to common belief but is not related to any legal rule. These processes show that social practices are not merely subject to unilateral legal steering, but have their own 'momentum' to create institutional facts. The tripartite conceptual framework offers a more sophisticated model to analyse the complexity of legal communication than the models of linear causality.

With the aid of this conceptual framework, the Eric O. case will be analysed. In the next section this case will be described in its relationship to shifts in meaning of the concept of war, new war terminology, new categories of war, and their unclear legal status.

A Case Study: The Eric O. Case and its Background

Shifts in the Concept of War

Decisions about war and warfare deeply affect the lives of citizens. In this context, the principles of democracy and the rule of law (legality) constitute a guarantee against governmental arbitrariness and political opportunism. This holds in particular for the declaration of war (Article 96 of the Dutch Constitution). The reasoning behind the definition of 'declaration of war' can be found in the work of Grotius. In Grotius' view, war and peace are to be distinguished as two mutually exclusive legal states. There must be a clear dividing point between war and peace: the declaration of war. Grotius' famous phrase *Inter bellum et pacem nihil est medium* is the basis for the idea that the declaration of war constitutes a precondition for the legitimacy of a war.[35] As the declaration of war initiates the legal state of war, the law of war binds the belligerent parties.

The period after the Second World War – when domestic law became dominated by the 1945 UN Charter's prohibition of interstate force – is an interesting phase because of the many changes that have taken place and are taking place. The attacks of 9/11, resulting in the 'war on terror', contribute to the dynamics of this era.

Article 96 of the Dutch Constitution (formerly, until 1953, Article 57) is important in this context. The meaning of Article 96 has changed fundamentally, whereas the textual amendment to the Article – in the 1953 constitutional revision – was minimal. In 1953, the Dutch expression 'de oorlog verklaren' (to declare war) in the former text of the Article was rephrased as a passive construction, viz. '*in* oorlog verklaren' (to declare [that the Kingdom is] *in* a state of war). The Charter of the United Nations (1945) was the cause for this minimal textual change. In the former Article 57 of the Dutch Constitution, the formulation 'to declare war' was constitutive in character. The declaration itself – a governmental

---

[35]   H. Grotius, *The rights of war and peace, including the law of nature and of nations,* with notes and illustrations from A.C. Campbell e.a. (Washington, 1993).

decision that needs the prior approval of Parliament – initiates *de facto* and *de jure* a state of war. This means that a war actually starts at the moment it is being declared and, at the same time, the legal consequences – the law of war – take effect.

It is obvious that the change in the meaning of Article 96 was in line with the international developments concerning the prohibition of force between states as a rule of positive law after the First World War. The Kellogg-Briand Pact (1927/28) explicitly condemned war as an illegal act of aggression between states. The UN Charter stated the prohibition of force in a stronger formulation.[36] The Netherlands and other UN member states are obligated 'to refrain in their international relations from the threat or use of force against the territorial integrity or political independence of any State, or in any other manner inconsistent with the purposes of the United Nations' (Article 2(4)). The most important exception to the prohibition of the use of force is the right to self-defence of a member state of the United Nations against an armed attack by another state (Article 51). The fact that the UN Charter leaves some room for a declaration of war in the case of self-defence means that such a declaration does not bring about a state of war, but *merely records its existence.*[37] The declaration of war in Article 96 of the Dutch Constitution should be understood in this restricted sense. The meaning of the declaration has thus changed from a *constitutive* statement that starts war *de facto* and *de jure* to a mere *declaratory* statement: the legal recognition of an already existing situation of war.[38]

---

[36]   H.G. de Jong, 'De oorlogsverklaring in het internationale en het nationale recht [The Declaration of War in International and National Law]', *RM Themis*, 3 (1990): 102.

[37]   H. van Schooten, 'The Declaration of War in the Dutch Constitution and Models of Legal Communication', *International Journal for the Semiotics of Law*, 14 (2001): 341.

[38]   Since the issue of the deployment of US cruise missiles and US army units in the Netherlands (1979/80), fierce debates have taken place about the question of whether Article 96 of the Dutch Constitution should be given a broader interpretation, implying a greater say for Parliament. Members of Parliament argued that the act of deploying cruise missiles (and the corresponding possibility of an actual launch of these weapons) could not take place without the prior approval of Parliament. However, the Raad van State [Dutch Council of State] stated that the term 'in oorlog verklaren' (to declare [the Kingdom] to be in a state of war) in Article 96 of the Constitution 'did not include the preparatory military actions, *not even if those actions were to result in a situation that the Netherlands would become involved in a war with another country*. Prior approval of the Staten-Generaal [States General] for putting troops and weapons into action is therefore not required under Article 96 of the Constitution' (Kamerstukken II [Parliamentary Documents], 1985/86, 192 90 (A) 6). By this statement, democracy has largely been reduced to *de facto* military actions. [Unless otherwise stated, all translations are my own.] *See* H. van Schooten and W. Werner, 'Democratic Control on the Use of Force under the Dutch Constitution', *Tilburg Foreign Law Review*, 10 (2002): 43-62.

New Terminology

Owing to the prohibition of force in the UN Charter, the terms 'war' and 'declaration of war' fell into disuse.[39] As a result, no declarations of war have been made since the First World War,[40] and the number of interstate hostilities *not* amounting to 'war' has greatly increased since 1945. Conflicts have been described as 'police actions', 'operations', or 'missions', or have been treated as civil wars in which the foreign party became involved to restore democracy.

For this reason, in each of the four Geneva Conventions (1949), it was explicitly stated that these Conventions would be applicable not only after a declaration of war, but also in the case of 'any other armed conflict' between two or more States, even when the 'state of war was not recognized' by one of the parties. For the same reason, in 1952, the Criminal Law in Wartime Act (*Wet oorlogsstrafrecht*) and the Dutch Penal Code *(Wetboek van Strafrecht)* were extended with identical provisions. Article 107(a) of the Penal Code states that the criminal offence of Article 102 – aiding the enemy in *wartime* – is also applicable 'in the event of an *armed conflict* that cannot be designated a war'. Here, a new category, next to war and peace, is introduced.[41] However, the terminology in the Military Penal Code (*Wetboek militair strafrecht*) was never changed to make criminal offences committed in 'war' and 'wartime' applicable in an interstate armed conflict.

With the revision (June 2000) of the Dutch Constitution concerning military defence and security (Articles 96-103), the description of the tasks of the national armed forces was modernized. Several provisions were replaced and reformulated to this end. Two phenomena in this revision are remarkable. Firstly, Article 96 remained unchanged, so the issue of the influence of Parliament on actual (*de facto*) involvement of Dutch military forces in international warfare was not settled yet. Secondly, the new Article 100, providing procedures concerning governmental decisions to send Dutch military forces to 'maintain or restore the international legal order' is, from a democratic point of view, weaker than Article 96. The prior approval of Parliament is not required under Article 100: government *only provides information* to Parliament. In parliamentary debates, the government stated that, although the procedure of Article 100 differs from the democratic

---

[39] *Notitie inzake het VN-embargo tegen Irak* [Government Memorandum concerning the UN embargo against Iraq] 1990/91, 21 664 (25), p. 9, states: 'Since the Second World War, the declaration of war at the beginning of an armed conflict between states has passed into disuse in international relations'.

[40] There is one exception. In 1989, Iran formally declared war against Iraq with which it had been engaged in hostilities since 1981.

[41] H. van Schooten, 'On War, Peace and Armed Conflict', *International Journal for the Semiotics of Law*, 17 (2004): 169-183.

procedures of Article 96 in the formal sense, it is similar in a substantive sense. This statement has been strongly criticised.[42]

The new war terminology – i.e., actions, missions or peacekeeping operations – and the new category of war – i.e., armed conflict – resulted in a confusing lack of clarity about the legal status of these 'war' situations. If these situations of 'war' are not recognized as a state of war, as a result of which the law of war is not binding, the question arises: what exactly is the legal status and what rules apply? Since the meaning of the terms and categories used is unclear and the legal consequences are uncertain, the legal status of an 'armed conflict' and a 'peacekeeping operation' have become blurred. The absence of the old clear-cut terms and categories affects the people who are involved in warfare. This became clear in several cases brought before courts concerning acts during the Gulf War, Operation 'Enduring Freedom' in Afghanistan, and the peace keeping operation in Iraq. In particular in the Eric O. trial, the question as to what rules apply during an international mission was central. The Public Prosecution Service declared the common Dutch Penal Code applicable and prosecuted O. for murder. The Court, however, pointed at international rules concerning the use of force that are binding for military units in the Iraq mission, legitimizing O.'s deadly shot.

The Eric O. Trial: New Terminology and Confusion in the Courts

The Facts of the Case

Eric O. took part in the Dutch military mission in Iraq, which was named a 'peace-keeping operation'. His rank was sergeant-major and he was attached to the operational group of the Royal Dutch Marines. As the commander of the QRF Battalion (Quick Reaction Force), Eric O. was ordered to recover a container that was stranded on Main Supply Route (MSR) Jackson between Al Khidr and As Samawa, on 27 December 2003. The goods in the stranded container (filing cabinets belonging to the force) had to be protected against plundering by Iraqi civilians. Several incidents had occurred on MSR Jackson, such as hijacking of civil vehicles and the use of deadly violence by criminal gangs. Containers as well as vehicles had to be protected against hostile and criminal attacks. The situation on MSR Jackson was dangerous, unpredictable, and explosive. The road was frequently patrolled. Patrols routinely anticipated hostile actions, a car bomb, or an attack by ambush.

Commander O. and his battalion – an armoured car with military personnel, an armoured ambulance with medical personnel, a hoisting-crane, and a flatbed trailer – arrived at 12:30 hours. Already at the moment of arrival, the situation was

---

[42]   P.P.T. Bovend'Eert, 'De inzet van strijdkrachten zonder instemming van de Staten-Generaal [The deployment of armed forces without prior approval of the States General]', *Nederlands Juristenblad* (1998): 1594-1500.

chaotic. The QRF Battalion was responsible for the security of the men who recovered the container. The armoured car and the ambulance were blocking the road in two directions, in order to get the work done. This led to a traffic-jam in both directions, and more chaos and agitation among the drivers. The agitation increased at the moment that a convoy of 25 American vehicles, flatbed trailers with prefabs, and an American convoy of 350 war prisoners from the direction of Al Khidr, tried to drive through the blockade. However, both American convoys were stopped. Agitated groups of Iraqi people standing beside the road tried to approach the container. The QRF Battalion was busy, blocking the road, recovering the container, and communicating by radio. Only three men were left to perform the protection tasks. As a result, O. had insufficient military personnel to adequately secure the persons that were hoisting the container on the flatbed trailer. The situation was threatening. Finally, when the container stood on the trailer, at 2:00 pm, about a hundred Iraqi people, standing in several groups, slowly approached the trailer, which was ready to leave. There was real danger that the Iraqis would surround the trailer, the trailer driver, and his men. In this foreseeable situation, the Iraqis would stand between Eric O. and the military men near the trailer, and O. would have lost sight of the situation. Radio communication was hampered by a malfunctioning radio. O. noticed that several groups of Iraqis continued to approach the trailer, creating the dangerous situation of isolating the men near the trailer. O. loaded his weapon slowly and visibly in order to show the Iraqis the gravity of the situation. The Iraqis were looking at O.'s action. However, they were not scared off and they continued to approach. At that moment, the Iraqi were at a distance of about 75 meters. O. fired a warning shot in the air. The Iraqis still did not stop, but continued to approach slowly. O. took his weapon again and aimed the barrel in the direction of the group Iraqis. He did not aim at the group. He looked through the sight and saw the man standing at the far left of the group at the far right of the picture. Then he turned to the left, saw nobody in the sight, and fired a second warning shot, aimed at the mud several meters before the group, in order to splash the sand, and to frighten and stop the group. At that moment, the group turned around and ran off. One Iraqi man stumbled and fell on the ground. This man (A.) was severely wounded. He was taken to the hospital in Al Khidr where his death was certified. Afterwards, A. was transported to the General Hospital in As Samawah for post-mortem examination. The post-mortem report gives a description of an oval wound of 3 cms diameter in the middle of the back and a bloody wound where his left eye would have been. From this description, it was not completely certain that the bullet had ricocheted.[43]

---

[43] These facts stem from the statements made by several witnesses, among them the crane driver, and from O.'s testimony. All statements were used by the District Court as well by the Court of Appeal. Both Courts stated that the accused did not give an unreasonable account of his actions and that the untruth of his testimony could only be established if the untruth of his testimony could be proved.

Eric O. was arrested as a suspect on 31 December 2003. He was directly flown to the Netherlands, where he was imprisoned and prosecuted for manslaughter on the basis of Article 307 of the Dutch Penal Code. Besides manslaughter, O. was accused of deliberately breaching the official instructions (*dienstvoorschriften*) with the result of life danger or death, as stated in Article 136 of the Military Penal Code. These official instructions were laid down in the *Aide Memoire for SFIR Commanders* (AM) and the Instructions on the Use of Force (IUF) (*Geweldsinstructies*).

The Legal Framework

The District Court's Conclusion

What rules apply in a situation which is a military mission, is called a peace-keeping operation, and is neither a state of war, nor a state of peace? The District Court in Arnhem (Military Division) rejected all demands of the public prosecutor, stating the following arguments for its conclusion.[44] The Dutch military mission in Iraq was based on Resolutions 1483 and 1511 of the Security Council, as well as on the missions as formulated in the Memorandum of Understanding (MOU) ratified by the UK and the Netherlands, among other states. The MOU declares applicable the Rules of Engagement (ROE) which are attached to the MOU. The ROE were written especially for the mission in Iraq. The ROE are clearly formulated and guarantee the military units in Iraq a sufficiently robust action.

The District Court stated that, in this case, the ROE applied. The ROE are official instructions in the sense of Article 136 of the Military Penal Code. The above-mentioned IUF and AM are only summarized versions of the most important rules and obligations set out in the ROE. The AM is a translation of the ROE for the level of the commander in the field, the IUF are a translation of the ROE for the soldier. Most important is that the IUF give the soldier autonomous power in case of self-defence; he can fire an aimed shot without further commands. Moreover, the AM regulates under what circumstances the use of force is permitted and refers to the ROE for further explication. The ROE were binding rules at the moment Eric O. was charged.

The ROE give guidelines and rules with respect to the use of force. They are a means to control the use of force by military personnel, by way of formulations of restrictions or by allowing particular forms of force. O.'s warning shot was legitimized on the basis of ROE 151, which authorizes 'the passing of warnings to any person by any means', if warnings are necessary for the execution of missions. This means that the use of a warning shot as an independent means of force, i.e., separate from the warning shot as the starting point for deadly force, is allowed.

The situation of the accused was one of potential threat and a hindrance for the execution of the mission. The warning shot, fired to avert the threat, is legitimized

---

[44]   LJN: AR4029, *Rechtbank Arnhem* [Arnhem District Court], 05/097011-03.

by ROE 151 if the accused's action meets the requirements of *necessity*, *proportionality*, and *subsidiarity*. The Court declared that O.'s conduct met these requirements. O.'s behaviour was necessary under the threatening circumstances, sketched by several witnesses (necessity requirement). He could not have acted in any other way, given the lack of military personnel in the threatening situation (subsidiarity requirement). Nor did he act out of proportion, giving the warning shots in order to remove the threat and the hindrance for the mission (proportionality requirement). The Court acquitted O. of the charge.

The Prosecution Department Appeals against the Court's Decision

The prosecutor appealed against the Arnhem District Court's decision. The attitude of the Public Prosecution Service was later on qualified by the Arnhem Court of Appeal as 'an attitude with a particular tenacity'. The public prosecutor's closing speech was long and consisted of 25 pages. The arguments concentrated on the term 'official instruction' (*dienstvoorschrift*) and the use of the ROE as an official instruction. The Advocate General, the public prosecutor of the Court of Appeals, argued that the term 'official instruction' as defined in Article 135 of the Dutch Military Penal Code had been interpreted in such a broad way – declaring the ROE as applicable rules – that the Court went beyond the legal basis of the facts of the charge, which is a violation of the legality principle, i.e., the rule of law. Furthermore, the Advocate General held to his demand of manslaughter, Article 307 of the Dutch Penal Code. To clarify the legal status of the Dutch mission in Iraq, the public prosecutor distinguished five situations as different categories of war:

(1) a state of war in which the Netherlands is involved as a belligerent;
(2) a state of war in which the Netherlands has not accepted war, but its allies have; in this case, the Netherlands is only in a state of war if it has empowered its military units to use force, based on the state monopoly on (the use of) force;
(3) a state of internal armed conflict between two or more sovereign states, or two or more sovereign states, on the one hand, and one or more parties with sovereignty claims, on the other;
(4) a state of external armed conflict between two or more sovereign states, or two or more sovereign states, on the one hand, and one or more parties with sovereignty claims, on the other;
(5) a state in which two competing parties without sovereignty claims fight each other, which has led to an internal state collapse, in which Dutch military units intervene on behalf of the UN or for the purpose of the International Criminal Court (ICC), for the enforcement of or for the purpose of on-site investigation.

The public prosecutor stated that, with respect to the situation of the Dutch troops in Iraq, only category 5. was applicable. On the basis of this argument, the use of force was excluded.[45] In this way, the accused was not a 'military component of a party involved', but an 'expert on mission'. The public prosecutor answered the question of whether the Netherlands, as a military party, was involved in a conflict in Iraq in the negative. If this statement is correct, what exactly *is* the legal status of the Dutch military units in Iraq, the Advocate General asked.

The public prosecutor concluded that the ROE were not applicable. The status of the Dutch military units was that of 'regular troops' responsible for 'non-military potential tasks'. For that reason, the law of the general Dutch Penal Code was applicable. As a result, the charge on appeal was again manslaughter.

The Court of Appeal's Conclusion

The Arnhem Court of Appeal (Military Division), like the Arnhem District Court, concentrated on the applicability of ROE 151 for the mission in Iraq. In its conclusion, the Court of Appeal repeated the essential arguments already stated by the District Court. The ROE, as official instructions, were applicable for the following reasons. The word *dienstvoorschrift* is defined in Article 135 of the Military Penal Code, which states:

> Onder dienstvoorschrift wordt verstaan een bij of krachtens algemene maatregel van bestuur dan wel bij of krachtens landsverordening onderscheidenlijk landsbesluit gegeven schriftelijk besluit van algemeen strekking dat enig militair dienstbelang betreft en een tot de militair gericht ge- of verbod bevat.[46]

Once again, the Court of Appeal concluded that the actions of the Dutch troops were legitimized by Resolutions 1483 and 1511 of the UN Security Council. In Resolution 1511, passed on 16 October 2003, it is clearly stated that the Security Council 'authorizes a multinational force under unified command to take all necessary measures to contribute to the maintenance of security and stability in Iraq.' In Resolution 1483, adopted on 22 May 2003, the Security Council welcomed 'the willingness of Member states to contribute to stability and security in Iraq by contributing personnel, equipment, and other resources under Authority.'

On the basis of these Resolutions, a number of states, among them the Netherlands, and the United Kingdom as lead nation, entered into a Memorandum of Understanding (MOU) with respect to participation in the Multinational Division (South East) (MND(SE)). This agreement was signed on 8 July 2003 on behalf of the Netherlands by the Minister of Defence. In this agreement, the ROE, laid down in Annex F, were declared applicable.

---

[45]   Here, the Public Prosecution Service referred to two cases in which the Court had rejected the existence of 'time of war' and its consequences, i.e., the applicability of the Dutch Penal Code and the Dutch Military Penal Code.

[46]   'An official instruction is defined as a written decision of general application by virtue of an order in council or a national ordinance or a national decree concerning any military service interest and consisting of orders and prohibitions directed at the soldier'.

For the evaluation of the Eric O. case, ROE 151 is essential. The MOU and Annex F are qualified 'confidential'. This means that, in principle, ROE 151 cannot be made public. However, the Dutch military units were actually familiar with the ROE. They were instructed about the ROE and had practised them. In this context, the 'need to know' principle had been used. The substantive meaning of ROE 151 had been recorded in the conclusion of the District Court, discussed in public, and published on the Internet. Moreover, ROE 151 had been discussed during the public hearing of the Court of Appeal. Under these circumstances, the Court of Appeal was of the opinion that the confidential nature of ROE 151 had to give way to transparency, also external transparency, an essential requirement for a fair trial, all the more since the conclusion of the Court of Appeal would not be comprehensible without information on knowledge of ROE 151.

Based upon this argumentation, the Court of Appeal was of the opinion that the ROE met all the requirements of an official instruction specified in Article 135 of the Military Penal Code. The fact that the ROE were in English was not a hindrance. The Court of Appeal's ample argumentation concentrated on the clarification of what rules were valid with respect to this specific military mission. In this context, the meaning of the words 'use of force' was analysed and elaborated. The ROE were rightly declared valid rules, being an Annex to the MOU, an agreement signed by the Netherlands. In this respect, the ROE count as valid rules, under a ministerial regulation. The Minister can exercise his power on the basis of Article 9, paragraph 2, under a, of the National Decree on Military Criminal and Disciplinary Procedure (*Rijksbesluit uitvoeringsbepalingen militair straf- en tuchtrecht*). In this sense, the ROE constitute a written decision of general application (*besluit van algemene strekking*), concerning the interest of military servicemen and women and including prohibitions, orders, and the division of powers.

According to the Court of Appeal, the ROE were evidently applicable, valid rules for the mission in Iraq. Therefore, it concluded that a breach of the legality principle, i.e., the rule of law, by going beyond the basis of the charge, had to be rejected. This basic principle had not been violated since ROE 151 was applicable. ROE 151 states:

> Passing of warnings to any person, aircraft, vehicle or vessel by any means in circumstances where MND(SE) forces or elements under MND(SE) protection or the mission are threatened or where the passing of warnings is necessary for purposes of execution of the mission is authorized.

The warning shot fired by O. could not be regarded as substantially imprudent, negligent, or careless. The Court of Appeal stated that, in general, shooting in the ground under the existing circumstances, was not more dangerous than a shot fired in the air. Based upon these arguments, the Court of Appeal, too, acquitted Eric O. of the charge.

Critical Considerations

After the final conclusion, some remarkable comments can be noted. Under the *obiter dicta*, the Court of Appeal strongly criticized the Public Prosecution Service as well as the Minister of Defence. Firstly, the Court of Appeal stated that judges, in the Dutch legal system, in conforming with Article 12 of the General Provisions Act (*Wet algemene bepalingen*) are obliged to take a reticent attitude with respect to the creation of new rules. Making new laws is solely reserved to the legislator. Within the separation of powers, the legislature has primacy over the judiciary. For this reason, the judge could not answer the legal questions posed by the Public Prosecution Service about the legal status of the situation in Iraq. Is it or is it not a state of war? If it is not a state of war, what then is the legal status? The Court of Appeal pointed out that these legal questions have to be answered by the Public Prosecution Service itself, in mutual deliberation and agreement with the military experts of the Ministry of Defence. The answers have to function as the basis of a balanced policy for instruction and prosecution. Unfortunately, there had not been such deliberation between the Public Prosecution Service and the Minister of Defence. Next, the Court of Appeal observed, much to its regret, that in the Eric O. case, the Public Prosecution Service had evidently been *insufficiently* prepared for the question of how to react to the described shooting incident. This had led to a far too severe assessment of the case and permanent damage to the serviceman involved.

The Court of Appeal noted that, in the meantime, a further elaboration of ideas had been initiated within the Public Prosecution Service, leading to a different procedure: a soldier who fires will no longer be regarded as a *suspect*, as a matter of course in accordance with the existing 'Instructions for police officers concerning the use of force' (*Instructies positie politiefunctionaris bij geweldsaanwending*). However, the Court of Appeal made the direct and clear statement that, in the comparison with similar rules, such as the 'Instructions for police officers', the fact that a military action during an international mission is *of a totally different order* had been completely ignored.

The Court of Appeal came to the conclusion that the Public Prosecution Service had prosecuted Eric O. with an attitude of excessive tenacity. The public prosecutor's statement about the District Court's breach of the principle of legality, the rule of law, was unjustified. Moreover, the Court of Appeal concluded that the Public Prosecution Service had a rather one-sided view on the principle of legality; it had been applied only to the detriment of the accused. In doing so, the Public Prosecution Service had ignored that, first and foremost, the function of the principle of legality is the protection of rights of citizens. In similar cases, in the future, the Public Prosecution Service's attitude could result in the absence of the necessary legal certainty for soldiers on international missions acting under dangerous circumstances. The Public Prosecution Service was told to work on its 'situational awareness'.

Meanwhile, a debate had been taking place in Parliament about this issue. The Minister of Defence reacted to this debate in a letter to Parliament in which he stated that, meanwhile regular deliberations had taken place between the Public

Prosecution Service and the Ministry of Defence. These deliberations involved (1) operational and legal questions concerning the Dutch rules for the use of force, (2) policy deliberations concerning the armed forces between a representative of the Arnhem Public Prosecution Service, the Legal Affairs Directorate of the Ministry of Defence and the heads of the Legal Affairs sections of the armed forces, and (3) a military three-way discussion between the chief public prosecutor in the district of Arnhem, the Legal Affairs Director and the Commander of the Dutch military police (*Koninklijke Marechaussee*). Furthermore, prior to all international missions, the Public Prosecution Service would henceforth be informed about the applicable rules on the use of force, the rules concerning the legal status of troops on missions and the mandate for the operation.

Applying the Institutional Framework to the Case Study

Two observations can be made on the basis of the case study sketched above. Firstly, the character of the Constitution, acknowledged as the rigid and unvarying basis of the whole legal system, suggests a solid guarantee for citizens' rights. This implies a strong belief in the law, in particular in the Constitution, as the basis for acting. The words of the Constitution are prior to governmental decisions. In other words, the Constitution determines governmental behaviour.

Secondly, although the Constitution, in particular the democratic procedures for war decisions laid down in Article 96, was not changed, the substantive meaning of the constitutional provision changed fundamentally. This transformation was the result of processes in political practice. 'War' is no longer declared. However, in practice, warfare continues under different names. The legal status of the new terminology is not unproblematic, as became painfully clear in the Eric O. trial.

What can we learn from applying the institutional framework to the case study? In Institutional Legal Theory, the essentials for the existence of a legal system are the interplay of a normative system with organizations and social proceedings which have an observable side, too. Law as a linguistic phenomenon and its relationship with social practices can be divided into three subsystems:

(1) the legitimate legal rule (the formal dimension), which comprises a message (the material dimension);
(2) the acts of the application of the rule by an official, and, in the case of a conflict, a judge (both testing factual behaviour against the rule);
(3) a degree of rule-conforming patterns of behaviour in social practice.

Given the relationship between words and reality described above, it has been concluded that, within these three categories only subsystems (2) and (3) are *discernible*: in subsystem (2) the acts of the official and the judge applying and enforcing the rule, are *perceptible*, both testing factual behaviour against the rule as fiction; and in subsystem (3) the rule-conforming patterns of behaviour are *observable* in social practices. The legal rule itself is an *indiscernible* construct; it is *thought* to be the basis of the two other subsystems.

Applying the analytical framework to the Eric O. case leads to the following observations. The problem concentrates on subsystem (2) in relationship with subsystem (1). Subsystem (1) involves a specific legitimate legal rule, which comprises a message. The message of the legal rule projects an imaginary reality, which can be distinguished in its perceptible application, see subsystem (2). In subsystem (2) of the analytical framework, factual behaviour (in this case, the behaviour of Eric O.), is tested against the message of a rule. However, in the case study, it is not so much the act of applying of one specific rule, but rather the uncertainty about the question of *what rules* apply and, as a result, about the conflicting opinions of the Public Prosecution Service and the Courts on the application of *two rules* which have an entirely *opposite* meaning. These rules are Article 307 of the Dutch Penal Code and Article 151 of the Rules of Engagement. In the viewpoint of the Public Prosecution Service, the specific situation, that is, the international mission in Iraq, is a regular situation, in which the Dutch Penal Code is valid law, since the mission is not a 'state of war', nor an 'armed conflict'. The situation is qualified as a peacekeeping mission, in which Dutch military personnel have to be seen as 'experts on mission', eventually to be compared with (the tasks of) police officers during their daily work. The judges, however, stuck to their standpoint that Eric O.'s act was not carried out under regular circumstances. The military forces operating in the situation in Iraq were not even similar to police officers. Even if the mission could have been qualified as 'peacekeeping', military actions during an international mission are of a totally different order, the judges stated. In this situation, Article 307 of the Dutch Penal Code is not applicable. On the contrary, under these 'war' circumstances, the Rules of Engagement, rules concerning the use of force, are valid and applicable law.

By way of this conflict about the question of which of the two opposite rules apply, we see that subsystem (2), expressing the act of applying one specific rule, is extended: the general rule 'Thou shalt not kill' (Article 307, Penal Code) has been turned into a rule with a complete different perspective 'Killing is authorized in "war" situations' (Article 151 ROE). This meaning became manifest, as said before, in subsystem (2), not just by testing the rules against the act of killing, but by testing the *specific situation* – 'war' practices, see subsystem (3) – in which the act took place. The observable and factual (war) practices caused the choice between the two rules. This means that, in the *actual* testing of facts against the mental picture of a rule, i.e., testing by the Public Prosecution Service, which is subject to court decisions, the meaning of the legal rule became manifest, including a strong influence of the circumstances of war *practices* as a decisive factor.

Final Remarks

The application of the institutional framework leads to the following final conclusion.

The processes described, express a strong 'bottom-up' influence on the determination of a rule. Although, in the classical 'top-down' view, the legal rule is the legitimate basis for the acts of officials applying the rule, as well as the legitimate basis for rule-conforming patterns of behaviour in social practice, the case study illustrates that the acts of officials and the facts of social practice influence the meaning of the rule. The facts of reality determine the fiction of the law. The message of the rule, projecting an imaginary reality, is determined by patterns of war practices, qualified as 'peacekeeping', and notably in such a strong way that the rule's projected meaning is turned into its opposite. Instead of the general prohibition of murder, killing is authorized under war circumstances. This means that the projected picture of a legal rule not only becomes manifest and clear in social practice, but also the reverse: social practice generates the meaning (or meaning transformation) of a rule. This constitutive process can even reverse the rule's meaning into its opposite.

From this analysis, it can be concluded that the Continental theoretical nation of the primacy of the legislature has to be put into perspective. This applies in particular with respect to such a solemn and rigid document as the Constitution. The character of the Constitution, acknowledged as the unvarying basis of the whole legal system, suggests a solid guarantee for citizens' rights and democracy. Constitutions are generally seen as democratic designs to constrain the arbitrary will of the rulers. The question arises whether the shifts in the concept of war, the development of new war terminology in political practices, and, as a result, the absence of a clear-cut distinction between war and peace as described, are in line with the traditional function of the Constitution, since the pertinent Article of the Dutch Constitution (Article 96) has remained unchanged.

Part III

LEGISLATION AND
THE DISCIPLINES

Chapter 8

Grounding Behaviour
in Law and Economics

Bruce Anderson and Philip McShane

*Bruce Anderson is Associate Professor of Commercial Law, Saint Mary's
University Mount, Halifax, N.S., Canada. Philip McShane is Professor Emeritus of
Philosophy, Mount St Vincent University, Halifax, N.S., Canada.*

Introduction

Most scholars interested in law and economics take a particular view of economics for
granted and they build their analyses of law and economics on that view. Today, the
version of economics that dominates analyses of law and economics is neo-classical
economics. But what if this portrait of economics is flawed? Would not this mean that
legislation concerned with taxation or trade for instance, and any studies of legislation,
grounded on such a view will also be flawed? The purpose of this chapter is to make
the point that the field of legisprudence must take into account the ground of particular
pieces of legislation. Our focus is law and economics.

This chapter contains four sections. A first section provides a broad context of
discussion, a context which goes to the root of present confusion regarding the
meshing of law and economics. The second section gives an outline of a missing
economic analysis: the startling fact of the absence of such an analysis is becoming
clearer as the dysfunctions of present economic and legal performances reveal
themselves in First, Second and Third Worlds. The third section presents some current
speculations that help grasp the problem of the ungroundedness of most present
thinking on the topic of law and economics. The fourth section draws some elementary
conclusions.

The Context of an Absent Definition of Sanity

Laws regarding criminally insane behaviour are acknowledged to be based on some
grasp of the meaning of sanity. One might expect, then, that laws regarding
dysfunctional economic behaviour would be based on some grasp of sane economic
behaviour. This, however, is not the case. Further, just as insanity comes under many
complex guises, so too does economic dysfunction. In both areas there are, however,

genera of dysfunction that can be identified with the aid of some elementary grasp of functional behaviour. In economics the dominant genus of dysfunction seems to be that which ranges over various myopic perspectives on pricing. Most obvious of these is the assumption that stock price variations are seriously indicative of economic functioning; less obvious are various Pareto optimization techniques. Most destructive, however, is the myopic view of the price called profit.

But none of these claims makes sense unless one has, or has been offered, some grasp of functional economics. Is there one on offer? Nicholas Kaldor, reflecting our generic problem, points to a warp in economic analysis that he pins down quite precisely.

> The difficulty of a new start is to pinpoint the critical area where economic theory went astray.... I would put it in the middle of the fourth chapter of Volume One of *The Wealth of Nations*. In that chapter, after discussing the need for money in a social economy, Smith suddenly gets fascinated by the distinction between money price, real price, and exchange value, and *hey presto*, his interest gets bogged down in the question of how values and prices for products and factors are determined. One can trace a more or less continuous development of price theory from the subsequent chapters of Smith through Ricardo, Walras, Marshall, right up to Debreu and the most sophisticated present-day Americans.[1]

The dominant figure between Smith and Keynes, definitely a price-man, is Leon Walras, who fathered a general analysis of the equilibration of prices in Western economics in the 1870s.[2]

There was another direction in economic analysis that sought to attend to production as a prior reality to pricing, a reality that would have natural and deeper demands than pricing, much as the nature of intelligence and its neural conditions lie deeper than lists of forms of insanity. For our purposes it seems best to note that three economists of the twentieth century sought to turn attention away from simple price or profit analysis to demands internal to rhythms of the productive process. These are Joseph Schumpeter (1883-1950) an Austrian economist who found his way to America, Michal Kalecki (1899-1970), a Polish economist who found his way to Cambridge, and the Canadian economist, Bernard Lonergan (1904-84), whose work of the 1930s and 1940s attracts present attention due to its recent publication.[3] Indeed, all three began to attract attention at the end of the twentieth century. Kalecki's main efforts coincide in time with those of Lonergan, but Schumpeter's key work goes back exactly one hundred years from the time of writing. His *Theory of Economic*

---

[1]   N. Kaldor, 'The Irrelevance of Equilibrium Economics', *Economic Journal*, 82 (1973): 1240-1241.

[2]   The key work is L. Walras, *Elements of Pure Economics*, trans. W. Jaffe (Illinois, 1954). Originally published in 1874.

[3]   For detailed consideration of the three economists and their interrelations *see* P. McShane, *Lonergan's Challenge to the University and the Economy* (Washington, 1976), chapters 6-8. Now available at <http://www.philipmcshane.ca>.

Development was the product of the first decade of the last century. In that work he brought forth the significance of creative and innovative behaviour in economics, something that found little place in the economics of the century that was to follow. The key significance, for our purpose here, is the manner in which major innovation has an inner rhythm that demands naturally – sanely, if one thinks of our initial parallel with deranged behaviour – a concomitant financial rhythm.

It is best to begin to think here of simpler innovations in simpler economic times. So, there was the idea of replacing the spade by the horse-drawn plough. Thinking this out in concrete detail shows the slow surging of the production of ploughs, with no extra consumer goods, the gradual surging of consumer goods, the stabilization of the production of capital goods, and the later stabilization of consumer goods. Concomitant to these surges are rhythms of prices, including those prices named profit and interest. In so far as there is an absence of concomitance between production and financial rhythms there is a departure from sanity.

While the problem of production of goods and financial rhythms keeping pace was a focus of attention in both Kalecki and Schumpeter, it was Bernard Lonergan who tackled successfully the necessary analysis.[4] But before we proceed it is important to return to our starting point, and to emphasize the principal demand. That demand is for grounded assertions in any law relating to economics and empirical groundedness in the economics that mediates such law. So, one might ask, for instance, what would ground a law demanding steady profit, or the optimization or maximization of some price-structure, in a economy that is naturally rhythmic in profit flow and price-flow?

The problem is that without the analysis that reveals and specifies those natural rhythms, the question remains rhetorical. But the key point must be up-front. Law based on the unanalysed cannot but be arbitrary. On the other hand, law based on an analysis of natural rhythms of economic behaviour requires not only a grasp of that analysis and its applications, successful and unsuccessful, but also a creativity internal to legal thinking. The latter task is not our focus here. It seems sufficient to make the general point, then to draw attention to the lines of the missing economic analysis. However, in a third section of this chapter we draw attention to two current positions on law and economics that appear clearly, in the light of the required analysis, to be groundless. In the next section we attempt a sketch of the missing economic analysis. A summary statement by Lonergan captures what we have been attending to here.

On classical analysis the economic mechanism is the pricing system. It coordinates spontaneously a vast and ever shifting manifold of otherwise independent choices of demand and decisions to supply. But man does not stand outside this machine, he is part of it, his choices and decisions are themselves the variables in the system. It follows that there is not possibility of setting down methodically, on the one hand, the exigences of the machine and, on the other, the consequent performance of man. A study of the mechanics of motorcars yields premises for a criticism of drivers, precisely because the motorcars, as

---

[4]   B. Lonergan, *For A New Political Economy*, Collected Works of Bernard Lonergan (Toronto, 1998), vols. 15 and 21.

distinct from the drivers, have laws of their own which drivers must respect. But if the mechanics of motors included, in a single piece, the anthropology of drivers, criticism could be no more that haphazard.[5]

A Sketch of Economic Dynamics

A Brief Sketch

The economic dynamics that we wish to sketch is difficult and outside present establishment thinking. For that reason, it seems best to proceed here in a somewhat popular fashion.[6] So we move from Lonergan's suggestion about the need to understand the mechanics of cars as distinct from the anthropology of drivers. This section consists in drawing an extended analogy between operating a car and operating an economy. That analogy is between the parts of a car and the parts of an economy, how a car works and how an economy works, the needs of cars and the needs of economies, the norms of driving a car and the norms of an economy, the role law plays in driving a car and the role law plays in running an economy.

What are the essential parts of a car? If someone was going to explain to you how a car works they might begin by naming those essential parts. For instance, there is the battery, starter, radiator, engine block, electrical wiring, gears, brakes, gas tank, tires, wheels, and so on. These are the sorts of things that if your car was missing any of them it would not work properly.

If someone was going to explain to you how an economy works the same question seems relevant. *What are the essential parts of an economy?* Broadly speaking, Bernard Lonergan's answer is that the main parts of an economy are (1) the productive process, the process of transforming raw materials into finished products and (2) exchanges (the sales and purchases of goods and services, for instance).

To be more specific, Lonergan sharply distinguishes between two types of goods and services: (1) consumer goods and services and (2) capital goods and services. Consumer goods are goods that are used up. They include food, beer, clothes, spy novels, DVD rentals, electricity for homes, home heating oil. Capital goods are goods that are used over and over again in a business in order to produce other goods which will be sold-computers of graphic artists, welding machines used by welders, refrigerators used by a grocery store.

Following from the idea that there are two distinct types of goods and services Lonergan goes on to sharply distinguishes between two types of exchanges. One type of exchange involves the sale of consumer goods. The other type of exchange involves

---

5   Ibid., p. 109.

6   Other presentations of this perspective include: B. Anderson and P. McShane, *Beyond Establishment Economics: No Thank-you Mankiw* (Halifax, 2002); P. McShane, *Economics for Everyone: Das Jus Kapital* (Halifax, 1998); P. McShane, *Pastkeynes Pastmodern Economics: A Fresh Pragmatism* (Halifax, 2002).

the sale of capital goods.

But Lonergan also identifies exchanges that are not connected to the production of new products. This type of exchange simply involves a change in ownership. The sale of land or secondhand goods are examples of exchanges not connected to the productive process. These are called *redistributive* exchanges.

Let me name and order the significant parts of an economy in more detail:

• The rate of payments–namely income, expenditure, receipts, outlay–related to the production and sale of *capital* goods and services in a particular time period. (These payments vary with changes in the quantity, price, and rate at which capital goods and services are produced and sold.)

• The rate of payments–namely income, expenditure, receipts, outlay–related to the production and sale of *consumer* goods and services in a particular time period. (These payments vary with changes in the quantity, price, and rate at which consumer goods and services are produced and sold.)

• The rate at which suppliers and sellers of *consumer* goods purchase capital goods and services in a particular interval. (This is the flow of money from the consumer circuit of payments to the capital circuit of payments.) Lonergan calls this flow of money a *crossover*. Examples include a carpenter buying a new bandsaw and a sailmaker purchasing a new automated machine to cut sailcloth.

• The rate at which suppliers and sellers of *capital* goods purchase consumer goods and services in a particular interval. (This is the flow of money from the capital circuit of payments to the consumer circuit of payments.) Lonergan also calls this flow of money a *crossover* circuit. Examples include the employees of a transport truck assembly plant buying groceries.

• The rate at which money leaves the *capital circuit* of payments and joins the *redistributive exchanges*. Conversely, the rate at which money leaves the redistributive exchanges and joins the capital circuit of payments. For instance, businesses that make dump trucks deposit their profits in the bank or buy shares. And such businesses also borrow money to buy more welding machines to build, for instance, ships.

• The rate at which money leaves the *consumer circuit* of payments and joins the *redistributive exchanges*. Conversely, the rate at which money leaves the redistributive exchanges and joins the consumer circuit of payments. Some people, for instance, deposit a portion of their salary in the bank or buy shares, and people also borrow money or use their credit cards to buy household goods.

• Also, there are choices and decisions concerning who is to produce what particular goods, who is to perform particular services, how many goods to produce, what price to set, whether or not to buy capital goods and services, whether or not to buy consumer goods and services, whether or not to save money, whether or not to borrow money, and so on.

How Do Cars and Economies Work?

How do the parts of a car fit together? How are the parts related? How does a car actually work? It makes sense that the next step would be to explain how the parts of a car fit together, what the different parts do. Now I do not know how a car works. I do know that cars have an electrical system, a drive-train, and a cooling system, but I do not have a clue how they are related. In fact, it takes a mechanic a couple of years' study at the community college to understand how a car works. At least I know that some people know how a car works.

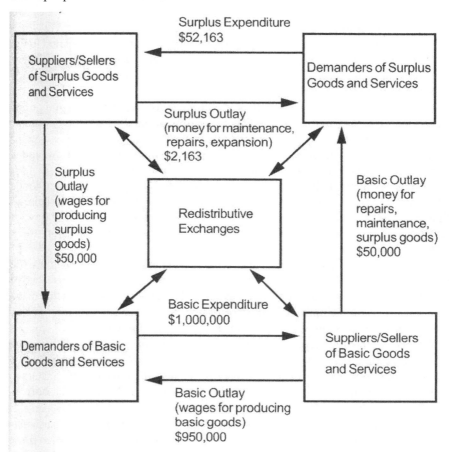

Figure 8.1 Structure of an economy

How do the parts of an economy fit together? You might suspect that how an economy works is more complicated than how a car works. Think about what would happen if we did not know how the parts of an economy fit together. We would probably have problems such as inflation, deflation, currency fluctuations, and poverty and our efforts to manage the economy would be haphazard and a matter of guess-work. We really would not know how the economy works. Imagine the state of affairs if we could not even identify the essential parts of an economy.

A compact version of Lonergan's explanation of how the parts fit together is the following:

- Goods and services should be divided into two distinct classes: (1) capital goods and services and (2) consumer goods and services.
- The productive rhythm of *capital* goods and services is related to a particular circuit of money consisting of expenditure, receipts, outlay, and income. The productive rhythm of *consumer* goods and services is related to its own particular circuit of money consisting of expenditures, receipts, outlays, and income.
- The velocity of money in these two main monetary circuits (that is the money related to the production and sale of capital goods and the money related to the production and sale of consumer goods) is tied to the velocity with which goods and services are produced and sold.
- In redistributive exchanges the velocity of money depends simply on how often owners change their minds and decide to buy or sell something, not on the production of goods and services. For instance, a house can be sold whenever a seller has a buyer. Shares in a corporation can also be sold whenever a seller has a buyer.
- When an economy is running properly the production of goods and services is subject to phases. The names of those phases are: capital expansion, consumer expansion, and steady-state.
  - During a capital expansion the economy devotes its resources to increasing the quantity of capital goods and services.
  - When the production of capital goods and services reaches its maximum, the resources of the economy should then be devoted to a consumer expansion – increasing the production and sale of consumer goods and services.
  - When the production of consumer goods and services reaches its maximum, the economy experiences a steady-state phase during which neither the production of capital nor consumer goods and services are increasing or decreasing.
- Raising the standard of living of citizens depends on realizing the basic expansion phase of the economic cycle.

The phases of production have their counterparts in the monetary circulation. Further, the phases of the productive cycle are possible only if variations in rates of payment keep in step with the phases of the productive cycle. In other words, the flow of money in the capital circuit has to vary concomitantly with the turnover of capital goods and services and the flow of money in the consumer circuit has to vary concomitantly with the turnover of consumer goods and services.

Successful acceleration of the capital circuit requires increments in the quantity of money added to the capital circuit and increases in the frequency with which money is added to the capital monetary circuit. The velocity of money in the capital and consumer circuits is tied to the velocity with which goods and services are produced. To be more precise, the velocity of money is understood in terms of how much money is required to complete a turnover. The concern is with how much money it takes and how long it takes that amount of money to initiate and complete the cycle from outlay to income to expenditure, to receipts, to outlay. For example, if the turnover of a supplier of welding machines is ten machines per month and they raise their turnover to twenty machines per month, the size of their circulating capital must increase proportionately or else they will not be able to increase production. They must be able to bridge the gap between payments made and payments received (ie. the gap between the initiation of the turnover and its completion) which depends on the size of their turnover and the price of the welding equipment. On the other hand, if the circulation of money in the capital circuit or the consumer circuit bears no relation to the velocity with which goods are produced, we will have inflation or deflation.

According to Lonergan, 'the rate of increase in circulating capital is the motive force of the expansion' of the economy. If money flowing from the redistributive exchanges increases it is possible to increase turnover size and turnover frequency. Hence a successful acceleration of the capital circuit is possible if money is added to it and if capital outlay, income, expenditure, and receipts keep in step. And a successful acceleration of the consumer circuit is possible if money is added to the consumer circuit and consumer outlay, income, expenditure, and receipts keep in step.

What Do Cars and Economies Need in order to Work Properly?

Cars have needs and so do economies. Knowing how a car works enables people to write the manuals car owners are supposed to read when they buy a new car. These owners' manuals are full of practical advice about running a car. In this context the concern is with what things have to be done to the car so that it will work properly. The key question is *What are the norms related to running a car properly?* Here are a few norms: Use winter tires in snow. Change the oil every 5,000 km. Use high octane gasoline. Inflate the tires to the stipulated pressure. Do not over-rev the car. Drive in first gear only at low speeds.

What are the norms of a properly functioning economy? What does an economy need in order to work properly? A few norms can be identified. Money has to keep pace with production of goods and services. For instance, in order to increase the production of capital goods there must be a proportionate increase in money used for the production and sale of those capital goods. The crossovers must be balanced; one circuit cannot expand at the expense of the other. For instance, if money is removed from the consumer circuit by taxation and spent on research and development there will be less money available to pay for the production of consumer goods and less money available to buy them. Money removed by taxation from either circuit must be returned to that circuit or else the particular circuit will shrink. Money leaving the economy to pay for imports must be replaced or else the economy will shrink.

In the sections above we have identified the needs of a properly functioning economy and have expressed them as norms. The car-economy analogy was drawn between what a car needs to function properly and what an economy needs to function properly. Now let us turn to the human factor in driving cars and managing economies.

What Must People in the Drivers' Seats of Cars and Economies Do?

Over the years norms of good driving have developed, been accepted, and are taught to beginners. *What are the norms of good driving?* The norms of good driving include: Use your right foot for both the gas pedal and the brake pedal. Drive slowly near children. Slow down by pumping your brakes, not slamming them on. Turn on your lights at dusk. Drive slowly in fog. Keep the car maintained. Drive safely. Do not drink alcohol and drive. Do not speed. Park close to the curb. No 'back-seat' drivers.

It is worth noting that legal penalties are connected to some of these norms, but most norms are taught in driver education programs and learned by watching and imitating good drivers.

What are the norms of properly running an economy? The norms have not been worked out in detail. In fact, one of the current problems is to sort out who should be managing an economy. Politicians, central bankers, stock brokers, business people, and economists compete for control. But in general terms relevant norms grounded on the analysis of how an economy works presented in this paper would include: A group of people must understand how an economy works and is working. The role of this group, and also citizens, is to make sure the economy works properly. Economic education is crucial for properly running an economy. Central controls are not the key to running an economy.

More particular norms would include: When an economy is in a steady phase do not add money to it. Support the shift from a capital expansion to a consumer expansion. During a capital expansion the wages of workers should not be raised. Artificially promoting a capital expansion should not be permitted. Transfer payments, from one part of a country to another for instance, should not be permitted unless it is known they will not adversely affect the circuits.

The key point is that in order to articulate suitable norms for a properly functioning economy we must know how a properly functioning economy works. The next section is concerned with whether such norms should be given the force of law.

What Is the Role of Law in Running Cars and Economies?

What type of laws cover car driving? The laws related to cars stipulate what types of behaviour are unacceptable. For instance, there are laws that set out fines, jail terms, and revoking drivers' licenses for drunk driving, speeding, and dangerous driving. The role of these laws is to take dangerous drivers off the streets and to punish them, and also to tell people what type of behaviour is not acceptable. We do not have laws that cover good driving. Good driving is an incredibly complex skill.

What type of laws should cover the economy? Good economic behaviour involves an incredibly complex array of knowledge and practical actions that would have to taken at the appropriate time. It would be impossible to legislate for such occasions. However, unacceptable behaviour can be identified and perhaps spelling it out and assigning legal sanctions would be useful. There might be a law fining or jailing anyone who destabilizes the monetary circuits of an economy by speculating on currency exchange rates. Laws that prohibit artificially maintaining a capital expansion and laws that prohibit raising wages during a capital expansion may be necessary. Perhaps anyone who hinders or frustrates the shift from a capital expansion to a consumer expansion should be penalized. A law against foreign money financing a domestic surplus expansion may prove necessary.

The point is that the norms for running an economy and judgments regarding the suitability of legislation cannot be grasped unless we know how an economy works. Otherwise any legislation concerning the economy is made blindly.

Economics and Law: Present Confusions

Posner's Economic Analysis of Law

It is probably safe to say that Richard Posner has framed the modern field of law and economics. He uses economics 'to explain the procedures, institutions, and substantive doctrines of the law' and he uses economics as the basis for proposing reforms in legal procedures, institutions, and doctrines. For instance, in the US the economic analysis of law has 'contributed to the deregulation movement' (particularly public utilities) and has 'played a significant role in orienting American law in a free-market direction...'[7]

How does Posner see the relation between law and economics? The starting point is that Posner believes that individuals are self-interested. Their interest is in wealth-maximization. For Posner this means that what counts as an improvement in economic welfare brought about by law will be a change that is potential Pareto superior – if the gains in money to a buyer and seller exceed the loss in money to a third party (a competitor for instance) adversely affected by the transaction, even if the third part is not compensated, then the transaction maximizes wealth.

Posner

> views law's aim as 'mimicking the market', which is to say bringing about the allocation of resources that the market would bring about if market transaction costs were not prohibitive (if they are not prohibitive, the market can be left alone to bring about the allocation, and so one important aim of law, particularly of property, contract, and tort law is to minimize market transaction costs)...[8]

Further, Posner writes that 'When potential Pareto superiority is applied in fields of law ranging from contract, tort, and property law, among public law fields, to antitrust, securities, labour, environmental, and administrative law, among public law fields, it

---

[7]   R. Posner, 'Law and Economics', *IVR Encyclopedia of Jurisprudence, Legal Theory and Philosophy of Law* (Berlin, 2005), <http://www.ivr-enc.info/en/>.

[8]   Ibid.

constitutes a regulatory system isomorphic with the economic system itself.'[9]

Joel Bakan on Regulating Corporate Wealth

Joel Bakan, a law professor at the University of British Columbia, recently published a book called *The Corporation: The Pathological Pursuit of Profit*. Also, a movie based on the book has toured mainstream movie theatres in Canada. Bakan argues that '[t]he corporation's legally defined mandate is to pursue, relentlessly and without exception, its own self-interest, regardless of the often harmful consequences it might cause to others'.[10] As a result, 'the corporation is a pathological institution, a dangerous possessor of the great power it wields over people and societies'.[11]

He blames this problem on the limited liability and separate legal personality of the corporation. Bakan believes that corporations have one mission, namely to increase shareholder value. He stresses that the legal duty corporations owe to shareholders is to make money, to make as much money as possible for their shareholders. This means not only that 'law inhibits executives and corporations from being socially responsible, but that it is also illegal to be socially and environmentally responsible'.[12]

Bakan claims that corporate culture is defined by greed and moral indifference and is obsessed with profits and share prices. Self-interest is valorized and moral concerns are irrelevant. For the corporation social goals and environmental goals are not ends in themselves, but are strategic resources to be worked in order to maximize profit. A corporation can be ethical so long as being ethical is good for business, that is good for profits. Corporations are morally blind and are programmed to exploit others for profit.[13] In fact, 'the corporation is "legally compelled", to externalize costs without regard for the harm it may cause to people, communities, and the natural environment'.[14] Cost-benefit analysis is the criterion for corporate decision-making, including whether or not to break the law. Workers, consumers, communities, and the environment are regularly harmed by corporate activity.

This state of affairs provokes Bakan's question 'What can we do now about, and with, the corporation?'[15] His answer is that 'The market alone cannot provide sufficient constraints on corporations' penchant to cause harm ... Corporate persons – institutional psychopaths who lack any sense of moral conviction and who have the power and motivation to cause harm and devastation in the world should [not] be left

---

[9]   R. Posner, 'Law and Economics-Ethics, Economics, and Adjudication', *IVR Encyclopedia of Jurisprudence, Legal Theory and Philosophy of Law* (Berlin, 2005), <http://www.ivr-enc.info/en/>.

[10]   J. Bakan, *The Corporation: The Pathological Pursuit of Profit and Power* (Toronto 2004), p. 2.

[11]   Ibid., p. 2.

[12]   Ibid., p. 37.

[13]   Ibid., p. 72.

[14]   Ibid., p. 73.

[15]   Ibid., p. 140.

free to govern themselves'.[16] On the contrary, Bakan believes that corporations should be regulated by the state in the interest of all citizens, not just the corporations themselves and their shareholders. Tinkering with corporate governance is not enough because they will not become more social and environmentally responsible. He supports the creation of enforcement agencies to monitor corporate activities, and deterring unwanted behaviour with the threat of fines, suspending and revoking corporate charters, and making directors and managers liable for corporate illegalities. Such regulatory activities would be based on the precautionary principle. More generally, he advocates cutting links between government and business such as the revolving door employment scenario and the influence of lobbyists on political decisions. Further he believes that proportional representation and publicly financed elections would help create a society in which corporations acted in the best interests of all citizens.

Some Concluding Comments and a Single Pointer

General Reflections

Our illustrative pair are opposites politically. Posner is politically on the right, with the standard attitude towards the free market, wealth maximization, and government regulation of business. Bakan is politically left. Further, he is anti-free market because the free market has failed regarding society and the environment.

While Bakan focuses on the need and methods for regulating corporate self-interest and profit maximizaton, he gets no further than vague generalities. Posner is concerned with regulating self-interest which means profit and wealth maximization in economics by the criterion of potential Pareto superiority, which is a vague mathematicized generality. A mathematical context, of course, adds the semblance of scientific seriousness, so Bakan's lighter view has more popular appeal, but makes it easier to note that he has no ideas about a properly functioning economy.

Posner focuses on exchange in economics and wealth maximization via transaction costs in law, but he wants law only as a last resort, and only to reduce prohibitive transaction costs. Profit maximization is portrayed by him in terms of wealth maximization/potential Pareto superiority. This is how he proposes to limit self-interest, and indeed how he comes to a view of the public interest. In the end then, vagueness prevails in his reflections.

In the context of Lonergan's explanation of how an economy works Posner's transaction costs would be considered part of the consumer or capital monetary circuits and in itself would not be considered one of the central issues in economics. In fact, Posner's assertion that exchanges should be potential Pareto superior would not be considered part of a scientific economics. Posner's view, expressed in terms of driving

---

[16]   Ibid., p. 110.

a car, would be that the real function of cars is teenaged racing.

Bakan takes it for granted that the driving force of an economy is the profit motive and he wants the government to regulate corporate self-interest and the profit motive in order to protect society and the environment. In terms of cars, Bakan takes it for granted that the real function of cars is teenaged racing and he wants to set speed limits.

By contrast, for Lonergan the real function of the economy is to provide the goods and services people need and to provide leisure time so people do not 'live to work.' The driving force of an economy is not profit maximization. Rather, it is properly running the economy – to keep productive and financial rhythms in step in order to provide the goods and services people need. So we come to our single pointer.

Success in Law and Economics: The Relevance of the Ground of Law

Today, a country's economy is judged a success if it exports more goods and services than it imports even if its exports destroy local markets in foreign countries. A business is a success if it gets bigger and bigger even if it puts local businesses into bankruptcy. And business executives receive bonuses even if revenues fall. Does any of this seem insane to you?

Would it not make sense to consider a business as a success if it provided things that people need and, in the process, it did not mess up the monetary circuits of the local economy or other economies. We might even get to the point where we condemn innovation simply for the sake of innovation and become content with a going-concern and a standard of living. Leisure rather than work might become our *raison d'être*. Our heroes of business might be the people who, through good ideas and invention, actually liberated people from work without lowering their standard of living. Imagine if technology actually freed us from work rather than simply enabling us to do more things at the same time.

The day may even come when politicians admit that they have no idea how an economy works, and is working. And someday, no political party, surely, will wish to take a stand on stupid interference with the dynamics of the economy. In fact, without a clear view on how an economy works political manoeuvrings about tax, trade, equality, progress, culture, values, whatever, are manoeuvrings in the economic dark. However, that new day depends on understanding how any economic unit works, and is working. A crucial part of that clear view is that there are two main sets or flows of payments in an economy – consumer and capital – and that without making that distinction you are in the field of guess-work and myth. And, further, any legislation that fails to take into account that distinction will be haphazard and arbitrary. Of course, any analysis of law and economics that neglects that distinction would be a move toward further irrelevancy.

The fundamental measure of success in the field of law and economics, then, is the measure of one's understanding of the normative demands of the economic process. Legislation would be, sanely, an overlay on such economic structures.

Chapter 9

Legislation and Informatics

Marie-Francine Moens
Katholieke Universiteit Leuven, Belgium

Introduction

We live in a society where *technology* plays an increasing role and is often used as an instrument for reducing the operational costs of governments and companies. The use of the Internet as a main communication medium is undeniable. We are confronted with an information overload and large quantities of information are stored on magnetic and optical discs. Our machines become more and more powerful and can perform complex computations at an increasing speed. Economical considerations play an additional important role in the use of information technology. Such an environment forms quite a challenging setting for reflecting on the format, the function, and the application of *legislation*.

This work starts from an analysis of the basic functions of legislation in our constitutional state and of the basic requirements to fulfil these functions. The confrontation with large quantities of legislative documents and the growing complexity of their content force us to get assistance from information technology when managing legislation. Moreover, legal sources are increasingly – or should we say exclusively – consulted online, making the use of information technology a necessity. In addition, the economic situation is a driving factor to 'technologize' law in many sectors of society as law becomes imbedded in the hardware and software of devices that we use in our daily life. This chapter aims at answering the following questions. What information technologies are currently available when managing digital legislation? What technology can we expect in the future? What are the advantages of using them? What are the side effects and what are the dangers?

An important focus is on how legal theory, and more specifically the study of legal reasoning, will help in building the information technology of the future. If we understand the cognitive behaviour of legal reasoning, comprehend how humans find argumentative knowledge in the legal sources, and are able to identify how legal argument and legal reasoning are explicitly and implicitly expressed in the sources, successful information technology can be designed.

Another key issue is the use of representations of legal sources as surrogates of their content in information systems. The legal source (e.g., legislation) is translated into a (mathematical) language, i.e., a representation that is readable and interpretable by the machine. The representations themselves are increasingly automatically generated based on the original sources. We illustrate the use of the representations with simple and more advanced search engine technology and with a situation where the applicable norms are imbedded in technology. This raises important questions with regard to the basic principles such as the definition of legal sources, their accessibility and their computability. In an era where digitalization of legislation is an irreversible process, these *reflections* are valuable.

In this article we will successively discuss the functions of legislation and the information technology for managing legislation with regard to both the technology that is in use today and the technology that very probably will be used in the near future. The second part reflects on the role of legal reasoning and on the validity of manual and computer-generated representations of the legislative sources. We will conclude with some important directions for future research.

Legislation and Informatics

Words have different meanings, so it is useful to define the meaning of the title words of this chapter. The main meanings of the term *legislation* according to the Merriam-Webster Online are (1) the act of making or enacting laws where laws or rules have the force of authority by virtue of their promulgation by an official organ of a state or other organization; (2) law enacted by a legislative body. In addition to sources of legislation that are officially promulgated, a lot of pseudo-legislation is being drafted (e.g., circular letters, contracts, guidelines distributed by governments). We restrict here the term legal source to a document that contains legal content mostly in the form of text and to which additional data (metadata) can be attached. The document can be published, exchanged between institutions and systems, and accessed by humans and by machines. The second term, *informatics,* refers to the collection, classification, storage, retrieval and dissemination of recorded knowledge treated both as a pure or applied science. In this chapter, we will often use the term information technology as a synonym for informatics.

No one doubts that we will increasingly rely on the science of informatics in order to retrieve legislation, to find answers to legal problems, to extract problem-solving knowledge from the legislative collections and to enforce law in certain situations. Let us first define the *functions of legislation* in order to better understand the setting in which informatics is active.

Firstly, legislation plays a central role in our democracy. Law enables us to live relatively peacefully and is a key factor in inhibiting further unregulated conflict. Legislation offers a guarantee for the citizen and informs him or her of rights and duties. It enforces norms that have been accepted by the society. Legislation registers and records conceptions of law that live in society. As such, it improves the legal security of the citizens and promotes legal unity. Secondly, legislation is an instrument for the government to set out a policy. Law becomes more and more an instrument that governments use in order to solve ad hoc problems. Furthermore, legislation offers a framework for the judge to settle disputes. And fourthly, legislation provides a standardized solution to public and private legal relations in a society.

It is important to note in the context of the remainder of this chapter that law is expressed in some *linguistic formulation* that humans understand. In order to have effect, this linguistic expression must contain implicitly the *seeds of legitimacy*. This is an important given that we have to keep in mind when considering the rest of this chapter. Legislation is a living instrument. It changes dynamically following social, economical and governmental evolutions in society. It is not an exception that legal norms are reinterpreted. It is not inconceivable that a certain social group gives its own explanation to legal norms. Modifications and interpretations are also commonly expressed in some linguistic form.

There are a number of *requirements* in order to fulfil the functions of legislation. First of all, there is the transparency of the law. Legislation and its collection in print and paper books and legal databases should not be a labyrinth for its users. One should easily find rules that can be applied in a certain case. Accessibility is another important requirement. The content of any rule or norm should be accessible by all citizens. Computability and reliability refer to the effect of the application of legislation. The effect should be computable and predictable, and these computations should be reliable. Finally, there is the requirement of applicability and the possibility of enforcement. One should be able to apply the law in real situations, maintain it and enforce it.

Current legislative sources are characterized by *large quantities*. As we see an exponential growth in content creation worldwide, legal content drafting does not escape this process. Society is changing rapidly and hosts a web of complicated phenomena. Law has to accommodate for this situation. A large number of ad hoc rules are drafted, for instance in case of acute problems or when a government aims at enforcing a certain policy. In the recent years we have seen a number of high-profile incidents of corporate accounting fraud, security violations, terrorists acts, disruptions of financial markets, environmental disasters and outbreaks of diseases to which law tries to give protection or a framework for conflict resolution. In addition, we are confronted with a semi-redundancy of the content. Some of this redundancy is wanted when it is created at different levels of authority or in the case of rules that are drafted by a higher authority are being adopted by a lower authority. For instance, some rule from a high-level regulation is copied in some executable decree. On the other hand, some of the redundancy is unwanted. Often, new rules are drafted, while ignoring the existence of applicable rules.

The more rules are drafted, the more the *complexity of legislation* grows and the bigger the chances are that some rules are conflicting, yielding situations that demand still more regulation or that have to be resolved by judges in court. The enormous quantities and complexities of the law jeopardize its quality also because of the many ad hoc regulations and of the consequent need for coordinating the multitude of ad hoc laws.

Another facet of our current society cannot be neglected. Law enforcement is in many cases expensive and difficult to practically realize, while an automated solution is often cheap and obvious when realized by means of technology. *Digital*

Rights Management protects content from unlawful copying by means of technology and is a good example of embedding norms into technology. Another example is given by *compliance management systems* that help businesses to fulfill their legal requirements by means of automated checking devices. A third example regards *e-voting systems* that turn codes of law into program code that governs the functionality of computer systems used in election processes. All these systems rely on formal (knowledge) representations of the law that are readable and interpretable by the machine.

Legislation is becoming a very dynamic constellation of content, characterized by frequent changes in content, additions and redundant content, thus increasingly demanding of automated tools that assist in the many processes in the lifecycle of legislation, which we will discuss in the next section.

Current and Future Technologies

Informatics can be used in different phases of the lifetime of legislation. Ideally, legislation should be born digitally and there should be *support from information technology* throughout the *complete life cycle*: from the drafting, throughout the process of approval and publication till archiving, the input and storage in databases, information retrieval and the use of legislation as legal knowledge components in rights and compliance management and other knowledge-based systems that incorporate the codes of the law.

We define a *legal drafting or drafting support system* as a computer program that automates (an aspect of) the construction of a legal source. Because of the growing belief that legal drafting systems should support a facilitated processing of the documents by the computer, recent drafting systems offer the possibility to format certain information with mark-up tags in a *mark-up language* that form metadata of the documents. Metadata are defined as data that describe other data. Metadata are used to structure the legal document in mandatory and optional components (e.g., the structuring of a statute in books, chapters, sections and articles) and possibly to describe the content of the legal document. Metadata are usually present in the document in the form of tags and although in most representational formats they will be invisible to the user, computer programs can use them to correctly identify or classify documents or parts of documents. Metadata are usually encoded in a standardized mark-up language, the most common being XML (Extensible Markup Language).[1] XML offers the advantage that the structure of a document type can be standardized and defined in a document grammar. The grammar exhaustively describes the structure of the document and how it can be constructed in terms of possible configurations of its metadata attributes and their possible values. In XML the grammar is called a Document Type Definition (DTD) or XML schema depending on the syntax used for describing the grammar. Based on such a DTD or XML schema the conformity

---

[1] <http://www.w3.org/>.

of a document instance to the grammar can automatically be verified. XML also allows customization of the tag set towards a specific application (the tag set is extensible). In addition, XML marked documents are in *text format* (i.e., using only standard character coding) and can thus be interpreted on virtually all platforms, thus ensuring maximal exchange possibilities given that the mark-ups are equally interpreted by the different institutions that exchange information, or that labels are used that can be easily and unambiguously translated.

For an overview of legal drafting systems, we refer to Moens.[2] We also learn that whereas early drafting support systems put the emphasis on producing qualitatively better texts and more uniform documents in order to increase the convenience of their manual use (such as their readability by humans), the focus of current drafting support technology is on *producing digital documents that can be read and interpreted by computer*, so that current information systems can offer advanced information services based on the document contents. This evolution is reflected by the functionality of the systems: early systems only provided informative help tools or offered some templates for text assemblage; the newer systems focus on enforced verification and translation of the content into formats readable by machines. In this way the legal documents can be more effectively processed by the machine and can conveniently be used in information systems such as an information retrieval system.

Once legislation is approved, it is usually stored in databases. *Retrieving legislation from legislative databases* is done by using typical information retrieval and database technologies. Information retrieval (IR) concerns the retrieval of documents or information from a database of documents that satisfies a user's query. Present-day retrieval systems commonly allow users to express their query with a set of key terms. The result of the search is a list of documents. They are usually sorted by relevance, which most of the time is simply computed as a function of the frequency of occurrence of the search terms in the legislative texts. The metadata can act as search filters and they make it possible that certain subsets of the database that comply with the requested restrictions can efficiently be searched. For an overview of legal databases and their requirements with regard to metadata and information retrieval we refer to Moens.[3]

In the following sections we discuss more in detail the technologies that search engines use, current information extraction technologies that can be used in describing (legislative) content with ontological concepts, and the integration of legislation in law compliance and enforcement systems and e-voting systems. These cases are illustrative for the points that we want to make at the end of this chapter.

---

[2]   M.-F. Moens, 'Improving Access to Legal Information: How Drafting Systems Help', in A. Oskamp and A. Lodder (eds.), *Information Technology and Lawyers* (New York, 2005), pp. 119-136.

[3]   M.-F. Moens, 'Legislative Databases', in M.-F. Moens (ed.), *Legislative Databases* (Bruges, 2003), pp. 149-173.

Commonly the texts of the legal documents (among which is legislation) are stored in one or several distributed databases. The databases are increasingly accessible via Web portals that are maintained by public and private institutions. *Search engines* are a primary means to access legislation. The legal information is usually searched by means of a full text search, i.e., (almost) every term in the texts of the documents can function as a search key. Users input a query composed of one or several search terms and texts that contain the query terms are retrieved and possibly ranked according to relevance to the query.

The search can be made more effective by selecting documents based on descriptors called metadata, attached to the documents (e.g., statutes) or to document components (e.g., articles, books, chapters), which reflect for instance, the domain of law, subject titles, institutions that issue a certain document, dates of enactment, regions in which an article in applicable, etc. Statutes or articles are usually retrievable when the query contains words that occur in these texts or the user of the search engine inputs or selects certain metadata values (e.g., the title of a statute or the number of an article) and the appropriate texts are retrieved upon their matching with the query based on the metadata.

In the domain of *legal informatics*, we see also a large interest in *ontology research* as a means of modelling the content of legislative documents and to improve the retrieval of information. With a Google-type word-based search, it is common that the words in the query of the user do not occur literally in the documents. This is especially true when interrogating legal documents where users of search systems might use legal conceptual terms that do not occur in the documents. Hence, there is the need to add additional content descriptors to the legislative documents by which they can be retrieved.

Legal concepts are usually defined by means of an ontology. Whereas philosophical work on ontology traditionally concerns questions about the nature of being and existence, in artificial intelligence communities ontologies refer to the general organization of concepts and entities found in knowledge representations, which are sharable and reusable across knowledge bases. When processing natural language texts, ontologies have been primarily used for modelling the semantics of lexical items. In legal informatics a common definition of the concept ontology is that the ontology provides a formal specification of concepts and their relations. An ontology is often defined for a specific domain of law. There are many initiatives for building legal ontologies and to manually relate ontological descriptors to legislative texts.[4] For instance, the concept 'employee' can be

---

[4]   A. Boer, T. van Engers and R. Winkels, 'Using Ontologies for Comparing and Harmonizing Legislation', in *Proceedings of the 9th International Conference on Artificial Intelligence and Law* (New York, 2003), pp. 60-69; J. Breuker, A. Elhag, E. Petkov and R. Winkels, 'Ontologies for Legal Information Serving and Knowledge Management', in *Legal Knowledge and Information Systems. Proceedings of the 16th Annual Conference* (Amsterdam, 2002), pp. 73-82; L. Dini, D. Liebwald, L. Mommers, W. Peters, E. Schweighofer and W. Voermans, 'Cross-lingual Legal Information Retrieval Using a WordNet Architecture', in *Proceedings of the Tenth International Conference on Artificial Intelligence and Law* (New York, 2005), pp. 163-167.

described with structural and functional properties. The structural properties involve, for instance, that the employee is a person and belongs to a certain enterprise; the functional properties specify that the employee has rights and works under certain conditions. These properties can be the labels by which certain content of the employee contract is labelled. More information on the meaning of ontological concepts and its relation with truth values can be found in Wintgens.[5]

The ultimate aim is to describe legal documents with standard descriptors in order to facilitate retrieval and to simplify the harmonization and comparison of law across different jurisdictions (and when the terms of the ontology are translated in order to be used in different languages) across languages and possibly cultures. These ideas are inspired by the idea of the *Semantic Web* that was originally expressed by Tim Berners-Lee.[6] The idea is to describe Web texts with standard concepts, which would especially benefit e-commerce on the Web. As seen above an ontology can be considered as a form of knowledge representation and special languages have been developed in the realm of the Semantic Web. Several formal languages have been drafted and implemented that allow reasoning with the concepts and the relationships provided by the ontology. A popular example is OWL (Web Ontology Language), which is a revision of the DAML+OIL (DARPA Markup Language + Ontology Inference Layer) language, and is, like DAML+OIL, a semantic mark-up language that builds on the RDF (Resource Description Framework) language. RDF allows the expression of propositions using formal vocabularies.

The manual assignment of ontological terms to textual content is labour-intensive and expensive, hence the current interest in using information extraction technologies to label content. Information extraction can be defined as the automatic identification, and consequent or concurrent classification and structuring into semantic classes, of specific information found in unstructured data sources, such as natural language text, providing additional aids to access and interpret the unstructured data by information systems. Information extraction has been researched since the 1970s in some of the earliest applications of artificial intelligence. With the growth of computer power, its application becomes more in the reach of commercial applications. Moreover, information extraction technology is currently being seen as a solution for assigning ontological knowledge to a (legal) document's content.

The above paragraphs describe the present state of the art of information technology. Let us have a look at the role of informatics in the management of legislation in the future. Giving the foregoing evolution, legislation will become a dynamic constellation of related texts, metadata and knowledge components.

The information overload causes the *traditional library paradigm* of information retrieval systems to be abandoned. A classical information retrieval system very much relies on keyword indices to search documents, after which the

---

[5]   L.J. Wintgens, 'Legisprudence as a New Theory of Legislation', *Ratio Juris*, 19/1 (2003): 187-209.

[6]   T. Berners-Lee, J. Hendler and O. Lassila, 'The Semantic Web', *Scientific American*, 284/5 (2001): 35-43.

documents are retrieved and consulted. This is pretty similar to searching, borrowing and consulting books in a paper and print library. Retrieval of documents contained in today's very large digital libraries often results in a large amount of possible relevant documents. Moreover, the user usually has no time to consult all retrieved documents in order to find the answer to his or her information need. When the library is becoming very large and the pile of potentially relevant books is immensely high, humans want more advanced information technology to assist them in their information search. This situation is not different when searching large legislative databases. So, we need to redefine the retrieval model paradigm. We expect the retrieval systems to more directly answer our information needs by information extracted from the documents and processed into a coherent and ideally synthesized answer to our information query, or at least to intelligently link information as the possible answer to the information query which allows the user to efficiently navigate through the retrieved information.

We foresee that future information technologies will much more incorporate *information synthesis* and *reasoning* when retrieving information, automatically answering questions and solving problems. If we are able to extract specific content elements and their relations from legislation, if we are able to translate content into ontological concepts and find the relations between them, we can make inferences with this knowledge, and such an information system acts like a real knowledge-based system. Instead of a simple search engine, we are then dealing with a proper problem-solving system. Users might input real problem situations and the system proposes solutions based on the content of documents that are stored in the databases.

These ideas are a further elaboration of current question-answering technology. In a *question-answering* (QA) system the information need is expressed as a natural language question and the answer is selected from one or more sentences of the text. Current question-answering systems are able to answer simple, factual questions based on the content of documents (e.g., 'What year was Mozart born?'). However, research predicts that more complex questions that require synthesis and reasoning with content will be automatically answered based on the content of natural language text (cf. the success of the yearly workshops on knowledge and reasoning for answering questions). Many implementations of question-answering technology could focus on information retrieval from databases that have an added value for society. Governmental databases contain much information that is vital to many citizens. Recent *e-government initiatives* are aiming to make this information generally available via the World Wide Web, but their databases are usually too large and too complex to search effectively. A question-answering engine could make the step towards online government services a lot easier.

A special governmental service could offer access to legal documents such as legislation. Governments, institutions, courts and businesses use this knowledge in decision-making. However, full text *searches* of large *legal databases* offer the user too little assistance in finding the right information for his or her problem. Alternative legal information systems are *decision support systems* or knowledge-based systems. A decision support system assists its users in finding a solution for a specific problem by reasoning with knowledge sources that are represented in a logical formal language. An important bottleneck in the development of legal decision support systems is the manual acquisition and implementation of the knowledge considering that the legal texts from which the knowledge is extracted are constantly revised and complemented (e.g., legislation). Moreover, a decision support system usually operates in a very limited problem domain, and lacks the flexibility of information-seeking in large databases.

One could think of a hybrid of an information retrieval system and a decision support system, which has the form of an interactive question-answering system for solving the above problems. An *interactive question-answering system* that is based on logical knowledge representation theory and reasoning might offer guidance in more precisely combining information that is distributed over different sentences and texts. Such a system might be capable of generating a more precise answer to the information need while guaranteeing the flexibility of the search.

Suppose the following question: 'When is hunting with fire weapons on roe goats open?'. The answer 'Hunting with fire weapons on roe game is open: on roe goats and calves: from February 1 to March 15' can be found in Art. 4 of the Decree issued by the Flemish Executive of 16 June 1993. The question 'Is the cultivation of Erythroxylon punishable?'. In the international treaty of 20 December 1998 against the illicit trade of narcotic drugs and psychotropic substances, we find the following definition: 'Coca plant means one of the species of the genus Erythroxylon' in article 1 and under the punishable facts in article 3 of the same treaty: 'The cultivation of papavers, coca plants or cannabis for the production of narcotic drugs contrary to the stipulations of the treaty of 1961 or the treaty of 1961 as modified.' An advanced information system might be able to extract these texts from which the user can infer the answer to the question.

This technology is not yet developed, but we already see the first signs of the evolution towards the above systems. The POWER project implemented by the Dutch tax administration is such an example.[7] POWER supports the quality of legislation from the drafting of legislation onwards to its implementation in legal knowledge-based systems. POWER aims at an automated control of the quality of legislation and simulation of its effects besides an automated translation in formal knowledge rules to be used in legal knowledge-based systems. Converting sentences and questions to formal representations is done automatically by using natural language-processing techniques.[8] Extracting normative and ontological

---

[7]   T.M. van Engers, R. Gerrits, M. Boekenoogen, E. Glassée and P. Kordelaar, 'POWER: Using UML/OCL for Modeling Legislation – an application report', in *Proceedings of the 8th International Conference on Artificial Intelligence and Law* (New York, 2001), pp. 157-167; T. van Engers and E. Glassée, 'Facilitating the Legislation Process Using a Shared Conceptual Model', *IEEE Intelligent Systems*, 16/1 (2001): 50-58.

[8]   T. van Engers, R. van Gog and K. Sayah, 'A Case Study on Automated Norm Extraction', in *Legal Knowledge and Information Systems. JURIX 2004: The 17th Annual Conference* (Amsterdam, 2004), pp. 49-54.

knowledge from texts is currently done in a semi-automatic way;[9] a complete automatic extraction is the topic of current research. In Kerrigan and Law[10] the information system generates questions from text sentences that are represented in first order logic predicates that are used in a compliance management system.

We may already be able to extract certain information and relationships from the text of legislation, the technology is still far away from automatically solving problems based on information found in text. Actually, in order to be able to perform this task, we have to extract information from the natural language sources, to translate the extracted information into a logical formalism (e.g., first order predicate logic), to fuse information and to reason with it.

Reasoning is typical for knowledge-based systems that are equipped with an inference mechanism and a knowledge base. Such systems were popular in the 1980s and 1990s, but the huge burden of inputting and maintaining the knowledge rules, i.e., the *formal representations* that can be read and interpreted by the computer, largely hampered their success. However, the use of formal representations of law has gained a renewed interest in rights and compliance management systems and other legal knowledge systems. They illustrate the growing use of knowledge that is embedded in technology. In electronic contracting the rights and duties are expressed in a Rights Expression Language that is readable and interpretable by the computer. This allows the machine to control the execution of the contract by the parties and possibly the enforcement of the execution of the contract. The proliferation of new regulations discussed above directly impact businesses. They face the daunting task of complying with an increasing number of intricate and constantly evolving regulations. There is a growing interest in modelling regulations and managing them at an enterprise level in compliance management systems. Examples can be found in Kerrigan and Law[11] and Giblin et al.[12] E-voting systems integrate intricate and voluminous codes of election law.[13]

---

[9]   For example, S. Kerrigan and K.H. Law, 'Logic-based Regulation Compliance Assistance', in *Proceedings of the 9th International Conference on Artificial Intelligence and Law* (New York, 2003), pp. 126-135; P. Quaresma and I. Pimenta Rodrigues, 'A Question Answer System for Legal Information Retrieval', in *Legal Knowledge and Information Systems. JURIX 2005: The 18th Annual Conference* (Amsterdam, 2005), pp. 91-100.

[10]   Kerrigan and Law, 'Logic-based Regulation Compliance Assistance'.

[11]   Ibid.

[12]   C. Giblin, A.Y. Liu, S. Müller, B. Pfitzman and X. Zhou, 'Regulation Expressed as Logical Models (REALM)', in *Legal Knowledge and Information Systems. JURIX 2005: Proceedings of the 18th Annual Conference* (Amsterdam, 2005), pp. 37-48.

[13]   R.T. Mercuri and L.J. Camp, 'The Code of Elections', *Communications of the ACM*, 47/10 (2003): 53-57.

Reflections

A first reflection regards the *importance of legal theory* in the development of adequate legislative information systems. The theory of legal reasoning has a primordial role to play in the development of intelligent information systems in order to comprehend how knowledge (concepts, conceptual relations, arguments, reasoning structures) is implicitly and explicitly expressed in legal documents. The study of legal reasoning also permits us to comprehend how humans reason with legal knowledge. Legal reasoning is extensively studied by Bench-Capon, Gordon, Prakken and Sartor.[14] These authors have built theoretical models of legal reasoning and represented argumentation structures in a logical formalism (e.g., propositional, first order predicate, deontic and defeasible logic, claim lattices). Many of the approaches model defeasible reasoning (i.e., an argument that is acceptable in itself can be overturned by counterarguments). So, the cognitive model of human legal reasoning is well-documented. In contrast to case-based reasoning, there is little research on how legal argumentation is reflected in legislation and on what argumentation structures can be found in the texts of legislation. It would be interesting to study legal reasoning from this angle and make an inventory of the types of discourse and the linguistic features that signal the reasoning patterns.

Currently, we consider as primary *legal sources* legislation, jurisprudence and doctrinal documents. A second reflection regards the validity of the translations – manually or automatically performed – as additional genuine legal sources. Intelligent information technology demands the translation of the sources into a mathematical/logical language. Natural language is not directly understandable by the computer. We need additional intermediary data structures in which the natural language is translated and that are read by the machine (e.g., XML, first order predicate logic, OWL), when required for instance in searching, reasoning or in problem-solving. This translation can be done manually or automatically. A second related issue regards the official promulgation of these derived sources. We will illustrate the issues with the following examples.

A first example regards the search technology that we use in our daily life and also when searching legal databases. Any regular *search engine* builds an inverted file of the texts (i.e. a dictionary of lexemes or words) as is shown in Figure 9.1. Each word has pointers to the address of the document identification code and the position where the word occurs. The words of a text as well as assigned descriptors or metadata can be represented in this way. As such, the vocabulary list represents the content of the source, although a list of words is a very simple translation of the real content of a text. Such a situation has as a consequence that if a document is not indexed with a particular word or term, the search engine will never find the

---

[14]   T.J.M. Bench-Capon, 'Argument in Artificial Intelligence and Law', *Artificial Intelligence and Law*, 5, 249-261; G. Sartor, *Legal Reasoning: A Cognitive Approach to the Law: Treatise* 5 (New York, 2005).; T.F. Gordon, *The Pleading Game. An Artificial Intelligence Model of Procedural Justice* (Dordrecht, 1995); H. Prakken, *Logical Tools for Modeling Legal Argument. A Study of Defeasable Reasoning in Law* (Dordrecht, 1997).

document, when users use only this term in their query. Or to say in stronger terms, the document does not exist for this particular query. In the legal field one tries to partly solve this problem by assigning additional content descriptors to the texts (see above). This is however an expensive process and the terms can often be inaccurately assigned both by humans and by machines. Humans make errors when indexing documents, and especially the information extraction techniques discussed above are not completely accurate.

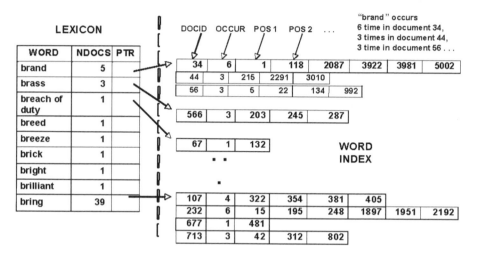

Figure 9.1 Example of an inverted file in a search engine

In examples of *advanced information searching* we automatically translate the natural language expressions into logical representations that can be interpreted by the machine, and that infer the answer to an information question. In this framework, the correctness of the representation is of primordial importance, if we want the system to deliver correct answers. In figure 9.2 we see a computer-interpretable representation of a norm. Here again, both humans and machines can be inaccurate when translating legislation into a formal representation, or during translating they might impose a certain interpretation upon the norms.

Users rely more and more on technology without posing themselves questions about the validity of the answers. We blindly trust search engines and other information systems. For instance, studies gave an indication that users of legal knowledge-based systems in public administration are insufficiently aware that the systems give them only a partial support.[15] Users too often rely on the outcomes of the systems without questioning the results.

---

[15]   H. de Bruin, H. Prakken and J. Svensson, 'The Use of Legal Knowledge-based Systems in Public Administration: What Can Go Wrong?', in *Legal Knowledge and Information Systems. JURIX 2002: Proceedings of the 15th Annual Conference* (Amsterdam, 2002), pp. 123-132.

If younger than 18 years, then minor.
minor(X)::= age(X) < 18.
Class (pp:employee partial restriction (pp:receives someValuesFrom (owl:Money)))
{youngerThan27YearsAndLargelySupportedByHim and DutchmanisDeemedToLiveInThe Netherlands implies areAlsoDeemedToLiveInTheNetherlands}

Figure 9.2   Examples of formal representations of norms

Above we have seen that legal sources offer transparency, accessibility and reliability, computability and reliability, and applicability and enforceability. In order to have effect, legislation must contain at least implicitly the seeds of legitimacy. If we use computer-readable and interpretable source representations, these requirements are also applicable to these representations.[16] Actually computer code or source code, among which are the data and knowledge structures that represent content in an information system, is considered as a form of persuasive speech by courts, social theorists, and technologists.[17] Should then the computer-generated and computer-interpretable representations be promulgated and enacted as a valid, official source of law? If this is not the case, law could be reinterpreted and it is not unthinkable that certain groups would take the opportunity to translate the sources into an interpretation that was not originally present in the original. One thinkable example is reinterpreting the law codes that are implemented in an e-voting system. Computer software is unique in the history of technology, because the choices imposed by it are not limited by physics, suggesting that social impact in the design can play a larger role than is the case with more constrained physical products. Software is both a sociological and a technological construct. The issue of the legal value of software representations was already raised when information of legal documents (e.g., of legislation) was manually translated into knowledge rules to be used in knowledge-based system technology. When the translation is done automatically, it is done on a much larger scale, thus making this question much more pertinent. When manually drafting rules for knowledge-based systems, it has been proposed to build knowledge rules that are isomorphic with the original text in order to facilitate the verification of their validity.[18] The need for validation is equally important when legal sources are automatically translated in a format that is convenient for computer processing.

---

[16]   L. Lessig, *CODE and Other Laws of Cyberspace* (Basic Books, 1999).
[17]   Mercuri and Camp, 'The Code of Elections'.
[18]   T.B. Bench-Capon, 'Exploiting Isomorphism: Development of a KBS to Support British Coal Insurance Claims', in *Proceedings of the Third International Conference on Artificial Intelligence and Law* (New York, 1991), pp. 62-68.

Such a situation minimally demands a serious involvement of the legal scholars and professionals in development of legal information systems.

A third reflection regards the increasing use of *law embedded in technology*.[19] As stated earlier, incorporating knowledge of rights and duties in electronic contracts and especially in contracts for the use and dissemination of digital content as in Digital Rights Management is convenient and economically accepted. For instance, the technology allows you to copy a music file only 10 times when you purchase it, i.e., it enforces you to obey a certain rule. Such simple and often successful examples open the door to many more applications and to the integration of more complex regulations into the technology. These regulations should be translated in a computer-readable formalism entailing the problems discussed in the previous section. We can make the following additional reflections. The compliance with the contract or in other cases with the law is controlled by technology. In some cases, the only attitude that the user of the technology can follow is to obey the law. He or she cannot anymore violate the law. The citizen is forced into a straitjacket, which can be seen as a form of totalitarianism that in a handy way makes use of technology. Given that governments increasingly use ad hoc rules in order to impose a certain policy, this might not always be a wanted situation.

Finally, it is interesting to incorporate some *lessons from history*. When we review history from the Roman empire until now, we witness that the nature of the available legal sources have had a powerful impact on legal change.[20] Low accessibility and poor quality of the legal sources and confusion on the real source of the law were often witnessed and recognized during history, but changes were not forthcoming for a long time. The desire for clarity in the law and for knowledge of its rules has been among the main forces driving for technical advancements in the form of an official codification. We see currently a similar situation: different forms of law exist next to each other and there is a need for transparency, accessibility, computability and reliability, applicability and possibility for enforcement. We hope that technology will bring us solutions for these requirements, but as was seen in history, it does not yet relieve the confusion on what is the real source of law. In the course of the history, after a codification initiative law sank back in complexity and ambiguity, thus the technological advancement did not offer a durable solution or provide only a solution that was accepted after a long period of time. Will this be the faith of law and informatics?

Conclusions

Informatics gives us many opportunities when managing the complete life cycle of legislation. But, we have to be aware of several side effects. Legal reasoning should be studied in the light of legislation management with information systems.

---

[19]   *See* chapter by Peter Wahlgren in this book.
[20]   A. Watson, *Sources of Law, Legal Change and Ambiguity* (Philadelphia, PA, 1998).

Moreover, we may not underestimate the consequences when representations of the law, whether manually or especially automatically generated, are being used by technology that is blindly used by the legal professionals, judges, legal scholars and citizens in their daily tasks. We do not yet know which durable solutions technology will offer in the management of legislation. What we do know is that there is an absolute need to involve legal scholars and professionals in technological developments that involve the management of digitalized legislation.

Chapter 10

Nulla Poena Sine Lege Parlamentaria? Democratic Legitimacy and European Penal Law

University of Lund, Sweden

'... Now to justify the bringing any such evil upon any man, two things are requisite. First, That he who does it has commission and power so to do. Secondly, That it be directly useful for the procuring some greater good...usefulness, when present, being but one of those conditions, cannot give the other, which is a commission to punish...'

John Locke[1]

Introduction: Questioning the Democratic Legitimacy of European Penal Law

In Western political systems it is elemental that legislation must have a democratic source in order to be legitimate. Above all, democratic legitimacy is regarded as important with reference to penal legislation, since penal power is paradigmatically the most intrusive form of political power. Therefore, it is generally acknowledged that punishment should be based on law enacted by a parliament, or at least that the parliament must be the principal, and in case of delegation, also the final legislative organ (*nulla poena sine lege parlamentaria*).[2] Hence, within penal law, democratic legitimacy is usually considered as intimately connected to parliamentary majority decisions.

However, some changes in contemporary penal law seem problematic with regard to the traditional claim of a parliamentary anchorage of penal legislation. Penal law is partly loosening its traditional foundation in the sovereign state due to a growing regulation of penal law at the international level. This development is most

---

[1] 'A Second Letter concerning Toleration', in *The Works of John Locke* (London, 1963; org. ed. 1823), Vol. VI, p. 112.

[2] *See* V. Greve, 'Criminal Law in the 21st Century', in P. Blume (ed.), *Legal Issues at the Dawn of the New Millennium* (Copenhagen, 1999), p. 53.

obvious within the framework of the European Union[3] where penal law to an increasing degree tends to become an object of decision-making at the EU level.[4] In some sense, a penal 'legislator' is already *de facto* operating at the EU level.[5] It is also credible that some kind of penal legislative competence in a foreseeable future will be formally entrusted to EU institutions. The problem is that when penal law develops into an object of decision-making at the international level, parliamentary control appears to be weakened. The tendency is that national legislators only execute penal law provisions which have been decided upon at the international level, where the parliamentary structure is at best incomplete.[6]

It is generally regarded as important to develop international penal cooperation. Criminality is today not easily confined within national borders and the states experience severe difficulties in fighting cross-border criminality alone. In order to deal with this international dimension of crime effectively, it seems necessary to develop some kind of international structures and institutions for penal decision-making. However, this development raises the essential question of whether it is possible to establish an (at least partly) international founded penal law and still uphold the claim for democratic legitimacy. Or to put it differently: *Can the ideal of democratic control of penal legislation be reconciled with the development of an autonomous penal decision-maker at the international level?* I will argue that this is possible, given that democratic legitimacy is separated from a state-based model of democracy and not *per se* identified with a claim that penal legislation must be

---

[3]   Hereinafter I will also refer to the European Union as 'EU'. I will use this reference either when I speak of the overall legal system of the European Union, or when I refer to the intergovernmental cooperation under the Treaty on European Union. In this article the focus is in this regard the judicial cooperation in criminal matters under the Title VI of this Treaty, i.e. the third pillar. I will refer to the European Community as 'the Community' or 'EC', and use this reference only when I specifically refer to the cooperation under the Treaty establishing the European Community, i.e. the first pillar.

[4]   For this development, *see inter alia*, M. Delmas-Marty, 'The European Union and Penal Law', *European Law Journal*, 4/1 (1998): 87-115; G.J.M. Corstens, 'Criminal Law in the First Pillar?', *European Journal of Crime, Criminal Law and Criminal Justice*, 11/1 (2003): 131-144; M. Kaifa-Gbandi, 'The Development towards Harmonization within Criminal Law in the European Union – A Citizen's Perspective', *European Journal of Crime, Criminal Law and Criminal Justice*, 9/4 (2001): 239-263; K. Nuotio, 'The Emerging European Dimension of Criminal Law', in P. Asp, C.E. Herlitz and L. Holmquist (eds), *Flores Juris et Legum: Festskrift till Nils Jareborg* (Uppsala, 2002), pp. 531-558.

[5]   *See* P.-A. Albrecht and S. Braum, 'Defiencies in the Development of European Criminal Law', *European Law Journal*, 5/3 (1999): 302; Kaifa-Gbandi, 'The Development towards Harmonization within Criminal Law in the European Union – A Citizen's Perspective', pp. 249-250.

[6]   *See* Albrecht and Braum, 'Defiencies in the Development of European Criminal Law', p. 302. *See also* A. Weyembergh, 'Approximation of Criminal Laws, The Constitutional Treaty and the Hague Programme', *Common Market Law Review*, 42/6 (2005): 1593-1595.

enacted through parliamentary majority decisions.[7] What matters in the end is the purpose, or underlying values, of democracy. The view to be outlined in the following is that the link between democratic legitimacy and penal decision-making at the international level is to be found in a non-state democratic theory, based on the autonomy-centred perspective of constitutionalism.

The focus in this article will, as signalled, be penal law as an object of interaction and cooperation between EU and the Member States, and the penal decision-making that is developed at the EU level. It should nevertheless be noted that the problem is of equal importance in the ongoing internationalization of penal law in other fora. The penal development within the EU is however, from a democratic perspective, of particular interest because it takes place within the framework of an international organization that in many aspects functions as an independent constitutional order. Thus, the penal law development occurring within the EU is not only concerned with international criminality as such, but also with the protection of the EU itself.[8]

The problem of the democratic deficit in the EU is by now well known. The European Union has over the years developed into a new kind of legal order, or an order *sui generis*, that to a significant extent exercises its powers directly over both states and individuals.[9] Especially due to the fact that the EU within the first pillar is formally endowed with legislative, judicial and executive powers, and that EC law is held to have supremacy over national constitutional law and as such preempts national competence, the question of whether the EU is compatible with democratic standards has often been raised.[10] It is evident that the democratic structure at the EU level is not at all comparable with the traditional model of state-based representative democracy, and the underlying question in the debate of the democratic deficit of the EU is whether norm-giving at the EU level can be democratic although the EU is not a state. Since the focus of this article is penal legislation, I will not enter into the more general discussion of the EU and democracy, but I will confine my arguments to the area of penal law. However, the problem of the democratic legitimacy of the

---

[7] Concerning the conception of the state, I rely on the notion recognized by general principles of international public law: A state is identified by a defined territory, a permanent population, a capacity to enter into relations with other states and, lastly, by effective control by a government, particularly by the claim of monopoly over the legitimate use of violence. *See further* P. Malanczuk, *Akehurst's Modern Introduction to International Law* (London, 1997), pp. 75-82. Although the EU could be viewed as an independent legal order, it is clear that it is not a state.

[8] *See* Kaifa-Gbandi, 'The Development towards Harmonization within Criminal Law in the European Union – A Citizen's Perspective', p. 240.

[9] *See inter alia* Case 26/62 *'Van Gend en Loos'* ECR [1963] 1; Case 6/64 *'Costa Enel'*, ECR [1964] 585; Case 106/77, *'Simmenthal'* ECR [1978] 585.

[10] For different perspectives on this question, *see inter alia* G. Majone, 'Europe's "Democratic Deficit": The Question of Standards', *European Law Journal*, 4/1 (1998): 5-28; G. Federico Mancini, 'Europe: The Case for Statehood, *European Law Journal*, 4/1 (1998): 29-42; J.H.H. Weiler, 'Europe: The Case Against the Case for Statehood', *European Law Journal*, 4/1 (1998): 43-62; N. MacCormick, 'Problems of Democracy and Subsidiarity', *European Public Law*, 6/4 (2000): 531-542.

penal decision-making at the EU level is an important part of the larger discussion, a part that has been relatively little analysed.

The European Union, Penal Law and the Challenge of Democracy

Legislative Power at the EU level?

There is a general agreement that formal legislative penal competence has not been entrusted to institutions at the EU level, since, according to the Treaties, no transfer of sovereignty has taken place in the field of penal law.[11] Even though the penal decision-making at the EU level is both extensive and far-reaching, penal legislation that emanates from the EU level and is applied by the national criminal courts throughout Europe is still, technically speaking, *national* penal law.[12]

However, as a part of the legal development of the EU, also penal decision-making is, as we shall see, to a great extent transferred from the states to the EU level. An important factor in this development is that penal law gradually becomes affected by the constitutional principles developed as a part of the 'operating system' of the Community. Especially due to the principles of supremacy, direct effect, implied powers, loyalty and preemption, penal legislative power is, at least partly, developed at the EU level.[13] This tendency is easily seen both within the first and the third pillar. It can generally be seen as a more common trend in the EU to focus on effective penal cooperation.[14] In this section, I will elaborate upon the tendency to develop penal legislative power at the EU level as an entry to the democratic problem that it carries with it.

Let us begin with the question of whether there is a development towards a legislative penal power within the first pillar. Even though the Treaty establishing the European Community (hereinafter 'TEC'), with a few exceptions, is silent on penal law, the influence of Community law on domestic penal law is today far-reaching. The last years there has been an increasing interest of penal matters within the first pillar, where especially the area of budget protection has been in focus.[15] The more the economic integration in Europe has been advanced, the harder it has become to leave penal law outside the reach of the Community law.[16]

---

[11]   *See* Delmas-Marty, 'The European Union and Penal Law', p. 87.

[12]   *See* Nuotio, 'The Emerging European Dimension of Criminal Law', p. 546.

[13]   Concerning the importance of these principles in the 'constitutionalization' of the EU in general, *see* J.H.H. Weiler, *The Constitution of Europe* (Cambridge, 1999), pp. 12-23, 221-238.

[14]   This is *inter alia* reflected in The Hague Programme, 'Strengthening Freedom, Security and Justice in the European Union', adopted by the Brussels European Council of 4/5 Nov. 2004, Presidency Conclusions, doc. 14292/1/04, 8 Dec. 2004.

[15]   *See* Delmas-Marty, 'The European Union and Penal Law', p. 87-88; Corstens, 'Criminal Law in the First Pillar?', p. 131.

[16]   *See* Corstens, 'Criminal Law in the First Pillar?', p. 131.

Since Community law to a large extent is implemented through the medium of national law, the dependence on effective national sanctions, among which penal sanctions have a unique position, is apparent.[17] The Court of Justice of the European Communities (hereinafter 'ECJ') has on this background, in the light of the principle of loyalty in Article 10 TEC and the doctrine of supremacy, affirmed that Community law has both positive and negative effect on the penal law of the Member States.

The negative effect is simply that the Member States must not enact penal legislation that is in violation of Community law. Thus, the competence of the EC is in this regard limited to decisions concerning when national penal legislation is *not* to be enacted. Even though this neutralization effect of Community law has a great influence on national penal law, one can hardly characterize this influence as penal power at the EU level. In this regard, the positive effect of Community law on national penal law is more interesting. To put it simply: According to the principle of loyalty in Article 10 TEC, the Member States are obligated to take all appropriate measures to ensure the fulfillment of the obligations of Community law. Using this article, the ECJ has identified an obligation of the Member States to sanction breaches of Community law. The sanctions have to be analogous to those applying to breaches of national law of similar nature and importance, and under all circumstances they have to be effective, proportionate and dissuasive.[18] Since the Community traditionally has been regarded as lacking competence to decide on penal matters, the choice of sanctions has *prima facie* remained at the Member State level, although the claim of Community law might indirectly oblige the Member States to use penal sanctions instead of administrative measures.[19]

However, the ECJ has recently pushed the development one step further. In a recent case, the court has claimed that the institutions under the first pillar, in the area of environmental law, have competence to require the Member States to introduce penal sanctions to secure the implementation of Community law.[20] To reach this conclusion, the court relied on Articles 10 and 175 TEC, and in relation to previous case law, it extended its view on implied powers into the area of penal law. The court also highlighted a clear overlap and integration between matters of Community regulation and matters of penal cooperation under the third pillar. It stated that penal law as a *general rule* does not fall within the Community's competence. However this does not prevent the Community legislature, when the application of effective, proportionate and dissuasive sanctions by the national authorities is an essential measure for combating serious environmental offences, from taking necessary

---

[17] On this matter, *see* K. Ligeti, 'European Criminal Law: Administrative and Criminal Sanctions as Means of Enforcing Community Law', *Acta Juridica Hungaria*, 41/3-4 (2000): 199-212.

[18] *See further* Case 68/88 *'Greek maize case'* ECR [1990] 2171. *See also* Case C-14/83 *'Von Colson'* ECR [1984] 1891.

[19] Concerning the positive and negative effects of Community Law on criminal law, *see further*, Corstens, 'Criminal Law in the First Pillar?', pp. 132-133; Delmas-Marty, 'The European Union and Penal Law', pp. 88-106.

[20] Case C-176/03, *Commission v. Council*, judgment of 13 Sept. 2005, nyr.

measures affecting the penal law of the Member States in order to ensure the effective implementation of environmental protection.[21]

By this ruling, the court makes a sudden inroad into previously forbidden country; that the EC is competent to make the involvement of national penal justice obligatory.[22] This ruling might function as a door opener in a development towards a general Community competence to decide upon penal sanctions. Provided that the Member States will support such a development, i.e. the representatives in the Council of the European Union (hereinafter 'the Council') will make use of the stated competence, norm-giving in penal matters will be a reality at the EU level.[23] Even though the competence in this regard will be annexed to community competences and therefore will not cover independent penal law-making, it is obvious that it will be far-reaching. If the EU institutions make use of a competence to decide upon penal matters this will also, in light of the principle of pre-emption, set aside conflicting national legislation and prospectively block the use of national competence in the relevant matter.

Penal decision-making, *sensu strictu* (not in the shape of EC law) takes place within the judicial cooperation in criminal matters of the third pillar.[24] However, although no transfer of legislative competence has taken place within this cooperation, it can be questioned whether penal legislative power is *de facto* exercised at the EU level. Since the implementation of the Amsterdam Treaty, the Council can adopt 'Framework Decisions' under Article 34 of the Treaty of European Union (hereinafter 'TEU'), in order to decide upon penal matters.[25] The Framework Decisions aim at the *approximation* of the laws and regulations of the Member States, in order to provide the EU citizen with a high level of safety, within an area of freedom, security and justice.[26] Through these instruments, minimum rules relating to the constituent elements of criminal acts and to penalties, can be enacted

---

[21]   Case C-176/03, para. 47-48.

[22]   *See* Case C-240/90 *Germany v. Commission* ECR [1990] 5383.

[23]   It should here be noted that the ruling goes against the advice of 11 Member States (Denmark, Germany, Greece, Spain, France, Ireland, the Netherlands, Portugal, Finland, Sweden and the UK).

[24]   Concerning this cooperation, *see* E. Denza, *The Intergovernmental Pillars of the European Union* (New York, 2002).

[25]   Framework Decisions are in their structure similar to the first pillar directives; they are binding upon the Member States as to the result to be achieved but shall leave to the national authorities the choice of form and methods. In contrast to directives they shall not entail direct effect. The adoption of a Framework Decision requires a unanimous decision. Framework Decisions are not the only means of approximation of laws under the third pillar. Laws can also be approximated and foreign decisions recognized through conventions. However, conventions lack the supranational features that characterize Framework Decisions, and hence they are not in focus of the democratic problem raised in this article.

[26]   Approximation is a model of legal integration, weaker than unification but stronger than coordination and cooperation, that implies adjustment of internal laws in order to meet specific objectives, *see further*, Weyembergh, 'Approximation of Criminal Laws, the Constitutional Treaty and the Hague Programme'.

in the field of organized crime, terrorism and illicit drug trafficking.[27] Although there is a limitation to three fields, it is noteworthy that the first of these subjects in particular is very wide. This is reflected by the fact that the approximation of laws on a wide range of subjects has been initiated by means of Framework Decisions during the last years, both within the area of substantial penal law and within the area of criminal procedure. [28]

The Framework Decisions create a binding obligation on all Member States to enact appropriate legislation according to their own constitutional arrangements.[29] Even though this obligation strictly speaking is of intergovernmental character it is not appropriately to characterize it that way, due to the institutional features and constitutional principles of the EU. The Framework Decisions are, according to EU law, binding as soon as they are adopted in the Council, and consequently they do not need the approval of the national parliaments for their validity. Even if the national parliament, according to national constitutional law, has to approve the adoption of a Framework Decision made by the representative of the government, the negotiations and discussions that results in the decision primarily takes place in the Council. The role of the national parliaments is thereby more or less degraded to 'yes or no' (in reality; very much degraded to 'yes'). To a great extent the penal decision-making in this regard takes place out of reach of the control of the national parliament.[30] It should also be noted that through Framework Decisions, the intended approach of the penal legislation in Member States could be the creation, reform or abolishment of crimes.[31] This leaves little or no choice for the national parliament to decide upon forms and methods for implementation.

This raises the question of whether the Council is *de facto* in possession of legislative powers within the field of penal law. To answer this question, it is important to see beyond a strictly formal-legal perspective since such perspective might not give an adequate picture of the functioning of penal law at the EU level. From a formal-legal perspective it is easy to argue that power exercised at the EU level within the third pillar is ultimately in the hands of sovereign Member States. In the absence of a formal legislative power at the EU level, the Framework Decisions

---

[27] Article 31(c) TEU.

[28] *See inter alia* Council Framework Decision of 13 June 2002 on the European arrest warrant and the surrender procedures between Member States, O.J. 2002 190/01; Council Framework Decision of 27 Jan. 2003 on the protection of the environment through criminal law, O.J. 2003, L 29/55; Council Framework Decision of 13 June 2002 on combating terrorism, O.J. 2002, L 164/03; Council Framework Decision of 28 May 2001 combating fraud on counterfeiting of non-cash means of payment, O.J. 2001 L 82/01; Council Framework Decision of 22 July 2003 on the execution in the European Union of orders freezing property or evidence, O.J. 2003 L 196/45; Council Framework Decision of 15 March 2001 on the standing of victims in criminal proceedings, O.J. 2001 L 82/01.

[29] N. MacCormick, *Who's Afraid of a European Constitution* (Exeter, 2005), p. 3.

[30] *See* MacCormick, *Who's Afraid of a European Constitution*, pp. 2-3, Albrecht and Braum, 'Defiencies in the Development of European Criminal Law', p. 302.

[31] *See* Kaifa-Gbandi, 'The Development towards Harmonization within Criminal Law in the European Union – A Citizen's Perspective', p. 249.

can certainly be characterized as legally binding measures that can be used by the Member States at the EU level in order to coordinate the criminal policy activities among them.[32] However, the important question is if penal power is actually exercised at the EU level with the prospect of directly affecting individual behavior.

It is hard to deny that such power is exercised at the EU level today. This view is, *inter alia*, strengthened by a relatively new case from the ECJ, where the court, in light of the principle of supremacy of EC law, extended the principle of loyal cooperation as well as the principle of conforming interpretation to Framework Decisions adopted under the third pillar.[33] According to this ruling, when applying national law, the national court that is called upon to interpret it must do so as far as possible in the light of the wording and purpose of existing Framework Decisions.[34] By this interpretation of the legal nature of the Framework Decisions, the ECJ has found a way around the absence of direct effect for Framework Decisions.[35] This ruling well illustrates the tendency to make the cooperation in penal matters subject to the above mentioned constitutional principles of Community law, and thereby also of a growing difficulty to strictly separate the cooperation of the first pillar from that of the third pillar (in favour of the former).

This general tendency to make penal law subject to legislative power at the EU level is also manifested in the 'Treaty establishing a Constitution for Europe' (hereinafter 'the Constitution Treaty'). If this basic legal text had been fully ratified, and thereby legally binding, it would explicitly have made penal law part of a legislative competence at the EU level. According to the Constitution Treaty, the structure of the three pillars was supposed to be abolished, and all matters of European integration to be dealt with under a common institutional framework, where penal cooperation would be an area of shared competences and as such subject to forms of majority decisions.[36] It also explicitly stated the supremacy of EU Law, and consequently also of penal norms enacted at the EU level.[37] To the extent that the institutions were to be endowed with power to decide upon penal matters, the Constitution Treaty gave a formal legal basis to decide upon penal legislation at the EU level.[38] The penal decision-making was intended to take place through European Framework Laws, corresponding to the existing directives. Even though the Constitution Treaty was turned down by some of the Member States, it is probable that the intended development of penal law will be gradually realized, a development that is actually provided for by the so-called 'passerelle' provision of Article 42

---

[32] Nuotio, 'The Emerging European Dimension of Criminal Law', p. 546.

[33] Case C-105/03, *Criminal Proceedings against Maria Pupino*, judgment of 16 June 2005, nyr.

[34] Case C-105/03, para. 43.

[35] Weyembergh, 'Approximation of Criminal Laws, the Constitutional Treaty and the Hague Programme', p. 1595.

[36] *See* respectively Articles I-14 and III-396 of the Constitution Treaty.

[37] *See* Article I-6 of the Constitution Treaty.

[38] *See* Articles III-271 and III-272 of the Constitution Treaty.

TEU.[39] This provision is testimony to a strong political will to develop and effectuate the penal decision-making at the EU level. Although in many areas within the EU there are deep controversies between the Member States, they are surprisingly harmonious concerning the cooperation in penal matters.

A lot more can be said about how penal decision-making at the EU level takes place and the question of its specific content could have been much more analysed.[40] However, the purpose here is not to analyse the content and functioning of this decision-making, but only to draw attention to the fact that the tendency points towards the development of penal legislative powers at the EU level. This fact is interesting from the aspect of democratic legitimacy, since it to some degree seems to cut the link between national parliamentary control and penal decision-making.

Intergovernmental Cooperation or Supranational Legislative Power?

In light of the constitutional character of the EU, the penal decision-making at the EU level could basically be approached from two different perspectives, and the implications for democratic legitimacy differ according to which perspective is chosen. Penal norms that are decided at the EU level could be regarded as part of an intergovernmental cooperation between sovereign states, and thus as a form of delegation of national penal decision-making (*the intergovernmental perspective*), or they could be viewed as a part of a supranational legal order and as such independent from the national penal systems (*the supranational perspective*). These opposite perspectives are well-known in the Community context, where the question is whether the Community is an independent constitutional order, or if it is subordinated to the constitutional orders of the Member States. Hence, the basic question is whether constitutional pluralism, i.e. the idea that distinct constitutional orders can coexist, is possible or not.[41] Although the supranational perspective presupposes the view that there actually is legislative competence on the EU level, the existence of such competence must not necessarily lead to a support of this perspective. Even though a formal penal legislative competence at the EU level would be approved, it is still possible to view this competence as ultimately subordinated to the constitutional system of the Member States.[42]

---

[39] According to this provision 'The Council, acting unanimously on the initiative of the Commission or a Member State, and after consulting the European Parliament, may decide that action in areas referred to in Article 29 [cooperation in penal matters] shall fall under Title IV of the Treaty establishing the European Community, and at the same time determine the relevant voting conditions relating to it. It shall recommend the Member States to adopt that decision in accordance with their respective constitutional requirements.'

[40] For more thorough analyses *see inter alia* Delmas-Marty, 'The European Union and Penal Law', pp. 87-115; Corstens, 'Criminal Law in the First Pillar?', pp. 131-144.

[41] *See* N. MacCormick, *Questioning Sovereignty: Law, State, and Nation in the European Commonwealth* (New York, 1999), pp. 97-121.

[42] In particular the German Constitutional Court has adopted this intergovernmental perspective, *see inter alia* 2BvR 2134/92 & 2159/92, judgment reported in Common Market Law Reports [1994] 1.

If the intergovernmental perspective is chosen, penal decision-making at the EU level must be viewed as a *delegation* of legislative power from the national parliament to the European institutions. The relevant perspective in this regard is the *Member State citizen* in relation to the exercise of legislative powers *in the Member State*. The problem of democratic legitimacy can thus be formulated as a question whether the decision-making at the EU level *could be a legitimate delegation of penal legislative power*.

In this case the focus is the delegation from the citizens, via the national parliament and the national government, to the decision-making representatives of the Council. It is obvious in this case that the link between the citizens and the Council is not of a direct character, since the Council is not composed of representatives directly elected by the citizens. The Council derives its mandate only indirectly. In relation to the traditional construction of indirect representation, the election of representatives in the Council is one step further away from the citizens. The person representing a Member State in the Council does not derive his or her mandate directly from the parliament, which is the normal construction of delegation, but only indirectly from a part of it, namely the part which forms the government.[43] If the penal decision-making should become subject to majority decisions at the EU level the link to the national parliament will apparently become even weaker. The question is whether this distant form of delegation is sufficient in relation to democratically legitimate penal decision-making.

If, on the other hand, the supranational perspective is chosen, the relevant perspective is the *EU citizen* in relation to the exercise of legislative powers at the *EU level*. Democratic legitimacy of penal legislation based upon decisions at the EU level can in this case not be sufficiently derived from the Member State. This is so because in the case of supranational exercise of power, *strictu sensu,* the question is of a *transfer*, not of a delegation of power, and the national parliaments do no longer have the final control (if the community ideal should be maintained) in relevant matters of legislation. In contrast, on this view, a decision enacted at the supranational level has supremacy over majority decisions of a Member State, since it represents the European citizens and not just a portion of these.[44] The problem of democratic legitimacy must thus in this case be formulated as a question of whether the EU has, or could have, a sufficient democratic foundation in itself.

Consequently, the focus is the link between the decision-making institutions at the EU level and the European citizen. The problem formulated from the parliamentary state-based model of democracy is that the EU is not a state, and consequently lacks a parliamentary structure similar to a state, i.e. a parliament with independent legislative powers, an executive responsible to the parliament and a

---

[43] *See* O. Zetterquist, *A Europe of the Member States or of the Citizens: Two Philosophical Perspectives on Sovereignty and Rights in the European Community* (Lund, 2002), p. 318.

[44] *See* Majone, 'Europe's "Democratic Deficit": The Question of Standards', p. 12; Mancini, 'Europe: The Case for Statehood', p. 41; D. Wincott, 'Does the European Union Pervert Democracy? Questions of Democracy in New Constitutionalist Thought on the Future of Europe', *European Law Journal*, 4 (1998): 417-418.

European popular election to appoint the members of the parliament.[45] At the EU level in general, the Council and the European Commission (hereinafter the Commission) are primarily responsible for legislation; the Commission holds the monopoly of legislative initiative and the assent of the Council is necessary for the passing of legislation. The role of European Parliament varies from a right to consultation to a power of co-decision.[46] In the area of cooperation in penal matters, the Council is ultimately responsible for the decision-making and the right to initiate decisions is shared between the Member States and the Commission. The Council shall consult the European Parliament before adopting any Framework Decision, Decision or Convention. However, the European Parliament has no more than a consultative role. Its opinions are not binding and therefore only have a limited influence on the Council's decisions.[47]

Due to this institutional structure, the link between the EU citizen and the decision-makers at the EU level, usually regarded as present in a parliamentary structure, is weak. It is an internal matter for the Member States to appoint members to the Council, as well as to the Commission, and there is no link of responsibility between these organs and the European Parliament. Accordingly, nor is there any clear link of responsibility between the penal decision-maker at the EU level and the EU citizens.[48] The question in this regard is whether penal decision-making can be democratically legitimate in a supranational structure falling short of traditionally parliamentary structures.

To summarize this part, it seems like the penal decision-making at the EU level is bound to be ridden with problems of parliamentary representation, both seen as a part of the constitutional orders of the states and seen as a part of the EU as an independent legal order. From the traditional, state-based view, this seems to create a strong presumption that this decision-making is also bound to be ridden with problems of democratic legitimacy. However, one should be careful to draw a conclusion in line of this presumption to rapidly. The meaning of democratic legitimacy must be analysed in light of the purpose and underlying values of democracy rather than only in light of conventional political models.

Penal Legislation and Democratic Legitimacy

What Purpose of Democracy? What Purpose of Penal Law?

Irrespective of whether the penal decision-making at the EU level is viewed as independent from the Member States constitutional orders or not, in order to analyse

---

[45] *See* Majone, 'Europe's "Democratic Deficit": The Question of Standards', p. 7.

[46] A. Dashwood, 'Issues of Decision-making in the European Union after Nice', in A. Arnull and D. Wincott (eds.), *Accountability and Legitimacy in the European Union* (Oxford, 2002), pp. 22-23.

[47] *See* Article 39 TEU

[48] *See* Zetterquist, *A Europe of the Member States or of the Citizens: Two Philosophical Perspectives on Sovereignty and Rights in the European Community*, pp. 316-317.

the issue of the democratic legitimacy of this decision-making, one must start with some conception of democratic legitimacy. Before entering deeper into the problem of the democratic legitimacy of supranational penal decision-making, it is therefore time to turn to the concept of democracy. I do not intend to analyse the meaning of democracy in depth, but only to emphasize some archetypal ideas concerning democracy that can serve as tools in the subsequent discussion.

The concept of democracy embraces the idea that political power is in the end derived, or delegated, from the individuals, and therefore also responsible before the individuals. Hence, the democratic legitimacy of political power in any political community is to be traced back to its citizens. Democracy, i.e. the power of the people, can be exercised directly, as in a referendum, or indirectly. In Western representative democracies the prevailing political model is that the citizens elect representatives that exercise powers on their behalf and that these representatives are controlled primarily through periodical elections. There might be a general agreement on this political model of democracy. [49] However, on a theoretical level, there are various – and conflicting – normative positions concerning the more basic *purpose* of democracy.

Western political thinking is traditionally centred around two different and ultimately incompatible ideological positions concerning the question of legitimate state power, and consequently also concerning the legitimate purpose of democracy. Those positions are represented by the theory of *popular sovereignty* and the theory of *constitutionalism*. Basically, the theories support different views concerning the purpose of the democratic state power, the possible scope of this power and, as a consequence of these, its institutional structure.[50]

According to the theory of popular sovereignty the purpose of democracy is to effectively *generate and articulate the will of the sovereign people*. This position is therefore characterized by the pure democratic principle, i.e. the idea of the unlimited, indivisible state power. The people are the *terminus ultimus* of all power, which consequently is not subject to any (external) limitations.[51] A starting point for this view on democracy is an optimistic view on state power – the fear is not abuse of state power, but rather of anarchy in the absence of such power. According to the theory of popular sovereignty, democracy is in its institutional structure intimately connected to the state. As an instrument for the articulation of a sovereign will, democracy presupposes constitutional monism, i.e. it presupposes a sovereign state.[52]

---

[49]   *See* J. Hampton, *Political Philosophy* (Oxford, 1997), pp. 104-105.

[50]   The strongest holder of the position of popular sovereignty is usually held to be Jean-Jaques Rousseau. However, central features of the position could be traced to Thomas Hobbes' political philosophy. The theory of constitutionalism seeks its roots in the philosophy of John Locke. For a through analysis on these positions and their relevance in the Community context, see Zetterquist, *A Europe of the Member States or of the Citizens: Two Philosophical Perspectives on Sovereignty and Rights in the European Community.*

[51]   *See* J.-J. Rousseau, 'Of the Social Contract', in V. Gourevitch (ed.), *'The Social Contract' and Other Later Political Writings* (Cambridge, 1997), ch. 2, p. 58 ff.

[52]   *See* Zetterquist, *A Europe of the Member States or of the Citizens: Two Philosophical Perspectives on Sovereignty and Rights in the European Community*, p. 238.

Institutionally, it is also closely linked to an accumulation of power to institutions that directly represents the people, i.e. the parliament, and consequently it is also linked to majority decisions.[53] In terms of representative democracy, the position of popular sovereignty therefore in its purest form requires the view that the parliament should have unrestricted and final control in reference to other institutions.

According to the theory of constitutionalism the ultimate purpose of democracy is the *safeguarding of the autonomy of the individual*. This position is based on the view that everyone is endowed with rights that cannot be placed at the arbitrary discretion of the state, people or majority. Or to put it differently; constitutionalism embraces a principle of equality, in the sense that political power must be reasonably justifiable to all persons as respecting their rights and serving the common interests of all.[54] Hence, the scope of democratic state power is limited – there is no sovereign, not even the people, since all power are subordinated to (external) common rules aiming at the equal protection of each individual. The idea behind constitutionalism is that state power is potentially dangerous and the threat of oppression is ever present. In terms of institutional structure, the theory of constitutionalism aims at the division and control of state power, since this power is limited and can never be absolute. Constitutional pluralism is possible, and indeed desirable, and hence democracy is not necessarily connected to the state. The basic element of constitutionalism is the existence of binding constitutional rules, which above all aims at rights protection.[55] Another core feature is the concept of the rule of law, in relation to which the doctrine of separation of powers and the existence of impartial and independent judicial control is essential. According to the theory of constitutionalism, the position of parliamentary representation and majority decisions is diminished in favour of constitutional control and minority protection.[56] Even though majority decisions most often are regarded as important, they are not the final point.

Contemporary Western democracies have made use of central concepts from both these ideal type models, which have both given valuable contributions to the development of our prevailing political paradigm. The idea of popular sovereignty has contributed with the strong emphasis on the value of the democratic process for the identification and implementation of important common policies. Constitutionalism, on the other hand has complemented this view with the idea of necessary restrictions on this power.

Today, the idea of popular sovereignty is clearly visible in the institutional structure of democracy throughout Europe. State power is mainly concentrated to parliamentary decisions and the balance between political and legal institutions still

---

[53] *See* 2BvR 2134/92 & 2159/92, judgment reported in Common Market Law Reports [1994] 1, p. 88.

[54] *See* D.A.J. Richards, *Foundations of American Constitutionalism* (New York, 1989), p. 258.

[55] *See* R.S. Kay, 'American Constitutionalism', in Larry Alexander (ed.), *Constitutionalism – Philosophical Foundations* (Cambridge, 1998), p. 19.

[56] *See* G. Sartori, *The Theory of Democracy Revisited* (Chatman, 1987), Vol II, pp. 287-297, 321-328.

favour the former. However, it is quite clear that democracy is not just a matter of ensuring that the will of the majority prevails. Today no society should be considered democratic if it is not offering protection of the autonomy of the individual, irrespective of the argued source of this protection.[57] In other words: The protection of human rights is to a great extent a prerequisite for the democratic legitimacy in contemporary political thought, and in this sense the ideas of constitutionalism have prevailed. The protection of individual autonomy is regarded as especially important in the penal law context, where the fear of abuse of state power is most articulated, and probably, with reference to historical facts, also most well-grounded. Therefore, this protection is commonly advocated as the essence, or basic purpose, of contemporary penal law.[58]

Considering the presence of the protection of the rights of individuals, both in international law and in practically all national constitutions of the Western world, the essential features of constitutionalism should be a starting point when discussing democratic legitimacy. The protection of individual autonomy should be viewed as fundamental in our legal paradigm, and thereby as the hard core of democracy. Thus, when discussing democratic legitimacy, the protection of individual autonomy should be the key perspective.[59] However, this does not mean a rigid commitment to the classical institutional structure of constitutionalism. My support of basic constitutional ideas can, in this setting, mainly be reduced to two points: The first point is that it is important to seek the roots of democracy beyond the state, and the state based model of democracy where the state is ultimately seen as the institutional mechanism for majority rule. Particularly when discussing democracy with regard to an international organization such as the EU, it is important to consider the values of democracy outside the conceptual framework of the state. In other words: The normative criteria and concepts of democracy must be reinterpreted for an international context.[60] In this regard the theory of constitutionalism is most suitable also because it favours constitutional pluralism. The second point is that it is important to view democracy not as an end in itself but as a means for the safeguarding of individual autonomy.[61] For this task, especially with regard to penal law, the basic features of constitutionalism are more appropriate as a normative starting point than those of popular sovereignty. It should however be noted that within such a view, elements of political participation, parliamentary representation

---

[57]   *See* G.F. Mancini and D.T. Keeling, 'Democracy and the European Court of Justice', *The Modern Law Review*, 57/1 (1994): 175-180, p. 181.

[58]   *See* Greve, 'Criminal Law in the 21st Century', p. 39; N. Jareborg, *Scraps of Penal Theory* (Uppsala, 2002), p. 93 ff.

[59]   *See* Sartori, *The Theory of Democracy Revisited*, p. 286; N. Bobbio, *Liberalism and Democracy* (New York, 1990), p. 31.

[60]   *See* Majone, 'Europe's "Democratic Deficit": The Question of Standards', p. 6.

[61]   *See* 'Democracy my friend, is not the end. Democracy too, is a means, even if an indispensable means. The end is to try, and to try again, to live a life of decency, to honour our creation in the image of God, or the secular equivalent. A democracy when all is said and done, is as good or bad as the people who belong to it. A democracy of vile persons will be vile', Weiler, 'Europe: The Case Against the Case for Statehood', p. 60.

and majority decisions could still be regarded as essential: Such elements are the simplest ways to safeguard individual autonomy since brutal oppression is generally speaking not a vote-winner.

Democratic Legitimacy – A Matter of Equal Individual Protection

When democratic legitimacy of penal legislation is defined in light of the priority of individual autonomy it is essential that the democratic model, all things considered, safeguards the equal protection of the individuals. From such a starting position it is not *per se* necessary that a parliament must be the principal legislative organ. Hence democratic legitimacy must not necessarily be understood in terms of parliamentary majority decisions. On the contrary, such decisions could in theory very well be in conflict with the interests to be protected. Neither is the traditional institutional structure of the state *as such* required to secure a democratic anchorage of penal legislation.[62] What is required is that the control of the legislative penal power, continuously and ultimately, lies in the hands of the individuals, in the sense that each individual can take part as an equal of every other and thereby secure his or her autonomy.[63]

In order to fulfil this basic requirement, the political model of democracy can probably be elaborated in many ways. However, given our contemporary conceptions of democracy, every model of democracy must at least fulfil two minimum standards, standards that are of particular importance in the penal law context. First, there must be a link of accountability and trust between the political power and the citizens, as a condition for approving legislation (*the criterion of accountability*). As far as we know, this is best secured if the legislator is appointed, and under continuous control, by the individuals governed. Therefore, democratic legitimacy requires that there are channels that make it possible for the individual to influence and check legislation, and in last resort to replace the legislators. Second, democratic legitimacy requires that the political power is subordinated to common constitutional rules, safeguarding human rights, and judicial control open to every individual subject under its authority (*the criterion of rights protection*).[64] It should be emphasized that both these criteria, from the supported view, are subordinated to the protection of individual autonomy, as the essential purpose of democracy.

---

[62] A crucial point here is how one conceptualizes the right to political autonomy/participation. If one take this right for only being sufficiently safeguarded in a state, one could argue that the separation of the discourse on democracy from the state model *per se* is unacceptable even if one embrace constitutionalism. Without elaborating on this further, I would only make clear that in my view the right to political autonomy/participation could be satisfied in more ways than through the democratic framework of a state.

[63] *See* MacCormick, *Questioning Sovereignty: Law, State, and Nation in the European Commonwealth*, p. 164.

[64] The notion of human rights refers to the basic set of political and civil rights, which for the European context is primarily represented by the European Convention on Human Rights. This instrument is clearly built upon the idea of individual autonomy, and is also a part of the constitutional orders of all the Member States of the EU.

For penal legislative power to be legitimate both the criterion of accountability and the criterion of rights protection must be met. In this regard it is important to see that democratic legitimacy is always a matter of degree, i.e. political power could be regarded as more or less democratically legitimate. There is neither any fixed limit between legitimate and illegitimate power, but the required minimum level of democratic legitimacy must be understood dynamically in relation to the desired scope of power. Thus, the more far-reaching scope of penal power, the higher degree of democratic legitimacy should be required. And reversely, the less degree of democratic legitimacy that can be obtained, the smaller the legitimate scope of penal power that can be acknowledged.

To start with the criterion of accountability, penal legislation should in regard of the intrusive character of punitive power, as far as possible be enacted by institutions that are directly controllable and answerable to the individuals, i.e. by a parliamentary assembly. (Still, one should not totally exclude the possibility that the participation of the individuals in the legislative process could be secured in other ways than by means of a parliament.) The argued presumption that a parliament directly representing the people should serve as the penal legislator, is based upon an idea that this is the best way to secure an equal individual protection in penal law, rather than if these decisions were to be left to the executive or to the courts directly. This is so, among other reasons, because the greater heterogeneity of views that are reflected in a legislative process, the better, since this better secures that the final decisions are more thought through. A greater differentiation of arguments therefore also ensures that the product of legislation better represents a fair protection of individual interests. A parliament is also a better forum for an important public debate and thereby gives better support to an interaction between the citizens and their elected representatives. In a more homogeneous group that only reflects a part of the population, and thus only a part of the views in society, the risk that the legal decisions do not take the minority into account is increased.[65] It is important that penal legislation is based upon arguments that not only reflect the views of a portion of the citizens, but that it is subject to a viewing and balancing of as many different arguments as possible.

However, provided that the ultimate control is still in hands of the citizens, delegation of legislative penal power, or other forms of weakened parliamentary control, is not as such contrary to democratic legitimacy of penal legislation. Yet, if penal legislative power is delegated, or the link between citizen and the legislative power is weakened due to other circumstances, this must be reflected in the permitted scope of penal power. If the criterion of accountability is diminished, it is also important to balance this shortcoming with an increase of rights protection, i.e. with the criterion of constitutional rights protection and judicial control. Still, no matter how strong this constitutional element is, some minimal level of accountability is always required. Punitive power must never be fully detached from the people.

As to the criterion of rights protection, this is an essential means for the safeguarding of individual autonomy. Therefore, democratic legitimacy requires the

---

[65]   *See* J. Madison, 'The Federalist', No. 10, in A. Hamilton, J. Madison and J. Jay, *The Federalist* (Guernsey, 1992), p. 47.

existence of a genuine protection of human rights, which has to be safeguarded by superior constitutional norms and by judicial control.[66] This criterion must always be met should punitive power in any form be exercised and is of particular importance if the penal power in question suffers from a low degree of accountability. A constitution is essential for the safeguarding of individual equality since it implements the rule of law and defines limits and principles for state power that cannot be amended by simple majority vote. As such a constitution ultimately expresses the democratically legitimate mandate of penal legislative power (and hence there is no contradiction between the idea of a constitution as a superior law and the view that the power derives from the people).[67]

Legitimate Penal Legislation at the EU Level: Proportionality, Subsidiary and Supranational Decision-Making as *Ultima Ratio*

From the conception of democratic legitimacy outlined above, the penal decision-making at the EU level could *in principle* be regarded as democratically legitimate, both as delegation of powers and as independent supranational decision-making. If the decision-making at the EU level is regarded as a delegation, it is democratically legitimate if it is exercised within the bounds of the national constitutions, if a link of accountability between the national legislator and the Member State citizen is present, and if national courts secure access to effective legal remedies, safeguarding individual rights. If the decision-making on the other hand is regarded as supranational and autonomous, the legitimacy is to be found in the constitutionally established mandate of the EU, i.e. the condition for legitimacy in this case is that the penal decision-making is mandated by the TEU. In this case a link of accountability between the decision-maker at the EU level and the EU citizen must be secured, and effective judicial control must be present at the EU level.

To be democratically legitimate, as stated above, legislative penal power must never be uncontrollable, i.e. the link between the decision-makers and the citizens must never be entirely broken. The possibility to agree upon binding penal Framework Decisions at the EU level makes the 'delegation model' problematic in this regard, a problem that, as stated above, will be intensified if the penal cooperation will be subject to majority decisions. The mere possibility to argue for the supremacy of these decisions over national constitutional law raises the question if the decision-making at the EU level could actually be regarded as a delegation or if it is actually a matter of transfer of legislative power.[68]

In case of delegation of legislative competence from the national level to the EU level, the final control of the legislative power should still be at the national level. Therefore, in case of delegation, the democratic legitimacy of the decision-making at

---

[66] *See* Mancini and Keeling, 'Democracy and the European Court of Justice', p. 181.

[67] *See* Richards, *Foundations of American Constitutionalism*, pp. 256-268.

[68] *See* Albrecht and Braum, 'Defiencies in the Development of European Criminal Law', p. 302; Kaifa-Gbandi, 'The Development towards Harmonization within Criminal Law in the European Union – A Citizen's Perspective', p. 250.

the EU level could be traced back to the individuals via the constitutional systems of the Member States. In case of transfer of legislative power, the control of this power is also transferred, i.e. a new legislator with an independent position is created. Since the decisions enacted at the EU level could reasonably be argued to be directly binding in the national constitutional orders, the penal decision-making at the EU level could, from the perspective of the individuals, be viewed as an independent legislative power. When the national parliaments are not in a position of final control of penal decisions enacted by the Council, the democratic link to the supranational decision-making via the national parliaments is severely weakened, if not broken. To uphold democratic legitimacy it seems like we must make a choice: Either the decisions made at the EU level cannot bind the national parliament, or we must give up the idea of delegated powers and establish democratic legitimacy at the EU level.[69]

The latter choice is both possible and, in the light of the ongoing penal development, better. The first choice seems unrealistic. It seems not even possible to reverse the penal development that has taken place, and in this situation the cold grip of the state-based model of democracy only prevents us from regenerating democracy in our contemporary penal context. If an independent penal decision-making is to be placed at EU level, then the democratic control should also be developed at this level. If penal decisions enacted at the EU level could be given priority over national constitutions it is not sufficient to trace legitimacy through these constitutions, but this legitimacy must also be derived from a constitution and constitutional control at the EU level.[70] It is important that full democratic accountability starts where the decisions are taken, and not only at the implementation stage. As long as there is legal obligation to give priority to EU decisions, it is from the individuals' point of view irrelevant whether the Member States prefer to view the EU as subordinated to their constitutional systems or not. If we take the protection of individuals seriously, it is necessary that we develop supranational democratic control as we develop supranational penal decision-making

To begin with, it is therefore important that the penal decision-making at the EU level is based on a clear constitutional mandate. In this respect it would have been preferable if the Constitution Treaty had been approved, so that the penal decision-making had explicitly become subject to a supranational constitutional structure, based on the rule of law and upheld by a court of law. This would be a better situation than today, where the competences empowered to the EU under the third pillar are stretched to their outer limits, and where a formally intergovernmental cooperation is *de facto* developing into a supranational creature. In addition it would have been preferable if the pillar structure were abolished, as the Constitution Treaty suggested, since this structure is a source of vagueness and conflict concerning the

---

[69] *See* Kaifa-Gbandi, 'The Development towards Harmonization within Criminal Law in the European Union – A Citizen's Perspective', p. 250.

[70] *See* 'Now, even if it is true that the democratic character of the Member States is sufficient to legitimate the intergovernmental component of the Union, such indirect legitimation cannot provide an adequate normative foundation for its supranational component.' Majone, 'Europe's "Democratic Deficit": The Question of Standards', p.12.

legal basis of the penal decision-making at the EU level.[71] If the Constitution Treaty would have been approved, the penal competences of the EU should also in a more visible manner have been traced to the individuals, through the assent to this Treaty, either through the enactment by the national parliaments or through referendums in the Member States.[72]

Even if penal decision-making at the EU level is, or will become, legitimately mandated by a constitution, and subject to constitutional control, the 'democratic distance' between the penal decision-making at the EU level and the citizens is still problematic. Even though it is not inconceivable that in a supranational constitution the security of the individuals may to some degree rest with a court of law to which the individual has access, rather than through a parliamentary assembly, the parliamentary control of penal decision-making cannot be totally neglected. In penal law an important guarantee against abuse of state power is, as stated above, that legislative power to the extent possible is exercised by directly elected representatives. This creates an argument for the strengthening of the role of the European Parliament in penal decision-making at the EU level. In light of the ongoing development, it is not at all satisfactory that the European Parliament only has a consultative role within the penal cooperation under the third pillar. This argument also supports the Constitution Treaty which intended to introduce essential improvements by strengthening parliamentary representation in this area.[73] It should here be noted that the support for the European Parliament is not a support for a sovereign assembly at the EU level. It should only be interpreted as a belief that the protection of individual rights is best secured in this way, since it increases the degree of popular participation in the penal decision-making.

However, due to the relatively low degree of parliamentary representation that one can realistically expect to obtain in the near future, even though the changes provided for by the Constitution Treaty will be implemented, the existence of a genuine rights protection and, above all, access to judicial control at the EU level is essential. This requirement is reinforced by the fact that the ongoing penal development, both on the national and the international level, reflects an increasingly repressive orientation. In light of this tendency it is of utmost importance that penal decision-making is not withdrawn from constitutional control, ultimately placed in the hands of the individuals.[74] Also in this regard, the adoption of the Constitution Treaty would have contributed in a valuable way, since it both required the access of the EU to the European Convention on Human Rights, and incorporated the Charter of Fundamental Rights of the European Union into primary EU law.[75]

---

[71] *See* Weyembergh, 'Approximation of Criminal Laws, the Constitutional Treaty and the Hague Programme', p. 1573.

[72] *See* MacCormick, *Who's Afraid of a European Constitution*, p. 46.

[73] *See* in particular Article III-396 of the Constitution Treaty, on this matter cf. Weyembergh, 'Approximation of Criminal Laws, the Constitutional Treaty and the Hague Programme', p. 1595.

[74] *See* Weyembergh, 'Approximation of Criminal Laws, the Constitutional Treaty and the Hague Programme', pp. 1588-1590.

[75] *See* Article I-9 of the Constitution Treaty.

The shortcomings of the representative structures of the EU should also, from an autonomy-focused perspective, be reflected in the scope of penal power at the EU level. In order to safeguard individual autonomy, penal decision-making at the EU level should take place only when it is absolutely necessary. This necessity should be judged in relation to the protection of autonomy of the individual, and not in relation to the effective implementation of EU policies as is a tendency in the current development.[76] The protection of individual autonomy should actually, at least in the penal law context, be viewed as the *res publica* of the EU.[77] This *res publica*, or common good, unites the European Citizens in a new political society of a *sui generis* character and therefore the legitimacy of penal power at the EU level should ultimately be understood from this basis.

To secure the required minimal exercise of penal legislative power at the EU level, the *principle of subsidiarity*, the *principle of proportionality* and the *principle of ultima ratio* should serve as constitutional principles in relation to penal decision-making at the EU level.[78] These principles are important with regard to democratic legitimacy as they simplify the ensuring of accountability and strongly contribute to individual rights protection. In particular the principle of subsidiarity helps to structure democracy since it attempts to tie decisions to those affected to them.[79] All three principles should be understood as instrumental to the protection of individual autonomy. The principle of subsidiary should thus be viewed as a vertical *ultima ratio* principle, i.e. the principle that penal law should be used as the last resort. Penal decision-making at the EU level is legitimate only when the protection of autonomy is better secured through common legislation, than through national rules. At the EU level the autonomy protection should be secured by means of penal law, only when no other means can be used, i.e. penal decision-making at the EU level should be used as *ultima ratio*. In this regard, it might be time for reflection on the current development, where there is a tendency to consider penal law rather as *prima ratio*.[80] The principle of proportionality should lastly serve as a key principle in order to

---

[76]   *See* G.P. Fletcher, 'Parochial versus Universal Criminal Law', *Journal of International Criminal Justice*, 3/1 (2005): 20-34.

[77]   *See* MacCormick, *Questioning Sovereignty: Law, State, and Nation in the European Commonwealth*, p. 93, who emphasizes the wider formulation of the obtaining of peace as the common good of the EU. However, in the penal context there are, in light of the character of punitive power, strong reasons to support a more narrow conception, i.e. the protection of individual autonomy, as the common good.

[78]   This view necessarily supports a perspective on the EU as a kind of federal legal order. However, it does not presuppose the view that the EU is as a federal *state*. The EU has developed into a new kind of constitutional order (*sui generis*) of a federal character. As in all federal systems there is, with reference to individual protection, a need for constitutional principles for allocating power between different levels according to which level is most appropriate for decision-making, *see further* Weiler, *The Constitution of Europe*, pp. 130-187.

[79]   N.W. Barber, 'The Limited Modesty of Subsidiarity', *European Law Journal*, 11/3 (2005): 323.

[80]   On this tendency *see further* Weyembergh, 'Approximation of Criminal Laws, the Constitutional Treaty and the Hague Programme', pp. 1588-1590.

secure a minimal practice of penal decision-making at the EU level. This principle, as developed within constitutional law, entails three sub-principles of *suitability, necessity* and *proportionality in its narrow sense*. In the context of constitutional rights a restriction of a right is proportionate, and thus legitimate, only if all sub-principles are met. In analogy, a penal decision should be made at the EU level only if the principle of proportionality gives an affirmative answer. [81]

Conclusion: Rethinking Democratic Legitimacy in the Context of European Penal Law

It is clear that the development towards a legislative punitive power at the EU level challenges the traditional view of democratic legitimacy. However, this does not mean that we are left only with a choice to either resist the ongoing penal development, or to leave the idea of democratic legitimacy of penal legislation behind. On the contrary, the ideal of democratic control of penal legislation can – and should – be reconciled with the development of an autonomous penal decision-maker at the international level. The tendency of contemporary penal law points towards supranational penal cooperation and decision-making. We ought to meet the challenge and provide for democratic legitimacy in the penal context. In this regard it is important to view the penal law development first and foremost from the perspective of democracy and not the other way around, i.e. we should allow penal power at the international level only when it is democratically acceptable. This requires that we define the purpose and values of democracy, and on this background, also define the acceptable scope of supranational penal power. In this article my intention has been to emphasize the protection of individual autonomy as an essential value of democracy, and to give a view on the re-setting of this value in a European, non-state, penal context. The conclusion is that penal legislative power, due to a low degree of parliamentary representation, should be exercised on the EU level only when this is necessary for the protection of individual autonomy. In my view, this is the most appropriate way to approach the relevant problem of democratic legitimacy. However, for an acceptable development of penal law, a continuous discussion on this matter, a public reasoning if one likes, is in itself essential.

---

[81] This test of proportionality should not be confused with the penal assessment of proportionality that primary aims at the proportion between the severity of the crime and the level of repression of the punishment, *see further* A. von Hirsch, *Proportionalitet och Straffbestämning* (Uppsala, 2001), p. 84.